ON THE ROAD FOR WORK

INSTITUTE OF SOCIAL STUDIES

SERIES ON THE DEVELOPMENT
OF SOCIETIES

VOLUME VII

INTERNATIONAAL INSTITUUT
VOOR SOCIALE STUDIËN - 'S GRAVENHAGE

ON THE ROAD FOR WORK:
MIGRATORY WORKERS ON THE EAST COAST OF THE UNITED STATES

G. Thomas-Lycklama à Nijeholt

MARTINUS NIJHOFF PUBLISHING

BOSTON/THE HAGUE/LONDON

Distributors for North America:
Martinus Nijhoff Publishing
Kluwer Boston Inc.
160 Old Derby Street
Hingham, Massachusetts 02043

Distributors outside North America:
Kluwer Academic Publishers Group
Distribution Centre
P.O. Box 322
3300 AH Dordrecht, The Netherlands

Library of Congress Cataloging in Publication Data

Thomas-Lycklama à Nijeholt, Geertje.
    On the road for work.

    (Series on the development of societies; v. 7)
    1.   Migrant agricultural laborers—Atlantic States.
I. Title. II. Series.
HD1525.T48   331.5′44′0975   80-12077
ISBN 0-89838-043-X

Printed in the United States of America

CONTENTS

PREFACE

Migratory farm workers provide the extra hands that are so badly needed during the planting and harvest season in the United States. Although these workers have been essential to the American agricultural system for more than a hundred years, our knowledge of them is limited and quite fragmentary; it can be divided roughly into two types of information. On the one hand, we have the statistical data collected by various censuses and the data gathered by agricultural economists to study the supply of and demand for farm labor. The economic aspects of farm labor generally predominate in such material. On the other, we have the scientific studies and journalistic descriptions that report on migratory farm workers by using a qualitative approach. The social scientists and journalists who have compiled these reports lived in the labor camps and have vividly described the dismal and oppressive conditions these workers must endure.

The drawback of the first type of data is that its orientation to economic problems makes it too superficial and one-sided. It fails to interrelate the diverse economic factors affecting the lives and work of all farm workers, and consequently presents a distorted and incomplete picture of migratory farm worker life. Also, because the migratory farm workers are quite elusive and usually keep a low profile, they are often underrepresented in such data.

The data gathered by using qualitative methods have the major disadvantage of being quite limited in scope. The descriptions of migratory farm worker life "from the inside out" give in-depth reports on the life and work of quite small and specific categories of migratory farm workers on the East Coast (usually the blacks), but provide no *comprehensive* picture of the migratory labor force and its role in agriculture in the United States — and thus no reliable generalizations that can be used in designing policies. They have also been criticized for seeming to describe only the very worst living and working conditions and only the workers in the weakest socioeconomic position.

This book aims to fill the gap in our knowledge of these workers and also combines the valuable aspects of both approaches: that is, it combines statistical data analysis with descriptive reports on the workers' lives and work. To do this, a fourteen-state sample of migratory and nonmigratory workers on the East Coast of the United States is used; this enables the analysis of one of the three major migratory streams in the United States agriculture *as a whole*.

This analysis approaches migratory farm labor essentially as a farm labor problem which is inherent in the agricultural production structure of the United States, and not as a migration problem. By revealing and quantifying relationships between the various socioeconomic factors affecting farm workers, by distinguishing four ethnic groups, and by comparing migratory to nonmigratory workers, a more comprehensive — and at the same time more general — picture of the migratory farm workers' position in agriculture is obtained.

After describing the farm workers' historical and social context, the kind of work they do, and their particular problems, the survey data is examined to gain an understanding of the actual impact of the most relevant aspects of the migratory farm workers' lives: mobility, low but highly differentiated earnings, and the lack of job security and opportunities compared to nonmigratory farm workers. The conclusions drawn from this examination are translated into policy recommendations in the last chapter, which addresses itself to problems in designing effective programs for these workers in order to improve their lot. The recommended programs call for bilateral cooperation between states, greater recognition of the significance of ethnic group membership in migratory farm work, the creation of a job structure in farm labor, and further research on the role of women in farm labor.

The conclusions and recommendations presented here underscore the failure of government policies to deal with problems in farm labor. This failure is related to the fact that the government bases all its policies on the premise that agricultural production cannot operate effectively unless it has easy access to a large supply of cheap (often foreign) workers, who are employed only during the peak period of the demand for farm labor in the agricultural production process. Clearly, a more comprehensive approach must be taken if the quality of the farm workers' lives is to be improved. Those in the places of power — political leaders and policy makers alike — must recognize the needs *not only* of the employers *but also* of the farm workers themselves.

The future of migratory farm workers in the United States is also touched

upon. It becomes obvious that unless the influx of new, economically dependent, foreign workers is halted, and unless the distribution of bargaining power
between agricultural employers and agricultural workers becomes more equitable, the future of the migratory farm worker is virtually hopeless. It is only
through effective government programs that these workers can be given the
rights and opportunities their fellow workers in other sectors have had for years,
and to which they — like all other workers — are entitled.

G.T.-L.à N.

ACKNOWLEDGEMENTS

This book has been written over a period of several years, during which I received help from a number of people. First I would like to express my gratitude to Professor Dr. G. Kuiper Hzn. of the Free University of Amsterdam. His wise suggestions and guiding comments were a great help to me in preparing the first drafts. To Professor Dr. C. Boekestijn I would like to express my appreciation for his interest in my research and for his contribution to a stimulating exchange of ideas on the subject.

I am grateful to Drs. S.M. de Boer, Dr. H. Thomas, Drs. H.J.W. Weijland, and Dr. F.C.M. Wils for reading the manuscript, and for giving their perceptive and useful comments. Their assistance undoubtedly helped to clarify the reasoning and improve presentation and readability.

This book could not have been written without the support of many people at Cornell University. I would particularly like to thank Professor Dr. W.W. Bauder for his continuing interest in my work, for his assistance during the various stages of completing this book, and for the stimulating discussions we had on this subject and on many others. I would also like to thank Professor Dr. C.A. Bratton and Professor Dr. D.E. Moore for their helpful suggestions.

I am also grateful to Don Manson, Joe Remes, and Suzanne M. Broderick for their help in persuading the computer to release the right tabulations and computations at the right time; to Peggy Ulrich-Nims and Edie Pigg for their support, moral and otherwise; to Millie Blomhert for the competent way she edited the manuscript; to Netty Born for the typesetting; and to Koos van Wieringen and Henk de Roo for drawing the maps and doing other technical work.

Finally, this study would never have been completed if Henk, Jurjen and Rixte Thomas had not taken a participatory view of housekeeping.

G.T.-L.à N.

1

THE PLIGHT OF THE MIGRATORY FARM WORKER

Very few people in the United States would disagree with the statement that migratory farm workers comprise one of the most deprived groups in American society. For decades civic organizations, politicians, and individual citizens have tried to arouse public awareness about the plight of these people and to introduce measures which would improve their position, but so far they have only had limited success. Migratory farm workers, like all agricultural workers, are not only excluded from most of the protective social legislation which is enjoyed by most other workers, but also must live and work under conditions which create a combination of hardship, insecurity, and poverty that is indeed unique. The facts of the farm worker's life portray a situation which is considerably worse than that of any other occupational category in the United States.

To some extent the lives and work of the migratory farm workers can be compared with that of the guest workers (*Gastarbeiter*) in Europe and the seasonal workers in developing countries. All of them do dirty work, have insecure job situations, are poverty-stricken, and in many cases they are separated from their families for long periods.

However, what makes the position of the migratory farm workers in the United States both so sad and so shocking is the tremendous wealth of the

---

Notes to this chapter may be found on p. 10.

1

country in which they live. Poverty is a relative concept: it has to do with one's living conditions as compared to those of the people in one's surroundings. In a country where a great part of the population is more or less wealthy, people begin to feel very uneasy when they consider the question of why the country's wealth is not being shared by the whole population. Too often this uneasiness has led the well-to-do in the United States to the simplistic conclusion that in a country of such great opportunity, poverty must be the poor man's own fault: that is, the migratory farm workers must be poor because they do not work hard enough and because they do not make good use of the opportunities offered to them. Approaching poverty from this viewpoint makes it extremely difficult to build up the kind of political pressure that will induce the government to initiate policies and programs that will be effective in changing the living and working conditions of these workers. Another hindersome problem is the lack of awareness among the American public about poverty in the rural areas: the United States is a huge country, and many Americans have simply never been exposed to poverty, either rural or urban.

1. THE UNKNOWN RURAL POOR

As recently as 1972 Rushing wrote: "Like most poor people in the United States, very little is known about farm workers." (1972:21)[1] This has been as much the case since the Depression as it was during and before it, in part because during the nineteenth century, before the frontier had been cleared to the West Coast, abject poverty was quite rare in the rural areas in the northern states. Farming was on a small scale and life was hard, but if a farmer was unsuccessful he and his family could simply move elsewhere and start over again, for land was abundant and cheap in the frontier states.

In the southern states the situation was quite different: a large-scale plantation economy had thrived there since the seventeenth century and was dominated by a small, privileged class of white aristocrats who owned slaves and managed plantation agriculture. Regulation of the investment of capital, the labor force, and the marketing of crops, as well as control of the economic, political, and social aspects of life were in their hands. Life in the South was viewed as a romantic existence of leisure and affluence. People were almost completely unaware — both before and after the abolition of slavery — of the poor rural whites who lived under the most dismal conditions in the more isolated parts of the southern states and worked the land as tenants and sharecroppers.

Because of this lack of awareness, the nation was greatly shocked when, during the 1930s, the wretched conditions of the tenants and sharecroppers of the South were brought to the attention of the general public by Margaret Bourke-White and Erskine Caldwell's dramatic photographic documentary called *You Have Seen Their Faces* (1937). Other documentaries,[2] one of which was Agee and Evans' *Let Us Now Praise Famous Men* (1941), followed later and showed that in a land of seemingly endless opportunity, whites in the rural areas of the South were suffering great poverty.

During the Depression the decline in cotton production and the drought drove many southern farmers from their land. In their search for work, many of these people — among them both blacks who were descendants of the slaves, and white tenants and sharecroppers — migrated to the East Coast. Work was scarce and they, like many other Americans, experienced abject poverty in the 1930s and had to travel to find employment. Some of them were absorbed into the migratory farm worker streams, but most remained jobless. The government programs for creating jobs and providing relief proved to be far from sufficient for the tremendous stream of poor and uprooted people on the move.

Soon thereafter the United States became involved in World War II. Unemployment decreased rapidly and the poor were quickly forgotten. When the war was over, growing concern for the poor developed again, especially in the 1950s and 1960s, but attention was focused on urban poverty and racial problems. The farm workers and the other rural poor were almost completely ignored: in fact, what little was written about these people dealt nearly exclusively with the migratory farm workers. By publicizing the dismal living and working conditions of these migratory workers, writers, journalists, and filmmakers again tried to stir the public conscience (Shotwell 1961; Wright 1965; Allen 1966; and the CBS documentary entitled "Harvest of Shame" (1960)).

The almost complete lack of documentation on nonmigratory farm workers certainly does not preclude the existence of poverty among them. It does, however, give the impression that their living and working conditions are assumed to be such that they would not provoke an outcry of protest. It is also possible that the publicity about migratory farm workers has created an image of farm workers which has simply been imposed upon nonmigratory farm workers as well.

2. PROBLEMS IN MIGRATORY LIFE

During the winter months most of the migratory farm workers reside — that is, they have a home base, which is usually a wooden shack without running water — in the southern part of the United States. The greatest numbers are concentrated in certain parts of Florida, Texas, and Puerto Rico. Unemployment is a well-known phenomenon during the winter, but some jobs in farm work, harvesting, packing, or canning can be found; the workers may also do odd jobs in the tourist industry or find (unskilled) work in the construction industry. When spring comes and job opportunities in the home base area become scarcer, these workers start to move northward in search of work. It is this mobility, this departure from the home base area to do farm work in another area, that characterizes these workers as migratory.

The mobility of the migratory farm workers during the summer months, the necessity to keep moving in order to remain employed, is the most dominant feature of their way of life, and it is to a great degree responsible for the hardship and insecurity they must face. Their seasonal movement has, for instance, serious implications for their children's education. Traveling from state to state during the school year makes it difficult for the children to continue their education, whether or not school facilities are available. Traveling also creates another problem: housing. As the periods during which the employer needs these workers are quite short, it is not worth his while to arrange adequate housing; consequently, the migratory farm workers usually live in crowded camps in which the sanitary facilities are often inadequate. In order to formulate and implement policies that will contribute to improving the deplorable living and working conditions of migratory farm workers, it is necessary to know how they live and work, and why. Such information about these workers is very limited and fragmentary.

Migratory farm work is part of the agricultural system in the United States. As in agricultural systems elsewhere, there is a tendency to view farm labor from the perspective of the employer. Farm labor problems are usually analyzed in terms of the demand for workers, i.e., what the employers need. The main question asked is: how can arrangements be made to have enough workers at the right place and the right time to harvest the crops? Because of this we know little about the migratory worker as an individual — except that he or she has a pair of hands and is willing to harvest the crops. We do not know whether the workers are white or black, young or old, men or women; nor do we know what their needs are, how much they earn, and how they live and work. The available information about them is (as we will see in the following chapters) more or less bits and pieces: it is limited in approach and deals with particular groups of farm workers, usually the black migratory farm workers in a certain area. The popular image depicts these workers as trekking from state to state — as people with "itchy feet" who are unable to stick to a regular job — but in fact we do not know how far and how often they move during each year.

Taking the mobility of these workers as a basis, three major questions will be dealt with in this investigation:

(1) what are the migratory patterns of these workers?
(2) how much do they earn, and what factors influence their earnings in the course of their yearly movements? and
(3) what distinguishes them from other — i.e., nonmigratory — farm workers?

(1) *Migratory patterns*. During the past thirty years social scientists have become more interested in migratory farm workers and have studied certain aspects of migratory farm worker life (see Persh 1953; Greene 1954; Metzler 1955; Brooks and Hilgendorf 1960; Marcson and Fasick 1964; Shostack 1964; Friedland 1967; Nelkin 1969; 1970; Friedland and Nelkin 1971; and Dunbar and Kravitz 1976). However, with the exception of one or two studies on a specific category of migratory farm workers, no detailed research has been done on the migratory patterns of these workers. Statistics indicating the number of migratory workers employed in a certain state during a certain period do exist, but what is not known is whether the migratory worker who moves to one state also moves on to other states — and if so, how many — during the seasonal journey northwards and back. Thus a main aim will be to find out more about the migratory patterns of migratory farm workers on the East Coast (Chapter 4). Taking a week-by-week analysis as a basis (see Chapter 3, section 4), data will show that these workers are far less mobile than the popular image would have us believe.

(2) *Poverty*. Mobility is not the only characteristic of migratory farm worker life: extreme poverty also typifies most of these workers. To understand how economically depressed these farm workers are, the level and context of their earnings will be investigated (Chapter 5).

While it is well known that migratory farm workers — and farm workers in general — are in one of the lowest paid occupational categories in the United States, little is known about the differences in earnings within this category. Although farm workers are considered to be unskilled or semi-skilled workers, there are indications that considerable differences in earnings do exist, not only between migratory and nonmigratory farm workers but also within these two groups. The earnings of these workers during a given year will be analyzed to find out how much is actually earned and what factors influence these earnings. By constructing an earnings function for migratory as well as nonmigratory farm workers, we will be able to get a clear impression of the earnings differences and the factors influencing these differences within the two occupational subcategories. A discussion of the two earnings functions will show that there are significant differences in the socioeconomic characteristics of the migratory and nonmigratory farm workers, which are related to the fact that the migratory farm worker has to travel to remain employed, works for a number of employers, has no job security, and often does not know if, and how much, he or she will earn each day. The nonmigratory farm worker, on the other hand, does not have to travel to remain employed, usually works for the same employer throughout the year, has a more secure job situation, and knows what he or she will earn for the work done.

(3) *A comparison of migratory and nonmigratory farm workers.* After investigating the two most significant aspects of migratory farm worker life — interstate mobility and low earnings — we will concentrate on a comparison of the migratory to the nonmigratory farm workers (Chapter 6) to find out what types of farm workers travel to do their work and what types stay home, and whether the migratory farm workers show certain characteristics which are responsible for their migratory status. Such variables as education, skills, and ethnic group membership will be related to the migratory status of the farm worker. We will find that it is ethnic group membership — and not education, skill, age, or social background, as would be expected — which is most determinant for whether or not a worker migrates.

In Chapter 7 the implications this investigation may have for formulating and implementing policies to improve the plight of these workers will be discussed, and the future outlook for the migratory farm worker will also be considered. A comprehensive investigation of these aspects of the migratory farm workers has as yet not been made. Apart from this, the quantitative methods used in the investigation, and the availability of a large sample of farm workers (instead of a subsample of, e.g., black migratory workers), make it possible to present generalizations about these farm workers and to put the existing fragmented source material based on participatory observations in a wider quantitative perspective. More important, they enable the formulation of policies which can be effective in solving the farm workers' problems.

3. MIGRATORY FARM WORKERS, MIGRANTS, AND MIGRATION THEORY

People who migrate are generally referred to as "migrants," a term that tends to suggest a change of residence with the intention of staying at the new location. However, "migratory farm workers," who usually have a different pattern of movement in that it is seasonal and thus more continuous, are often also referred to as "migrants." Because the difference between the two kinds of migration has not been fully recognized and appreciated, the migratory farm workers are often quietly excluded from the definitions of migration which are used in theories focusing on migration as a permanent change of residence. In the United States, use of the term "migrant" is particularly confusing because it may mean either a person who changes his residence permanently, or a person who annually travels to the North and then back to the South, doing (farm) work while migrating (Ducoff 1951:217-224). The term is also used ambiguously in Europe with reference to the guest workers.

Since Ravenstein's laws of migration were published (1885:167-227; 1889: 241-301), migration has been studied by scholars from various disciplines. In the United States the field of internal migration was dominated by demographers; quantitative research was the main focus and little attention was given to the development of theory. Sociologists have complained about the lack of a general comprehensive theory of migration (Mangalam 1968:1-7; Jansen 1969:60; Albrecht 1972:2-3), which may to some extent be due, in the United States at least, to the predominance of demographers in the field. The demographic studies have dealt with three main subjects: migration, mortality, and fertility. The field of demography has been defined as follows:

The primary tasks of demography are (1) to ascertain the number of people in a given area, (2) to determine what change — what growth or decline — this number represents, (3) to explain the change, and (4) to estimate on this basis the future trend. In explaining a change in numbers the populationist begins with three variables: births, deaths, and migration. He subtracts the deaths from the births to get "natural increase" and he subtracts the emigrants from the immigrants to get "net migration".... It is clear that any factor influencing the number of people must operate through one or more of the variables mentioned. In no other way can a population be changed. For this reason we may call the four variables (fertility, mortality, immigration, and emigration) "the primary demographic processes." They represent the core of population analysis. (Davis 1949:551-552)

Thus there was a strong emphasis on counting the number of people involved, and little interest in developing a theoretical framework for explaining the qualitative facts and the changes in those facts. As was observed, "it [demography] has few unique concepts and theories that would explain 'why' a particular demographic situation exists at a particular moment or what forces underlie an observed change in demographic status." (Bogue 1969:5) A demographer depends heavily for his quantitative analysis on census data and other official statistics, and it is therefore not surprising that the migratory worker is too elusive for his approach. A move has to be a permanent one in order to be properly recorded because: "Theoretically, the term 'migration' is reserved for those changes of residence that involve a complete change and readjustment of the community affiliations of the individual." (Bogue 1959: 489).

Some demographers have stressed the need to study the qualitative aspects of demography, especially social mobility (Bogue 1969:1-2; Schnore 1961: 407-422). A well-known attempt to formulate a comprehensive and general theory of migration was made by Lee, who defined migration "...as a permanent or a semi-permanent change of residence" (1969:285) and considered four groups of factors to be relevant to the field of migration: factors associated with the area of origin, factors associated with the area of destination, intervening obstacles, and personal factors. This definition is broad and general in that it places no restrictions on the distance of the move or the nature of the migration, i.e., whether it is voluntary or involuntary. However, one aspect of this definition is, as far as migratory farm workers are concerned, not broad enough: "Excluded, for example, are the continual movements of nomads and migratory workers, for whom there is no long-term residence, and temporary moves like those to the mountains for the summer." (1969:285) This implies that migratory workers keep on moving and excludes the possibility of considering migratory work as an intermediate step in a more permanent change of residence.

In addition to approaching migration from the demographic viewpoint, social scientists have also studied it in a socio-psychological framework, investigating motivation, decision making, adaption, and absorption. A study on the absorption of immigrants in Israel (Eisenstadt 1955) emphasized that the prospective migrant's feelings of frustration in his original setting are part of his or her motivation to migrate. Such socio-psychological concepts as role expectation and the adjustment to and absorption in the new country were also dealt with. Findings of a study on attachment to one's area of residence (Boekestijn 1961) have also been interpreted in terms of a theory of migration with three main elements: (1) attachment to one's home area, (2) information concerning alternatives elsewhere, and (3) the social comparison process (i.e., comparison with the least different, next higher group). A typology of individual migration patterns (Holden 1968:15-28) was worked out by dichotomizing and combining three socio-psychological variables: (1) the skill of the migrant in assimilating the social system of the destination area, (2) the degree to which the migrant identifies with the social system in the destination area, and (3) the degree to which the migrant considers dissociation from his or her previous social system to be final. The nature of the decision to migrate is considered to be the crucial characteristic in defining "individual migration." Theoretically, these socio-psychologically oriented migration theories could indeed be applied in analyzing the position of migratory workers, but this has as yet not been done: most of these socio-psychological studies deal with migrants in the sense of a more or less permanent change of residence and leave aside those who move only temporarily.

In more recent attempts to work out a migration theory (Mangalam 1968; Mangalam and Schwarzweller 1968-69:3-16; Startup 1971:177-190; and Albrecht 1972), a sociological framework was used which also has some applicability to the case of the migratory farm worker. Migration was defined in terms of sociological concepts, and the use of the term was not restricted to permanent changes of residence.

The arrival of guest workers in the developed European countries has emphasized the need for a general migration theory that is not restricted to people who make permanent changes of residence, but includes those who move temporarily, intending to return to a home base.

It should be noted here that such phenomena as counterstreams of migration and stepwise migration have recently been given increasing attention. Studies of migration to the United States during the nineteenth century have revealed that the migratory process was less permanent than it was thought to be; in fact, there were cases of a regular pattern of migration back and forth between the native country and the United States.

Although the concept of migration has become more comprehensive, the use in the United States of the term "migrant" is still strongly associated with a rather permanent change of residence. For this reason the term "migratory farm worker" (see Ducoff 1957:217), rather than "migrant," will be used for those workers who move temporarily according to a seasonal pattern to find (farm) work. The seasonal character of their search for work and the return to a home base area distinguish their movement from what is generally understood to be migration.[3] These two distinguishing features also explain why migration theory, as it now stands, is of only limited use for the approach taken in this analysis. Because of this, the life and work of the migratory farm workers will be viewed not as a migration problem, but primarily as a *farm labor problem*.

NOTES

1. Rushing is obviously referring here to the lack of knowledge among academics, for writers, journalists, and photographers made quite an effort, both during the Depression and after World War II, to inform the general public about the plight of the rural poor.

2. Erskine Caldwell wrote his famous book, *God's Little Acre* (1949), which is the story of a poor southern farmer and his family digging for gold on their farm land. John Steinbeck told the story of migratory farm workers on the West Coast in *The Grapes of Wrath* (1939). The Dutch sociologist A.M.J. den Hollander, who was one of the few social scientists to become concerned with the rural poor whites, wrote an extensive and well-documented historical and socioeconomic account of them (den Hollander 1933).

3. In a comparative article, Burawoy (1976: 1050-1087) studied two migrant labor systems: one in South Africa (mine workers) and one in California (farm laborers). He focused on the nature of the external coercive institutions and the mode of organization through which these migrant labor systems are maintained. Burawoy used the term "migrant labor," but in his descriptions of the migrant labor force in California the term *"migratory* labor" was reserved for domestic workers who migrate from place to place in search of employment.

2

MIGRATORY FARM WORKERS:
THEIR HISTORY AND SOCIOECONOMIC CONTEXT

An explanation for the appearance of a large group of migratory farm workers on the East Coast — and elsewhere in the United States — is provided by the particular way in which agricultural production has come to be organized in this country. Large, specialized farms that grow perishable crops require many extra pairs of hands during the harvest. "Crop specialization has shortened the seasons of farm activity, reduced the need for a year-round hired hand, but it has created the new need for a large labor supply available for short seasons of cultivation or harvest. Thus we have the migrant." (U.S. Congress, Senate, Committee on Labor and Public Welfare 1960:6)

In order to make a comprehensive study of the migratory farm workers, an examination of the historical and socioeconomic context in which they do their job is essential. We will therefore first examine some of the dramatic developments in agriculture in the United States during the last century, emphasizing those aspects which are directly related to the position of migratory farm workers. The ways in which the government has managed to ignore farm workers all over the United States when formulating social legislation will also be recounted. The role of the foreign migratory worker in agri-

---

Notes to this chapter may be found on pages 47-48.

culture in the United States will be explained, and the conflicting interests of the employers and the labor organizations will be considered. Lastly, an overview of the migratory stream on the East Coast of the United States will clarify how this migratory system has developed and how it operates, and a description of the living and working conditions of the people involved in it will be given.

1. THE AGRICULTURAL REVOLUTION

Traditionally, the American farmer has been viewed as a family farmer who ran his farm with the help of one or possibly two hired men. (This was not the case in the South, where slavery was prevalent until 1865.) Labor relations in the country were stereotyped: the farmer, his family, and the farmhand worked together as a unit, sharing the same interests and problems, eating at the same table, attending the same place of worship, and sending their children to the same school (Schwartz 1945:4). The farm provided most of the food and other commodities which were needed, which meant that there was a great diversity of related jobs and chores that had to be done. Because of this, a more or less equal amount of work had to be taken care of throughout the year, and the farmer and his co-workers were kept busy all year-round.

Great changes have taken place in agriculture since the middle of the nineteenth century: mechanization and specialization were introduced into the agricultural production sector, and a new term, "agribusiness", came into usage. It may be defined as "the total of all activities involved in supplying agricultural production inputs, producing food and fiber, and processing and distributing the raw material and consumer products." (Taylor and Berkey 1970:1) A number of large corporations was established and purchased vast tracts of land, acquired the necessary equipment and machinery to farm them, and operated food processing plants and chain food stores (National Sharecroppers Fund 1971:2). While these corporations did not completely take over farming in the United States,[1] they did cause the number of farms that were owned by individuals to decrease and the size of the average farm to increase, as is shown in Table 2.1.

Table 2.1. *The Number and Size of Farms in the United States since 1900*[a]

Year	Total number of farms (in millions)	Average size (in acres per farm)
1900	5.738	148
1910	6.362	138
1920	6.518	147
1930	6.546	151
1940	6.350	167
1950	5.648	213
1960	3.962	297
1970	2.662[a]	387[a]

[a] Estimated by projecting the rate of change between 1960 and 1964 on the years up to 1970.
Source: Ball and Heady 1972:43-44.

Although it has been predicted that the number of farms will decline to even below one million (Taylor and Berkey 1970:1), a recent analysis of how scale and structure are determined in agriculture has shown that it would be premature to assume that agricultural production will become concentrated on fewer and fewer farms, and that the typical family farm will soon disappear, for "price rises and definitional problems have seriously distorted what is really happening to both farm numbers and farm size." (Gardner and Pope 1978:302) Counting the number of farms has become particularly difficult because the 1969 and 1974 censuses defined farms differently from the 1964 and earlier censuses. In the earlier censuses, all farm units with sales exceeding $50 were included, while in the later ones only those farms with gross sales exceeding $2,500 were counted. The escalation in prices of farm products during the 1970s has also affected the number of farms counted in the 1974 census (Gardner and Pope 1978:295).

The figures in the 1969 and 1974 censuses show that in terms of numbers, the position of the family farm is still strong: in the 1969 census 85 percent of all commercial farms were classified as individual or family farms; in the 1974 census this figure was 89 percent (Gardner and Pope 1978:299). Furthermore, various tax laws that have recently been passed (in 1969 and 1976) may also be seen as indications of the strength of the family farm. As to future developments, the agricultural analysis mentioned above suggested that "farms may be becoming small and more numerous at lower acreages, but larger and fewer at large acreages." (Gardner and Pope 1978:297) In that analysis, which is rather reassuring about the future of the family farm, the large share which corporate farms have in the total sales of certain products (see note 1 of this chapter) was unfortunately neglected.

Mechanization brought revolutionary changes to agriculture in the United States. Until 1831 farmers used techniques which were not very different from those used by farmers two or three thousand years ago (McWilliams 1942: 307). Between 1831 and 1900 such machines as the reaper, the steel plow, the threshing machine, the cultivator, and grain drills were introduced. All of these machines were completely dependent on animal power, and this period may therefore be referred to as the "mechanical" revolution (McWilliams 1942: 307). When, at the beginning of the twentieth century, tractors were introduced to replace animal power, agriculture came to be more closely related to industry, and thus began what may be referred to as the "industrial" revolution in agriculture (McWilliams 1942:307). During this period the tractor and the gasoline engine freed the farmer from his dependence on animal power. The time when the owner or tenant farmer had an advantage over the large estates because of the availability of cheap labor provided by his family had passed. What the farmer needed was the new, labor-saving machines that could plant, weed, and harvest. In order to purchase these, huge investments had to be made. The capacity to buy these machines thus became an influential factor in determining the scale of farm operations, and farming on a small scale soon ceased to be financially feasible. America began to witness – and continues to witness today – the merger of the small farms into larger ones.

Another technological development which was significant for agriculture in the United States was the refrigerator truck, which made it possible to transport perishable crops over great distances. Chemical preservatives and food-freezing techniques also greatly changed agriculture: together, these de-developments enabled the farmer to specialize in certain crops and to effectively control the conditions under which they were marketed.

As the farmers discovered the advantages of large-scale, specialized production, many of them switched over to using most of their acreage for this purpose. This had important consequences for their farmhands because work was no longer spread evenly throughout the year: many workers were needed during certain periods, while virtually no work was available during others. It was to fill the temporary high demand for labor that the migratory farm workers appeared. As badly as they were needed during the hectic harvest season, there was simply no work for them during other periods, so they had to travel on to find employment elsewhere.

This situation was not, however, the case on all farms, for there is a great variety in farming and not all types of farms need the help of temporary farm workers to the same extent. On a dairy farm, for instance, the work is spread quite evenly throughout the year. On farms that specialize in fruit or nuts, on the other hand, many workers are needed at certain times, while a few workers can take care of the farm chores during the rest of the year. The impact of the type of farm on the need for farm labor can be illustrated by some estimates based on the data collected in fourteen of the states included in a fifteen-state unemployment insurance survey made in 1970.[2] In these fourteen states, 40 percent of the agricultural employers were dairy farmers, while only 9 percent of the employees worked on dairy farms. Conversely, only 11 percent of the agricultural employers were fruit and nut farmers, while 27 percent of the employees worked on such farms. On dairy farms the average number of employees per employer was estimated to be four; on the fruit and nut farms the average was estimated to be forty-two. The dairy farms and the fruit and nut farms represent the two extremes as far as the use of farm labor is concerned; all the other types of farms fall between these two.

Migratory farm workers not only have to cope with the lack of job security, but also must live on very low wages, like all farm workers in the United States, generally speaking. The 1970 United States census showed that the median yearly earnings of male farm workers aged sixteen years or older was $2,597, compared to $4,647 for workers doing work other than farm work (U.S. Department of Commerce, Bureau of the Census, 1970b:398, Table 94). Thus daily wages for farm work are lower than those for nonfarm work. For many farm workers the low pay, together with the irregularity of the job and the days of partial or no employment, result in an extremely low yearly income.[3]

Although such revolutionary developments in agriculture as mechanization and specialization brought farming closer to other industries, the benefits provided to farm workers were nonetheless far less than those provided to industrial workers. This difference appears to exist even today, although there have been a few minor improvements (see Chapter 2, section 2, and Chapter 3). So far the farm workers in the United States, who comprise one of the few groups of wage earners that in general has not succeeded in organizing into trade unions, have not gotten the kind of pay and working conditions that other wage earners in American society have had since the 1930s, when the federal government introduced social legislation.

2. EXCLUSION OF FARM WORKERS FROM SOCIAL LEGISLATION

Social legislation in the United States has, throughout the years, continually managed to bypass the agricultural worker. While other workers have been given the right to unionize and to bargain collectively, and while they have had the benefits of workers' compensation,[4] a minimum wage, unemployment insurance, and all the schemes designed to guarantee an income, virtually none of these benefits has been extended to farm workers. To find out why, one has to go back to 1937, when the National Labor Relations Act was passed by the United States Congress to regulate relations between workers and employers. It required employers to discuss grievances and participate in bargaining with the workers' elected representatives, and it also prohibited employers from interfering with the workers' efforts to organize and from discriminating against workers who were active in unionizing. At the same time, it required that the trade unions act according to certain fair practices: for instance, they were not allowed to threaten nonmember workers with the loss of their jobs if they did not support the union's activities. In the original draft of this act, which was written in 1935, farm workers were included; however, when the bill left the Labor Committee, farm workers had been excluded, and no adequate justification was given. "The Senate report stated 'administrative reasons', and the House was equally vague." (National Advisory Committee on Farm Labor 1967:10)

This event has had a great influence on the living and working conditions of the farm workers. It has meant that an employer is permitted to ignore the existence of a farm workers' union and that he is not required by law to negotiate with the workers through a union. When strikes are touched off by such issues as wages, working hours, and other working conditions, the real concern is not the workers' demands, but whether the employer is willing to sit down and negotiate with the union which the workers have chosen to represent them (National Advisory Committee on Farm Labor 1967:10). This is the struggle of Cesar Chavez and the United Farm Workers Organizing Committee. Events which occurred during the Delano grape strike in California in 1965 show how difficult that struggle is:

The growers responded in traditional fashion by returning registered union letters unopened, hiring strikebreakers, denying the existence of a strike, and harrassing pickets. Trucks and tractors were driven near to choke the pickets with dust. Picket signs were riddled with bullets and the strikers sprayed with insecticide. Injunctions to limit picketing were secured and groups were arrested for unlawful assembly. Workers who had lived for years on grower property were evicted. (National Advisory Committee on Farm Labor 1967:49)

Farm workers are also specifically excluded from most of the programs and laws which were part of the "New Deal" of the Roosevelt Administration. For instance, while the intention was that all workers should be covered by the workers' compensation laws, most of the states that adopted these laws specifically excluded agricultural workers. In terms of the purpose of social legislation in general, it would seem rather illogical that farm workers are denied accident insurance, because agriculture is one of the more hazardous industries (U.S. Congress, Senate, Committee on Labor and Public Welfare 1960:61); but when one considers the cost to employers, the reason becomes clear. Even in 1965 only eight states provided the same kind of protection to farm workers, through compulsory workers' compensation, as they provided to other workers (Rushing 1972:27). Traditionally, responsibility for workers' compensation laws has been almost entirely in the hands of the state governments, but during the 1970s pressure on the federal government to prescribe federal minimum standards for state laws began to mount. In 1972 the National Commission on State Workmen's Compensation Laws described workers' compensation as a national problem. Since then the states have improved their programs, but in 1976 not a single state had complied with all nineteen of the recommendations which were cited as "essential" in the Commission's report (see Hribal and Minor 1977).

Under the Social Security Act of 1935, farmers and farm workers were excluded from old age and survivors' insurance and from unemployment insurance.[5] Under the Fair Labor Standards Act of 1938, minimum wage laws did not apply to farm workers. Furthermore, while this act prohibited children under the age of sixteen from working in establishments producing goods for shipment in interstate or foreign commerce, it did not — and still does not — forbid child labor in agricultural employment on the days and during the hours when the child was not legally required to attend school.[6] Of course there were and still are many violations of such a law, for large numbers of children work in the fields (see pages 117 and 118).

Since World War II some progress has been made in enacting social legislation which benefits farm workers. Nevertheless, the federal laws are still few, and they often cover only a small part of the agricultural labor force. In 1951, for example, social security was extended to regular full-time hired farm workers, and in 1954 it was extended to all farm workers who earned $100 or more in cash from a single employer during a given year. Two important changes were made in 1956: (1) workers who were paid $150 during a calendar year by a single employer, or who were employed for twenty days or more during a year by a single employer, were entitled to receive social security benefits; (2) crew leaders were considered to be employers whenever they were responsible for supplying the labor and paying the workers (U.S. Congress, Senate, Committee on Labor and Public Welfare 1960:64).

In 1966 an important change in the social legislation for farm workers was brought about through amendments to the Fair Labor Standards Act. The federal minimum wage was extended to those farm workers who worked on farms where 500 or more man-days of hired farm labor were used in a calendar quarter. This amendment only covered about 535,000 farm workers and 30,700 farms, which amounted to a little more than 2 percent of all farms with hired farm workers (*Manpower Report of the President* 1971: 125). Although the coverage was very limited and the wage standard maintained was far below that of nonfarm workers,[7] extending a minimum wage to a group of farm workers was an important step towards extending to farm workers the rights that other workers had enjoyed since the 1930s. In 1974 the Fair Labor Standards Act was amended again because the 1966 amendments had left a great discrepancy between the earnings of farm workers and nonfarm workers; these amendments were incorporated into the Federal Wage-Hour Law, which provided for a gradual correction of this discrepancy, as Table 2.2 shows.

Table 2.2. *Federal Minimum Hourly Wage Rates*

Minimum wage rate	Date effective				
	1 May 1974	1 January 1975	1 January 1976	1 January 1977	1 January 1978
Agriculture	$1.60	$1.80	$2.00	$2.20	$2.30
Industry	$2.00	$2.10	$2.30	$2.30	$2.30

Source: Fisher 1974:1.

Again, the law covered only those farm workers who worked for employers who had used more than 500 man-days of agricultural work in any calendar quarter of the preceding calendar year (Fisher 1974:1). Further amendments were made to the Fair Labor Standards Act in 1977 and resulted in an increase of the minimum wage to $2.65 per hour on 1 January 1978, to $2.90 per hour on 1 January 1979, and to $3.10 on 1 January 1980; it also provides for a raise to $3.35 as of 1 January 1981. The amendments made no distinction between farm and nonfarm work, and the rates were minimum wage rates which applied to both the farm and the nonfarm workers who were covered (see Elder 1978:9-11).

Although farm workers were excluded from the National Labor Relations Act, they have managed to gain some rights and benefits through laws passed during the 1970s. Responding to the increasing impact of collective bargaining, especially on large corporate farms, several states (Idaho, Kansas, Arizona, and California) have passed laws regulating farm labor relations, while others (Wisconsin and Hawaii) have provided coverage to farm workers under general statutes which regulate labor relations. The California Agricultural Labor Relations Act has come to be quite well known because of the publicity surrounding its enactment in 1975. Thanks to it, farm workers in California may freely choose the union which is to represent their interests when they are bargaining with employers. Furthermore, the act is designed to maximize the opportunities for seasonal workers to participate in union elections by shortening the period between filing an election petition and voting to only a few days. This aspect of the act is unique: none of the acts passed by the other three states includes similar provisions (for a comparison of the four laws see Koziara 1977: 14-18).

As far as migratory farm workers in particular are concerned, some legislation aimed specifically at providing better protection for them was also enacted during the 1960s and 1970s. Under the Migrant Health Act of 1962, grants were given to government-financed and nonprofit agencies to pay part of the costs of health services for migratory farm workers and their families. In 1963 the Farm Labor Contractor Registration Act, designed by the government to protect (primarily migratory) farm workers from the crew leaders' unscrupulous practices, was enacted. It required that crew leaders register at a government office and secure licenses, that vehicles used for transporting migratory farm workers meet the standards of the Interstate Commerce Commission, and that crew leaders give accurate information on prospective jobs, wage rates, and working conditions; it also stated that the crew leaders' licenses will be revoked if dishonest practices were ascertained. The Economic Opportunity Act of 1964 provided for resources which may be allocated to programs for improving the housing, sanitation, education, and child care for migratory farm workers and their families. In 1974 the Farm Labor Contractor Registration Act was amended: coverage was broadened, the employer's responsibilities were increased, certain violations became criminal offenses, and the maximum fines to be paid for such violations were increased (Fisher

1975:1). But as with all legislation dealing with migratory farm workers, effective control remained — and still remains — a serious problem (U.S. Congress, Senate, Committee on Labor and Public Welfare 1960:65; Friedland and Nelkin 1971:261-262).

Although some significant laws aimed at protecting farm workers have been passed, especially during the 1960s, many more are urgently needed if farm workers are to attain a socioeconomic position comparable to that of industrial workers. Far too often, when farm workers have been included in social legislation, the coverage has been too limited and too many farm workers have simply been excluded.

The idyllic picture of the farmer, his family, and the farmhand working together as a united team has had considerable influence on employer-employee relations in agriculture in the United States (Schwartz 1945:4). Because it was assumed that good personal relations existed between those involved in agriculture, regulation of their labor relations has been deemed unnecessary. However, the history of the farm workers in the United States shows that the situation of most farm workers could in fact hardly be described as idyllic: the farm worker is generally in an extremely disadvantageous position compared to the industrial worker.

The question is, *how* did the farm worker get into this position? One event which was extremely instrumental in creating this situation was the exclusion of farm workers from the National Labor Relations Act, which meant that farm workers were denied the right to organize into unions and bargain collectively. Prevented by law from organizing, the farm worker was quite unable to deal with the powerful and well-organized farm employers because the law did not, and still does not, require these employers — as it does industrial employers — to discuss and negotiate wage rates and other working conditions with their workers. The fact is that when employers harass farm workers who are trying to organize themselves into a union, they actually have the law on their side in most states! Farm employers are also well armed with justifications for their objections to social legislation aimed at benefiting the workers. The argument they most often use is that agriculture is very different from other industries, and weather conditions and perishable crops make farming, especially growing fruit and vegetables, a very risky undertaking. They claim that the cost-price squeeze makes it impossible to increase the cost of labor either through paying higher wages or through paying the higher costs that would result from better social legislation. If labor costs were to get too high, they say, harvesting would become unprofitable and crops would be allowed to rot in the fields, thus endangering the adequate supply of food in the United States. The final result has been that time and again, when social legislation is enacted, the interests of the farm workers are brushed aside in order to make room for the interests of the farm employers. The agricultural employers' lobbies in Congress have played a significant role in creating and maintaining this situation (see page 52).

Another reason for the farm workers' lack of success in forwarding their interests through social legislation is their own vulnerability. Harvesting crops is often the only way they can earn a living. No harvest work means no money, and this makes it very difficult for the workers to cooperate in organizing strikes for better working conditions. The strikes, once they have been organized, are seldom successful: in Texas and California, for example, cheap Mexican labor can easily be imported to operate as a strikebreaking force (see the next section). An unsuccessful strike deters, rather than stimulates, unionization. The relative lack of education among workers is a further drawback in attempts to unionize, as are the migratory movements of a considerable number of farm workers and the relative isolation of the nonmigratory farm workers, who often work on farms located far out in the country.

3. FOREIGN FARM WORKERS IN THE UNITED STATES

The position of the farm workers in the United States cannot be fully understood unless the role of the foreign farm worker is explained. This is as true now as it has been over the past two hundred years of American history. Foreign laborers have always tilled the soil owned by Americans — or rather by other foreigners, or offspring of foreigners who happened to have migrated to the United States several years or generations earlier.

3.1. *Importing and Exploiting Ethnic Groups in Farm Labor: 1776 through the Depression*

In 1776, when the American colonies declared their independence from Britain, large numbers of blacks were being imported from Africa and sold as slaves. This had been going on for years. In the South the plantation system had come to depend completely on slave labor: the Southerners had developed their own culture and way of life, based on the relationship of master to slave. In the

North, in the meantime, an expansive capitalistic industrial development had taken place in which slavery had gradually been abolished.[8] In 1865, with the end of the Civil War and the ratification of the Thirteenth Amendment to the Constitution, slavery was abolished throughout the United States.

The end of slavery did not mean that from then on, workers would not be brought from other countries to fill the demand for cheap agricultural workers. The first foreign workers to be imported in large numbers were the Chinese, who comprised the main group of cheap workers during the 1870s. They were particularly numerous on the West Coast, and history explains why. In 1850, after about twenty years of ferocious squabbling between the pro- and the anti-slavery factions in the United States, California was allowed to enter the Union as a "free" state (i.e., one in which slavery was prohibited). However, in order to develop California's enormous agricultural potential, a large supply of farm labor was needed. Because the landowners could not own slaves, they were forced to find another solution to their labor problems and turned to bringing in Chinese workers to fill the labor vacuum.[9]

Efforts to incorporate a system of indentured labor into the legal code failed, but the search for a labor supply which would be specialized to the needs of California agriculture continued. What was not possible legally could be roughly duplicated socially. Neither slavery nor indenture could be introduced as a legal system, but its social equivalent was found in the employment of alien labor rendered occupationally immobile by color, language, and custom, and organized into gangs under "boss men" or contractors, who spoke both languages and could move between both cultures. (Fisher 1953:21)

The Chinese worked for very low wages and began to be a threat to the American farm workers. The labor organizations which existed at that time started to agitate against them, and in 1882 two federal immigration laws were passed: the Chinese Exclusion Act and the first general Immigration Law. The Chinese Exclusion Act effectively decreased the number of Chinese immigrating to the United States (Husband 1926:168), but did not apply to other Oriental groups. The Immigration Law was more selective than restrictive: it only denied admittance to foreign lunatics, convicts, and other persons who were likely to become a burden to the government. This meant that healthy, non-Chinese workers had no difficulties in entering the United States. The result was that the gap left by the Chinese was filled by Japanese workers, who were well organized and often improved their positions by becoming landowners themselves. But because the Japanese workers preferred to work for Japanese employers, and because a "Gentlemen's Agreement" was reached between the governments of Japan and the United States to restrict the entry of new workers, a need for extra hands during the harvest season was soon felt again.

Around the turn of the century, Mexicans began crossing the border; they were attracted by high wages (at least in comparison to the wages in their own country) and were often contracted and transported by private employment agencies. At the same time, another group of foreign workers, the Philippinos, entered the agricultural labor market in the United States. Unlike the Mexicans, they were well organized, worked in groups, and managed to arrange strikes and demand higher wages.

Another, more diverse group of foreigners also joined the farm work force during this period: these were the predominantly European, unskilled immigrants who had just arrived in the United States and worked or lived in or near the big cities. Unlike the foreign workers described above, who were brought to the United States temporarily to do farm work and usually were imported under government contracts or by private growers or employment agencies, these people had no plans to return to their native countries and no contracts. They were often the first to be fired when times were bad, in which case the seasonal jobs available in the fruit and vegetable gardens near the big cities offered a welcome supplement to their families' incomes. At the end of the nineteenth century, first Irish and German immigrants, then French Canadians, Poles, and Italians were employed in the market gardens around Boston. Many of the Slavic immigrants who worked in the steel industry did farm work in the lakeshore fruit and vegetable area in Ohio. Italians from Philadelphia usually worked on the berry and vegetable farms in southern New Jersey and Delaware during the summer weeks: the mothers and children came first, and the fathers joined them when they became unemployed. Because these immigrants usually did not speak English, a labor contractor or *padrone* functioned as a middleman, and the employers, who employed vast numbers of workers, gladly left all the labor relations problems to these contractors (Schwartz 1945:38-39). This arrangement of course invited corruption and cheating because the new immigrants were often considerably disadvantaged not only by the language barrier but also by other cultural barriers.

In 1917 a new Immigration Law was passed to restrict the influx of unskilled immigrants from Europe. This law threatened to disrupt the influx of cheap Mexican labor, but as a result of the outbreak of World War I the restrictive rules were lifted, and Mexicans were permitted entry into the United States for temporary employment. During the 1920s one million Mexicans were absorbed into American society.

Of all the foreign workers who came to the United States to do farm labor, the Mexicans were considered by the employers to be the most desirable, because they generally did not strike or demand higher wages. As the manager of the Agricultural Department of the Los Angeles Chamber of Commerce said in 1929: "No labor that has ever come to the United States is more satisfactory under righteous treatment [than the Mexican]. He is the result of years of servitude, has always looked upon his employer as his patrón, and upon himself as part of the establishment." (Shotwell 1961:73)

The Immigration Act of 1924 further regulated immigration into the United States by establishing a system based on the national origins of the American people. Under this system a quota was established for each country outside the Western Hemisphere, taking the national origins of the United States population in 1890 as a basis. Because vast numbers of immigrants from the countries in northern and western Europe had immigrated to the United States during the nineteenth century, large quotas were assigned to these countries (see Warren 1977:36-41).

During the Depression years, the United States experienced a tremendous process of internal migration. When the dustbowl refugees from Arkansas and Oklahoma moved to California, job opportunities for the one million Mexicans who had crossed the border decreased, and about half of these workers returned to their country (Shotwell 1961:74). This large-scale movement of the poor and jobless has been documented extensively (see, for instance, Webb 1935; 1937; Webb and Brown 1938; Brown and Cassmore 1939; Lively and Taeuber 1939).

Up to the outbreak of World War II this system of quotas, together with further restrictions made by the United States after 1924, proved to be quite successful in limiting the influx of unskilled foreign workers.

World War II created an agricultural labor shortage because the domestic agricultural workers were absorbed by better-paid jobs in the military services and the defense industry. The farm employers did not increase wages to compete with industry; instead, they put pressure on the government to allow the importation of cheap foreign labor, and the government gave in. In 1942 the governments of the United States and Mexico signed an agreement permitting Mexican nationals to come to the United States to do farm work. Thereafter, similar agreements were negotiated with the governments of, for instance, Jamaica, the Bahamas, Canada, and British Honduras (Shotwell 1961: 74).

It is interesting to note that although Puerto Rican workers were readily

331.544   T368n
C.1

available, they were not brought to the mainland in this emergency situation. The main reason seems to be that the employers considered them to be less desirable because they had the same rights as American citizens. The president of a Florida employers' association described this drawback to the Secretary of Agriculture as follows:

The vast difference between the Bahama Island labor and the domestic, including Puerto Rican, is that labor transported from the Bahama Islands can be diverted and sent home if it does not work, which cannot be done in the instance of labor from domestic United States or Puerto Rico. (Shotwell 1961:75)

3.2. *Regulating Farm Labor: World War II and Thereafter*

In the years following World War II, the close relationship between the demand for cheap labor in agriculture and the (legal or illegal) immigration of foreign workers continued to be significant. Government policies, quotas, and other restrictions were only one part of the story of immigration; concern about the increasing number of illegal immigrants who were entering the United States was another. Exactly how many "undocumented aliens" (as these immigrants are called) are presently residing in the United States is not known, but the estimates range from two to twelve million (Office of the White House Press Secretary, 4 August 1977; quoted in Warren 1977:41). It seems quite apparent that most of the undocumented aliens are Mexicans: the long border with Mexico makes it fairly easy to enter the United States unnoticed, and agricultural (and some nonagricultural) employers in the United States eagerly await these illegal − and thus cheap − workers. Furthermore, these Mexicans (called "wetbacks" because they must swim across the Rio Grande River to cross the border) are known for their docility and are therefore very welcome seasonal workers, especially in California and Texas.

At the end of the war, the United States government wanted to terminate the emergency program it had set up in order to import farm workers, but this of course was against the wishes of the agricultural employers. As a result, a prolonged conflict developed between, on the one hand, the employers and employer organizations and, on the other, organized labor and several citizens' groups that were concerned about the living and working conditions of the farm workers and their families. For lack of an adequate policy to deal with immigration, the situation at the Mexican border became uncontrollable and chaotic. The United States government had functioned as the prime contractor between 1942 and 1947, subletting contracts for Mexican laborers to individual farm employers, but from 1948 onwards it played a less direct role: the importation of Mexican workers and labor relations between workers and employers were determined by intergovernmentally negotiated individual work contracts. This situation lasted until 1964, and although the Mexican and United States governments tried to regulate the stream of Mexican farm workers who crossed the border during this period, effective control of legal and illegal immigration on the 1600-mile border proved to be virtually impossible. From 1947 to 1954, many more wetbacks than braceros (Mexican workers who enter the United States under contract) entered the country: in fact in 1951, United States immigration officials discovered and deported approximately half a million wetbacks, while only 191,000 braceros were working in the United States (Shotwell 1961:75-76; only the wetbacks who were deported were counted; many others undoubtedly managed to evade deportation).

In 1951 the importation of Mexican workers was put under the jurisdiction of a new law, called Public Law 78, which was enacted as a temporary measure in response to the pressure of labor shortages caused by the Korean War. This law was intended to ensure that the importation of these workers would not be disadvantageous to American farm workers. Employers were only allowed to apply for Mexican workers if they could prove that there was a shortage of domestic workers, and if the use of Mexican workers would have no adverse effect on the wages and other working conditions of the American farm workers. As it turned out, the employers and employer organizations were very imaginative in finding ways to evade the law, and the government seemed willing to cooperate with them. The wages offered by the employers were often so low that the American workers refused to apply for the work, with the result that the shortage of labor which the law required was created and requests for braceros could be made and were granted by the government (*Migratory Labor in American Agriculture* 1951:42-46, 56-64; National Advisory Committee on Farm Labor 1967:34). The presence of braceros in the United States had a bad effect not only on wage rates but also on other working conditions of the domestic farm workers. At the same time, the Mexicans' working conditions did not meet the standards that were negotiated by the Mexican government:

Since braceros left their families in Mexico, barrack housing for single male workers largely replaced the family housing needed by U.S. workers. Working conditions for the imported workers resembled those of slave labor. The Mexican government, negotiating in behalf of its workers, insisted on minimum standards covering wages, food, shelter, medical services, and the like. But once the workers were in the United States, isolated by language and culture, and unfamiliar with their surroundings, they were unable to present grievances effectively; the Mexicans also knew that if they complained they would be deported. Thus the protections negotiated for them — ironically, the protections systematically denied American workers — were seldom enforced. (National Advisory Committee on Farm Labor 1967:35)

Together with the regulations for importing Mexican workers provided under Public Law 78, the Immigration and Nationality Act of 1952 allowed temporary visas to be issued to foreign workers for employment in agriculture in the United States if and when domestic workers were not available, as stated in Section H-2 (also known as Public Law 414). The H-2 program required that a contract be arranged between an employer in the United States and the immigrant worker before a visa could be granted. Under this program, approximately 20,000 foreign agricultural workers have entered the United States yearly with temporary visas. The majority of the workers with such visas were — and still are — West Indian sugarcane cutters and fruit harvesters who work in Florida or in other eastern states (see "The New Braceros" 1977). The H-2 program has resulted in the institutionalization of the legal use of cheap foreign labor and thus has weakened the bargaining position of the domestic farm workers.

Again and again, organized labor has accused the United States government of giving in to pressure from the employers and helping them find cheap foreign workers. Meanwhile, attempts by domestic farm workers to organize strikes for better working conditions have usually been undercut by Mexicans and other foreign workers who were glad to take over the strikers' jobs. This surplus of readily available cheap labor has effectively prevented any improvement in the working conditions of all farm laborers. The employers, on the other hand, have insisted — and to this day they still insist — on both the special character of agriculture, which they claim makes wage raises impossible, and on the special problems involved in marketing their produce, which require quick action and a sufficient labor supply at the right time. In 1964 Congress finally came under such mounting pressure from labor, religious, and civic organizations to terminate the importation program that enough support could be mustered to have Public Law 78 abolished on 31 December of that year (National Advisory Committee on Farm Labor 1967:43). This, however, did not put an end to the stream of Mexicans who were entering the United States illegally.

The enactment of a new Immigration Act in 1965 marked a major change in the national immigration policy. The quota system based on the national origins of the American population was abolished and substituted by a system that restricted the number of immigrants from each country each year to 20,000, with an overall restriction of a total of 170,000 for the countries outside the Western hemisphere. Furthermore, immigration from countries in the Western hemisphere was restricted for the first time, with a total of 120,000 immigrants being allowed each year. The act also gave more preference to immigrants with close relatives who were American citizens and to direct relatives of resident aliens. Later, on 1 January 1977, the restriction allowing 20,000 immigrants per country, which since 1965 had applied to all countries outside the Western hemisphere, was applied to countries in the Western hemisphere as well. The overall result of the policy change made in 1965 was a sharp decline in immigration from Europe and Canada, while immigration from Asia and Mexico showed a considerable increase (Warren 1977:37).

During the summer of 1973, the press again focused its attention on the corrupt and chaotic situation at the Mexican border (see, for instance, *Newsweek*, 23 July 1973; and the *New York Times*, 4 and 21 May 1973). A team of investigators from the Department of Justice collected evidence of widespread corruption in the branches of the Immigration and Naturalization Service located in the southwestern part of the United States (Walsh 1973). These findings showed that immigration officials had cooperated in smuggling aliens into the United States, in selling entry documents, and in supplying illegal Mexican laborers to large ranches in return for hunting privileges and cash payments. The following statement illustrates how unfairly the Mexican farm workers were treated:

It was time for one of the big Texas ranchers to harvest a crop. He hired a crew of illegal aliens, and notified the chief of that particular Border Patrol sector of his action. The chief patrol agent saw to it that the ranch was not raided during the harvest.

When the crop was in, the rancher notified the sector chief and, before the Mexicans were paid, the patrol arrested them and sent them back across the border. The rancher got his crop out of the field, the chief patrol agent got year-round hunting rights on the ranch, and the Mexicans got nothing. (Walsh 1973:20)

There was no doubt that the Mexicans would come back because, as one Mexican farm worker put it, "Since farming here is very difficult, jobs are scarce and the pay in the United States is much higher than for the same work in Mexico." (*New York Times*, 4 May 1973)

The immigration officials who are in charge of deporting the illegal immigrants have often complained about the lack of resources to do the job effectively: "They should either give us the tools we need to really get rid of the aliens," said Los Angeles deportation officer Noel Doran, "or admit that we want them in the U.S. as slave labor." (*Newsweek*, 23 July 1973:24).

The job of the United States immigration officers is indeed not an easy one: in 1976 alone, the Immigration and Naturalization Service located 875,915 deportable aliens, which was an increase of 14 percent compared to 1975. The Carter Administration has recently considered some highly controversial measures for solving the problem of these illegal workers, including sanctions against the employers, intensification of the measures preventing entry, and limited amnesty for undocumented aliens already living in the United States (Warren 1977:39-40; "Immigration, Carter's Anti-Labor Plan" 1977). Enforcing these measures will not be easy: the second measure, for example, will (as mentioned above) certainly run into difficulties because effective control of the long border between Mexico and the United States is almost impossible. Nonetheless, the employers are concerned that the Carter Administration's plans will limit their access to cheap foreign labor and they have therefore started to put increasing pressure on the government for expansion of the program for importing foreign workers provided for by Section H-2 (Public Law 414; see "The New Braceros" 1977:4-9). The agricultural employers' growing concern can easily be explained by the diverse aspects of the agribusiness and by the kind of work that has to be done. The problem is that while mechanization has taken over a large amount of the work in agriculture, the employers are still completely dependent on a cheap, docile labor force in the peak periods of the harvest. This is in part because machines are fallible: sugarcane cutters, for example, have a tendency to sink into the mud and uproot the stalks, and apple shakers can "pick" apples off a tree very quickly but can also bruise the apples badly. Illegal migratory workers are more than willing to do such heavy, dirty work for extremely low wages and will usually not threaten to strike at crucial moments in the harvest season. When the illegal foreigners become less readily available, employers will try to find foreign contract workers, whom they prefer to domestic workers because they have the same opportunities for intimidation with foreign contract workers as they have with illegal foreigners. It is the employers and the employers' organizations who determine the terms of the foreign worker contracts: the worker has no say. Furthermore, since the employers arrange the contracts with individual foreign workers, they can select only the youngest and most able workers and can conveniently bypass workers with a background of political and/or union activities. The countries from which these workers are imported are trying to solve their own unemployment problems by exporting contract workers to the United States, and they are hardly in a position to demand good conditions for their workers. Once the foreign contract workers are in the fields, they are under the complete control of the employers: those who protest against the living and working conditions are threatened with deportation; if they are deported their names are put on a blacklist, which makes it very unlikely that they will ever be contracted to work in the United States again. Given these circumstances, it is quite understandable that the employers continue to lobby for the expansion of the H-2 program.[10]

The situation at the Mexican border is undoubtedly a unique one: on one side of the border is a poor, underdeveloped, agricultural country with tremendous employment problems; on the other side is an affluent, developed country which needs large numbers of farm workers at certain times during the year. The extremely chaotic and uncontrollable immigration of Mexican workers has developed out of this discrepancy. The situation is quite different on the East Coast: there, the nature of the borders makes entrance by illegal foreigners much more difficult, and illegal foreign workers therefore play a far less significant role in farm work in this region. It is the foreign contract worker, and not the illegal worker, who has a depressing effect on the wages and other working conditions of farm workers in the East.

4. THE EAST COAST STREAM OF MIGRATORY FARM WORKERS

Having discussed the role which foreign farm workers have played — and continue to play — in farm work in the United States, let us focus on the geographic mobility of the migratory farm workers and examine in particular the patterns of migration on the East Coast. To do this we must look into the history of the East Coast migratory stream, the backgrounds of the people involved, the operation of the migratory system, and the working and living conditions of the workers.

4.1. Migratory Patterns in the United States

The United States has always been a country of migrants. Great numbers of people from all over the world have left their own countries for various reasons and have migrated to the land of freedom and opportunity. The chances of building a better future seemed endless, and once these migrants had reached the United States they generally did not stop traveling, but continued to move westward. If a farmer ran into difficulties in one place, he could move elsewhere and try again. Land was available, abundant, and cheap. The nature of farming was such that it required — as it does today — extra hands during certain stages of the production process. At that time it was not always easy to find the necessary extra farm workers because there were ample opportunities for people to buy their own land and work on it, and this made them reluctant to till the soil for others. If they did so, it was usually only to accumulate the necessary capital and experience to start farms of their own. Farming in the United States was therefore initially rather small-scale, except in the South where a plantation system based on slave labor had developed. As the American frontier was pushed farther and farther westward, cheap, unexploited land became less easily available, and the number of farm workers that could be hired began to increase.

The size of the country and the climatological differences between the various regions enable farmers to grow different crops in different parts of the country and to have the same crops ready for harvesting in the different parts of the country at different times of the year. A very meager living can be earned by providing the extra pairs of hands which are temporarily needed during the labor-intensive stages of agricultural production. The migratory farm workers do this work: in order to remain employed, they must leave home temporarily and travel to follow the crops.

Most of the workers have a home base in the South, where they spend the winter. They start moving northwards in the spring and return to their home base in the autumn. Three main streams of migratory farm worker movement can be distinguished in the United States: the West Coast stream, the mid-continent stream, and the East Coast or eastern seaboard stream. Figure 2.1 clearly shows that the state which supplies the largest number of migratory farm workers is Texas. Workers based there usually travel to the Midwest and the West Coast, but some may branch off to Florida and move into the East Coast stream.[11]

4.2. Development of the East Coast Stream

Exactly when migratory farm workers started moving up and down the East

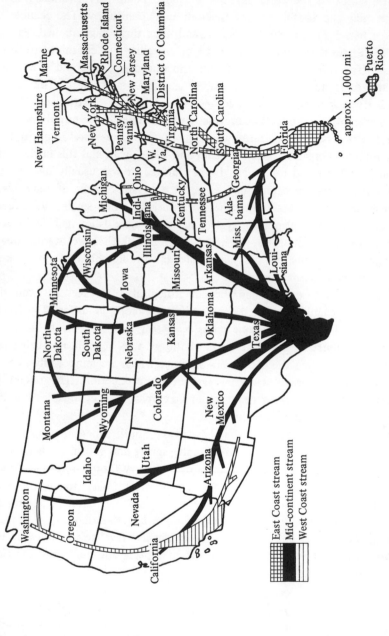

Figure 2.1. *Migratory Farm Workers: the Three Main Streams of Movement*

East Coast stream
Mid-continent stream
West Coast stream

Source: Based on a map prepared by the U.S. Department of Labor, Bureau of Employment Security, in 1961 and published in "Farm Workers: a Reprint from the 1966 Manpower Report" (U.S. Department of Labor, Manpower Administration, Washington, D.C.), p. 119.

Coast is not known. Although farming in the United States was generally on a rather small scale (except in the South, as mentioned above), nonlocal labor was employed even before 1900. In 1901 the Industrial Commission reported that blacks from the South were working on farms in the New England states: "For years prior to 1901, Negroes were imported each season by steamers from Norfolk to Rhode Island to work in the fruit and vegetable fields." (McWilliams 1942:168) A New Jersey agricultural employer testified before the Commission that "We depend almost wholly on Southern labor...in the fruit, berry, and garden-truck districts, it is mainly colored labor, coming from the South, and returning when the crops are gathered." (McWilliams 1942:168)

In the South, the sharecropper and tenant systems were developed on the plantations after slavery was abolished. The presence of the tenants' and share-croppers' wives and children guaranteed an extra supply of labor during the crucial cotton-chopping and cotton-picking period (Schwartz 1945:18). During the 1930s the economic situation, as well as the drought and the decline in cotton production, forced many of these people to leave the land they had worked on for generations and try to make a living elsewhere. While this was happening, an important government plan was implemented in the south-eastern part of Florida: a federal drainage project reclaimed the mucklands in Florida and transformed this swampy area into a fertile winter garden (McWilliams 1942:168). This project created opportunities for more or less year-round employment for migratory farm workers on the East Coast. Such opportunities had become increasingly scarce, as mechanization and special-ization had greatly reduced the need for year-round farm labor, but had in-creased the demand for workers during certain short periods of the year (sec-tion 1 of this chapter). Thus the sharecroppers and tenants who had been forced to leave their farms were able to find employment throughout the year in the migratory stream which moved up and down the East Coast. In the winter (from January to May), large numbers of workers could find work in, for example, the fruit and vegetable areas in Florida, and from May to September/October work was available in the states farther North.

4.3. The People Involved

Any attempt to estimate the number of workers who are involved in the yearly migrations up and down the East Coast is a kind of guessing game. Mention was made in 1949 of 58,000 workers (Metzler 1955:5), and in 1958 it was reported (by Pollitt and Levine in U.S. Congress, Senate, Committee on Labor and Public Welfare 1960:8) that 50,000 blacks left Florida for the summer to work in the northern states and nearly 20,000 persons from Mississippi, Georgia, Arkansas, Missouri, and South Carolina joined this migratory stream. The *Farm Labor Fact Book* (U.S. Department of Labor 1959:126) estimated that 50,000 workers were involved each year in migration on the East Coast and acknowledged that the exact number was not known. Another source (Friedland and Nelkin 1971:3) claimed that some 50,000 people traveled up and down the eastern seaboard. Estimates based on the data collected for the unemployment insurance survey made in 1970 showed a total of about 66,000 migratory workers on the East Coast (Bauder 1976a:35). The discrepancies among these figures are largely due to the fact that the mobility of migratory farm workers makes them so elusive that it is extremely difficult to find out exactly how many workers there actually are.

There is a great variety among the people who move up and down the East Coast doing farm work, but the black migratory farm workers comprise the dominant group. This is not surprising, for these blacks are the descendants of the slaves who later became the sharecroppers and tenants of the South. Their social and ethnic background makes them ill-equipped to find steady employment in a quickly modernizing society in which education, training, and a white skin are the keys to a successful career; they have therefore had to resort to work in the lowest paid occupational categories.

In the years immediately following the World War II, Puerto Ricans began to join in the East Coast stream:

Farmers searching for new sources of labor found that the tapering off of the sugarcane harvest in Puerto Rico coincided with their need for workers. The first intermediaries between the farmers and the workers were private, fee-charging agencies and labor contractors who appeared on the scene to capitalize on this new-found opportunity. In these first years, the private agents ran the program exclusively in their own interests. They charged the employer for securing a worker; they charged the worker for getting him a job; they acted as travel agents and collected a commission on tickets sold to the workers. (U.S. Congress, Senate, Committee on Labor and Public Welfare 1960:9)

The Puerto Ricans soon discovered that the working conditions of the migratory farm workers in the United States were very different from those mentioned in the attractive job descriptions provided by the private recruiting agencies. In 1948 the Puerto Rican government tried to put an end to the exploitation of its workers employed on the mainland by passing legislation that prohibited the recruitment of farm labor unless it was arranged through the Puerto Rican Employment Service. In order to bring farm workers to the mainland, employers were required to sign agreements with the Puerto Rican workers which were arranged through the Puerto Rican government and guaranteed certain minimum standards for work opportunities, pay, and housing. These contract workers were covered by old-age and survivors' insurance and a group insurance plan that paid for hospitalization, surgical and medical care, and also provided temporary disability and death benefits (U.S. Department of Labor 1959:136-137; U.S. Congress, Senate, Committee on Labor and Public Welfare 1960:9). Thanks to these guaranteed minimum standards, as far as the conditions written into their contracts are concerned, the Puerto Ricans are now generally better off than other domestic workers in terms of rights and benefits. However, their situation is in fact just as dismal as that of the other migratory workers (see "Puerto Ricans on Contract" 1977).

At present the Puerto Rican contract program is regulated under Public Law 87, which was passed in 1962 and gives the Puerto Rican Secretary of Labor the authority to establish the minimum requirements which are to be met by all employers outside Puerto Rico. Under this law the Puerto Rican Secretary of Labor annually negotiates the terms of the standardized "Agricultural Agreement between Employers and Puerto Rican Agricultural Workers" with employers in the United States. The Puerto Rican workers have no say at all in these negotiations, and in this sense their position is as bad as that of the other foreign workers from the West Indies (Jamaica or the Bahamas, for instance). The employers generally have all the advantages: they determine in large part the conditions of the contract and are able to select the workers they want, easily bypassing the others (see page 30). The only advantage the Puerto Ricans have over other foreign workers is that they are United States citizens and consequently cannot be deported.

In negotiating standardized contracts with employers in the United States, the Puerto Rican government is in the same position as the governments of other West Indian countries and of Mexico. The high unemployment rate in their countries forces them to export contract workers to the United States in order to curb social unrest. Employers are well aware of the weak negotiating position of these governments and skillfully exploit it (see "Puerto Ricans on Contract" 1977). Experience has shown that many regulations are often violated and that the foreign authorities lack the means and the will to enforce them.

Despite this, the Puerto Rican contract workers are less docile than other foreign contract workers: they have organized strikes, attempted to unionize, and in certain cases of gross violations of the contracts they have filed lawsuits against the employers. This has made the employers increasingly reluctant to employ Puerto Rican workers under government contracts. Between 1967 and 1969 more than 21,000 Puerto Ricans were brought to the United States under contract each year, but since then the numbers have declined steadily: between 1970 and 1975 an average of only about 12,000 workers came to the United States, and between 1975 and 1977 the average was only about 5,000 ("Puerto Ricans on Contract" 1977:19).

In addition to the Puerto Ricans who come to the United States under government contracts, there are others who are illegally imported by the employers. All the terms of employment for these workers are established by the employers exclusively. Thousands of Puerto Ricans also come to the United States on their own, without contracts. Estimates of the total number of Puerto Rican workers entering the United States each year to do migratory farm work range from 60,000 to 200,000 ("Puerto Ricans on Contract" 1977:19).

Besides the blacks and Puerto Ricans, the East Coast migratory stream comprises several other smaller groups, the largest of which is the Mexicans. Although most of the Mexican workers in the United States originally worked almost exclusively in the West Coast and mid-continent streams, some have also found their way to the East Coast. They are probably so-called "Texas-Mexicans" — that is, American citizens of Mexican or other Latin American descent whose home base is in Texas (*Migratory Labor in American Agriculture* 1951:2; U.S. Congress, Senate, Committee on Labor and Public Welfare 1960:9). White workers, workers from Jamaica and the Bahamas, American Indians, and a few Canadians are also found in the East Coast migratory stream.

4.4. *Operation of the Migratory System*

During the winter months, farm work is available in the vegetable, fruit, and sugarcane areas in Florida. While the tourists are crowding the beaches and other resort areas, the migratory farm workers are concentrated in the southeastern part of Florida around Lake Okeechobee and along Route 441. Most of the work they do is arranged on a daily basis. Events in the town of Belle Glade serve as an example. Each winter morning, the central square is the site of bustling activity: workers, labor contractors, buses, and trucks gather early and arrangements are made for the day's work. The contractor functions as a middleman in the daily recruitment process, which is called the "day haul": he picks out the workers he wants to do the job, negotiates the wages, and ensures that the employer will have enough workers in the fields for that day (U.S. Department of Labor 1962). Job security is unknown in this kind of employment, and wages are offered on a "take it or leave it" basis.

By May most of the farm work in Florida has been done. Jobs become scarce and the migratory farm workers head northward. Some workers travel on their own, while others join crews. The workers may know the crew leader they join up with,[12] or they may simply join a crew that happens to pass through their town on its way North. Their motivations for joining the migratory stream are varied:

There are some who see the trip as a way to expand their horizons. Some are sucked into the system for the first time, believing the extravagant promises made by the crew leader. Others are restless and prefer the loose schedules of migrant work to the routine of more regular employment. Many are unable to hold other types of jobs. Some are physically handicapped, others are alcoholics or have jail records. Most have no alternative. They must subsist during the summer when there is no work in Florida. Most claim that their decision to come on the season was made spontaneously because the opportunity presented itself at a convenient moment. (Friedland and Nelkin 1971:20)

The decision to go North may be taken at the last moment and is often quite casual and unplanned (Friedland and Nelkin 1971:19). Most workers have no illusions about what they are getting into: they move northwards out of economic necessity. A few set out with a specific goal in mind, such as buying a car, but saving to buy anything is very difficult in the labor camps. As the season progresses, it becomes increasingly difficult to "break even," and dreams of saving to buy a car or anything else vanish into thin air (Friedland and Nelkin 1971:186-191).

While recruitment may be a casual affair for the worker, planning ahead is important for the employer, who must have enough workers at precisely the right time — and the right time for certain crops is sometimes no more than a week or two. The Farm Labor Services in each state assist employers with this planning. These agencies were established in 1933 under the Wagner-Peyser Act as part of the Bureau of Employment and Security and were intended to bring workers and employers together when there were labor shortages or surpluses. Through a system of labor clearance, the agencies act as intermediaries between the workers and employers and coordinate — usually at the employer's request — the supply of and demand for farm labor in cooperation between the states.

During World War II a shortage of workers who could harvest the crops developed and caused strong competition among the employers for the available workers. While this situation was to the advantage of the workers, it certainly was not what the employers wanted, and in 1944 the employers and the Farm Labor Services in ten East Coast states decided to work together to make the best possible use of the available workers. Since then, these states have cooperated in the following way: each year, before the harvest season starts, an assessment is made by each state of the number of farm workers that are needed. The states which will need a supply of out-of-state labor during the summer and fall send representatives to Florida who meet with the crew leaders. With the assistance of the Farm Labor Services and on the basis of the demand for labor, plans are worked out for each crew or group of workers in order to ensure continuous employment during the season. This voluntary scheduling procedure has spread to other states and has come to be called the Annual Worker Plan.

Occasionally the demands for labor overlap: for example, workers may be badly needed in the northern states while harvesting is still going on in Florida. The states that work together on the East Coast have an agreement that prohibits the recruitment of workers before the peak season in Florida is over. Local employment offices in Florida decide when the crews which have committed themselves to jobs in Florida may be released to do work in other states (Metzler 1955:5-7; U.S. Department of Labor 1959:102-104, 118-121).

In Florida the number of farm workers hired by each agricultural employer is relatively large: the 1970 unemployment insurance survey (Bauder *et al.* 1976) showed that an estimated average of sixty-five workers were hired per employer in Florida, fifty-four of which were seasonal. In Ohio and the mid-Atlantic states (New York, Pennsylvania, New Jersey, Delaware, Maryland, and West Virginia), the employers were estimated to have hired an average of nine to ten workers, seven to eight of whom were seasonal. In the New England states (Connecticut, Massachusetts, Rhode Island, Vermont, New Hampshire and Maine), they hired an estimated average of around fourteen workers, eleven of whom were seasonal (Bauder *et al.* 1976:32-34).[13] These differences are not surprising if we take into account the fact that only 5 percent of the agricultural employers in Florida were dairy farmers, while 28 percent were fruit and nut farmers (Bauder *et al.* 1976:50, Table 2.11; 53, Table 2.13): as mentioned above (page 15), dairy farmers use considerably less farm labor than fruit and nut farmers.[14]

Compared to the other thirteen states in the survey area, Florida employed on the average the largest number of workers per farm, which indicates that corporate farming is more widespread there than in the other thirteen states. Nevertheless, only 2 percent of the agricultural employers in Florida were corporations with ten or more stockholders. In Connecticut this percentage was estimated to be 1, and in the other states it was estimated to be less than 1. Estimates also showed that only 1 percent of the agricultural employers in the fourteen-state survey area as a whole were corporations with ten or more stockholders (Bauder *et al.* 1976:44, Table 2.6; 45, Table 2.7). The estimated average number of workers hired per corporate farm was 160, compared to fifteen for noncorporate farms. The estimated overall average of workers hired in the fourteen-state area per agricultural employer was seventeen (Bauder *et al.* 1976:36, Table 2.1; 44, Table 2.6; 45, Table 2.7).

Thus it is a combination of factors — on the one hand the fact that employers in Florida hire large numbers of seasonal farm workers, and on the other the fact that the peak and slack seasons in Florida complement the seasons in the northern states — that makes Florida the state which supplies harvest workers to the northern states.

Employers, employers' organizations, government officials, and crew leaders are involved in the preseason procedures for planning where and when the migratory farm workers will be hired during a season. They make all the decisions on wage rates and other working conditions: the workers do not participate in any part of this planning process. Migratory farm workers who do not join up with crew leaders, but go North on their own, are not calculated into the annual plan for migratory work. These "free-wheelers" usually have their own arrangements with certain employers, or they may simply try their luck and find work as they travel. At various points along the routes taken by migratory workers, the State Farm Labor Services operate information offices which assist crew leaders and free-wheelers by informing them about weather and crop conditions. These offices also make arrangements for last-minute adjustments of preseason schedules, which are often necessary because the exact day on which a certain crop needs to be harvested depends upon many factors and is rarely predictable. The Farm Labor Services have, through the Annual Worker Plan and the information offices, contributed to better planning and scheduling in the migratory farm labor system.

Without these services, the system would be even more inefficient than it is now: many more migratory farm workers would have found, upon their arrival in a certain area, that the crop they had come to harvest was not ripe, or that enough workers were already doing the job and their help was not needed. These information offices have made it possible for the workers to keep themselves informed about the availability of work.

4.5. *Work in the Fields*

In Florida most migratory farm workers work on a daily basis (pages 36-37). Some contractors recruit for a certain employer throughout an entire season, while others recruit only for single jobs, and still others recruit for a given period of time. Rather than using contractors, some employers go to the loading ramps and recruit the workers themselves.

Harvesting fruit and vegetables and cutting sugarcane are some of the jobs done by migratory farm workers (the latter is done primarily by British West Indians; Shabecoff 1973:24). Harvesting vegetables is dirty work and often involves crawling through the mud. There are frequently no toilet facilities in the fields where the work is done, and arrangements for food and fresh water are often minimal. The buses which transport workers to the fields leave early in the morning and sometimes have to ride long distances to reach the work sites. The work is irregular and delays are usual. Changes in the weather affect crop conditions, and this in turn affects the availability of work. Most workers usually do only three or four full days of work each week (Friedland and Nelkin 1971:6).

While they are in the North, the migratory farm workers usually live in camps. A worker's arrival in a camp does not, however, guarantee that he or she can start on a job right away. To assure the presence of enough workers at the right time, the employer and the crew leader quite often arrange for the workers to arrive well ahead of time, with the result that they are idle for several days. Since no work means no wages, and since the crew leader takes care of providing for food, for which the worker must pay, the worker is often in debt to the crew leader even before he begins working. As in Florida, most of the work done by migratory workers in other East Coast states is harvesting (usually beans, potatoes, onions, peas, tomatoes, lettuce, apples, cherries, etc.). Between harvests such jobs as weeding, haying, packing, loading trucks, weighing, and driving tractors or trucks may be done. The organization and supervision of the work is generally delegated to the crew leader, who acts in his (or sometimes her) own interest, showing little concern for either the employer or the worker. Because the crew leaders lack training in labor management, poor planning and labor wastage are common phenomena in the migratory farm labor system (see Friedland 1969:48-53; Friedland and Nelkin 1971:71-76).

When labor wastage occurs, it is the worker who suffers the most. If the bus that brings the workers to the field breaks down, the time wasted reduces the number of hours for which the worker is paid; if the crop which is to be harvested is still wet, the worker has to wait for hours without pay until the crop is dry; if the tools needed for a certain job are not at the work site, the time wasted by waiting for them to be collected is also not paid; if, when the workers arrive at the field, the crew leader still has to confer with the employer about which fields are to be picked, or still has to negotiate the wages, the workers must again wait but get no compensation for the time wasted.

The migratory farm workers' wages are usually calculated on a piecework basis. Comparison of these rates is almost impossible because units of measurement and of time vary: for example, six different units of measurement and three different units of time were observed in potato harvesting (Metzler 1955: 48). A combination of a piecework rate with an hourly wage rate is frequently used in harvest work. Such jobs as haying, weeding, and driving a tractor are paid by the hour. The migratory workers receive their pay at the end of the day or the end of the week and are paid either by the employer directly or by the crew leader, who gets a lump sum from the employer and takes care of payment. (This arrangement obviously offers the crew leader optimal opportunities for cheating the workers.) Sometimes the employer and the crew leader agree to a certain piece rate per unit harvested, in which case the largest portion goes to the worker and a certain percentage per unit is paid to the crew leader. Occasionally the employer pays the crew leader a daily or weekly wage, with or without a commission for the number of workers he recruits or for the crew's productivity. The great variety in rates and methods of payment makes earnings in migratory farm work very difficult to evaluate or compare, and it also invites exploitation of the workers: for instance, a crew leader may deduct social security from the workers' earnings without asking the workers for their social security numbers (Friedland and Nelkin 1971:190; Wright 1965:140).

The work done by each worker is recorded on punch cards or by handing out tickets. At the end of the day or week, the cards or tickets are exchanged

for cash. In certain extreme cases the crew leader keeps only a mental record
of how much work each worker has done. Observations have shown that,
regardless of how the work done is recorded, great uncertainty exists among
the workers about how much they have actually earned (Friedland and Nelkin
1971:71-96).

It is not only in the fields that the crew leader has control over the workers;
back at the camp, he also has effective means for exercising control (as the
next section shows). In this sense the labor camps are a kind of trap: they
are quite isolated and there is usually no way for the workers to get away
from the camp, from the other workers, and from the crew leader, even in
their free time.

4.6. *Life "on the Season"*

During the winter months the migratory farm workers in Florida live either
in camps, or in the black neighborhoods of such towns as Belle Glade and
Pahokee, or in scattered settlements in the areas around Lake Okeechobee and
along Route 441. The appalling living conditions of migratory farm workers in
Florida were reported as early as 1942:

The typical Negro migrant lives in a single $10'$ x $10'$ stall in a long shed or barrack....
Barracks are usually built around a central court in which there is a common toilet, often
indescribably filthy, and a community spigot or wellwater connection. (McWilliams 1942:
172)

In some of the older camps in Florida, it was observed that "migrants still
live in wooden shacks, most of which have no running water or heat." (Friedland and Nelkin 1971:4) Undoubtedly serious illnesses — such as typhoid,
which became a major epidemic in a camp in Dade County in 1973 — have
been caused largely by the lack of adequate sanitary facilities in the camps
(*New York Times*, 6 March 1973).

An article about the British West Indian cane cutters in Florida, that was
published in the *New York Times* (Shabecoff 1973), confirmed how dismal
conditions in the labor camps are. It described the Saunders Labor Camp,
which is run by the Glades County Sugar Cooperative Association, where
cane cutters live in unfurnished wooden shacks or barracks with no running
water or toilets and only a communal toilet located at least one hundred yards
away.

Talking to the sugar workers themselves to get at the facts of the situation is not easy. The West Indian labor camps are tucked away in the middle of the cane fields, which stretch mile after mile across the flat landscape where ripe cane – twice as tall as a man – rustles endlessly in the wind. The planters surround these camps with wire fences and discourage visitors by setting up no-trespassing signs and watchful supervisors. Not long ago, a young reporter for a Palm Beach newspaper, John Purnell, was charged with trespassing after he visited he Saunders Work Camp, the camp with the toiletless wooden barracks, and attempted to talk to workers. Once inside these camps, it is difficult to get the workers to talk. Almost to a man they fear they will be deported if caught talking to strangers. "I need this work, man" said a cutter from Jamaica at the Saunders camp. "There are no jobs, no money at home and I have six children." (Shabecoff 1973: 24)

The British West Indians are afraid because their individual contracts with the employers or employers' organizations contain a clause stipulating that workers who are unwilling to work or have misbehaved in any way will be sent home at their own expense (*Migratory Labor in American Agriculture* 1951:46-47). Domestic migratory farm workers who live in camps owned by the employers or employers' associations are also made well aware of the power of the employer. They do not have to pay rent, but are usually not allowed to work elsewhere without permission from the employer who owns the camp; if they do so they are threatened with eviction. The employer is thus assured of having enough workers, but the workers are entirely dependent on the arrangements and provisions the employer makes – or neglects to make. Some employers go to quite surprising extremes to interfere with the workers' private lives: for example, one employer evicted workers from a camp because they joined an adult education program (Friedland and Nelkin 1971:5).

Educating the workers' children is also a problem. Children of migratory parents receive most of their schooling in Florida, where some of the larger camps have their own schools. The children who live in the smaller camps or settlements, which are usually located on the outskirts of a town or village, attend school in the nearest community. Studies of education and school enrollment among migratory children have shown that in the East Coast migratory stream, although the relatively long period at the home base provides a good opportunity for the children to attend school, the children tend to miss too many weeks at the beginning and the end of the school year (Marcson and Fasick 1964:37-39; Greene 1954:52-67). In the mid-continent and West Coast streams the periods spent at the home base are shorter, and the children's education suffers accordingly (Marcson and Fasick 1964:39; Greene 1954:55).

The harvest season in Florida comes to an end in May, as does the tourist season, and the scarcity of work forces the farm worker to move northwards. Some workers pack their families into the old family car and simply leave, hoping that they will find work; others join crews (page 37). In both cases the trip North is long and uncomfortable. The crew leaders transport their workers in buses or trucks that are overcrowded and often dangerous. The family car is rarely in better condition than the crew leaders' means of transport, and there are accidents every year during the trip northwards and back.

Upon arrival in the North, the migratory farm worker goes to a labor camp. Some camps are in good condition, but the great majority are not; moreover, the town nearest to the camp is usually several miles away, and if the worker does not have a car, he or she must depend on the bus or truck owned by the crew leader or employer to make shopping trips and other visits to town. The only alternative is to buy the provisions which are sold in the camp, for the employer or crew leader often makes arrangements with the nearest shopkeeper to have food and other products available; however, the goods sold to the migratory workers are generally very expensive (Friedland and Nelkin 1971:11, 36, Wright 1965:104-105). By supplying transportation, giving the workers credit when there is no work, and providing the workers with both food and work, the crew leaders and employers make the workers completely dependent on them.

Housing in the labor camps leaves little space for privacy. Barracks, trailers, cabins, or shacks are provided for sleeping, while the "juke," a separate building or room, is intended for social life in the camp. The workers can usually buy their meals and have drinks in the juke, or play cards, gamble, talk, and dance to the music of a "piccolo" (a jukebox). This means that the migratory workers are together throughout the entire day: they spend all their working hours as well as all their leisure time with the same people. Monotony and boredom are typical of camp life: when there is no work, the laborers kill time by telling stories and jokes, playing cards, gambling, and, especially during the weekends, drinking (Friedland and Nelkin 1971:149-172). Outsiders usually do not have free access to the camps because no-trespassing signs and barbed wire surround them and discourage strangers (du Fresne and McDonnell 1971: 284-285).

The hygienic conditions in most of the labor camps do not encourage personal cleanliness. Many migratory workers are disgusted by the inadequacy of the showers and toilets and by the generally bad conditions in the camp. They carefully maintain their own rooms (Friedland and Nelkin 1971:104-

109) and consider the rest of the camp to be hopelessly dirty. It was observed that:

Personal health practices vary widely. Some migrants come north to take advantage of the better medical services available in certain northern states. Others are apathetic and show conspicuous self-neglect about their health. Attitudes in the latter group are fatalistic; doctors and conventional medicine are mistrusted.... (Friedland and Nelkin 1971:109)

In Florida the migratory children can attend school when they are at their home bases, but in the North they can only attend school at the larger camps which have summer school and day care arrangements. This means that the parents must often choose between taking all the children to the fields or leaving the small children behind in the camp under the supervision of an older child. This choice can be a difficult one because eight- or nine-year-old children are able to supplement the earnings of the parents substantially, while four-teen- and fifteen-year-olds can work as hard as the adults (Marcson and Fasick 1964:230). In many states the laws prohibiting child labor either do not apply to the children of migratory farm workers (e.g., because they work with their parents; see note 6 of this chapter) or have many loopholes. In the cases where they do apply, they are often not enforced because the state authorities are usually more concerned about the crops than about those who harvest them, and this leads to much neglect in enforcing the laws. Thus the children who are obliged by law to attend school are often sent to the fields, where they help their parents to earn a meager living. This is an ambivalent situation for the migratory family because sending the children to school means that badly needed extra money cannot be earned, while keeping the children out of school greatly decreases their chances of breaking out of the migratory farm work stream when they grow up. Moreover, if the migratory worker works in several camps during the summer, it hardly seems worthwhile to put the children in school for such short periods of time, and the children are seldom able to fit into the school programs already in progress.[15]

Thus in terms of transportation, housing, education, and hygiene, as well as in terms of getting away from the camp or having some privacy within it, the migratory workers live under deplorable conditions. These have been described in much greater detail than the nature of this investigation would allow in a number of studies that use the participant-observer method. One of them, Friedland and Nelkin's *Migrant: Agricultural Workers in America's Northeast* (1971), provides a particularly extensive and valuable body of information on the living and working conditions of the black migratory workers on the East Coast.[16] It is unique in that it gives a description of migratory life "from the inside out," for the students who worked on the study experienced the camp life of the workers by living with them as participant-observers for several months. Critics of this study have claimed that the situation is not as bad as it is portrayed to be, that the study only describes specific extreme cases, and that the results cannot be generalized for the whole East Coast migratory stream. A more recent study on the migratory workers' living and working conditions (Dunbar and Kravitz 1976) has provoked the same criticism.[17]

The investigation presented here takes a quite different approach: it attempts to *quantify* the dismal conditions of the migratory workers on the East Coast so that such information can be used effectively in policy making. The large sample of farm workers taken for the 1970 unemployment insurance survey (Bauder *et al.* 1976) provides a unique opportunity for presenting more general findings based on the data collected on these workers, and may thus undercut the argument that studies using the participant-observer method present only the extreme cases. The figures on interstate mobility, earnings, and the factors influencing earnings (Chapters 4 and 5) clearly show that the information gathered on migratory farm workers through participant observation does *not* present a biased view of the plight of these workers. On the contrary, it proves that *in general*, the migratory farm workers live and work under the most distressing conditions. The comparison of the migratory to the nonmigratory farm workers (Chapter 6) underscores the hopelessness of the migratory workers' situation.

NOTES

1. In the 1969 agricultural census (U.S. Department of Commerce, Bureau of the Census, 1969:123-134), corporations accounted for 1.2 percent of all farms, 8.8 percent of all land in farms, and 14.1 percent of total agricultural sales. In the total sales of some agricultural products, however, the corporations accounted for much higher percentages, for instance 50 percent of nursery and greenhouse products and 31.7 percent of vegetables, sweet corn, and melons.

2. This survey comprises the research base for this investigation (see Chapter 3, note 7). These estimates were computed from Bauder *et al.* 1976: Chapter II, Tables 2.1, 2.2, 2.8-16, which gave estimates of the number of employers in the fifteen-state study area surveyed in 1970 to find out what impact the extension of unemployment insurance would have on agriculture. The estimates were given for the survey area as a whole, for the regions, and for the states separately. All the states except Texas were in the eastern part of the United States. The data on Texas were extracted from the fifteen-state data to get estimates for the eastern states (page 71). The number of workers was measured by wage item, which was defined as the employment of one worker by one employer during any part of a given year.

3. U.S. Department of Agriculture, Economic Research Service, 1970:15, Table 7, estimated the average wages earned in farm work to be $11.10 per day, and in nonfarm work $16.35 per day. This table also showed that only 12 percent of the 1970 hired farm work force did farm work for wages for 250 days or more; 69 percent did farm work for wages for less than seventy-five days (the workers were either unemployed or employed in another sector during the rest of the year).

4. In the United States, workers' compensation laws generally cover cash benefits, medical care, and rehabilitation services for those who have work-related diseases or injuries.

5. For a more detailed discussion of farm workers and unemployment insurance, see Chapter 3.

6. U.S. Congress, Senate, Committee on Labor and Public Welfare 1960:64. In addition to these regulations, amendments made in 1974 to the Fair Labor Standards Act prohibit the employment of children under twelve years of age except on their parents' farm or with their parents' consent, or on farms which are not required to pay the minimum wage. The amendments also prohibit the employment of twelve- or thirteen-year-olds unless their parents have consented or unless they work on the farms where their parents are employed (see Elder 1974:33-37).

7. In 1970 the farm wage rate of $1.64 per hour amounted to only half the average hourly earnings of workers in manufacturing. Furthermore, workers in such traditionally low-paying service industries as laundering and dry cleaning earned, on the average, 53 cents more per hour than farm workers. *Manpower Report of the President* 1971:125-126.

8. A very interesting study on the slave civilization in the South, the developments that led to the Civil War in 1861, and the question of whether that war could have been avoided appears in Genovese 1965.

9. Shotwell 1961:72. The description on pages 22-25 is based on the historical accounts in McWilliams 1942; Fisher 1935; U.S. Department of Labor 1959; U.S. Congress, Senate, Committee on Labor and Public Welfare 1960; and Shotwell 1961.

10. For an overview of the impact of foreign contract labor on wages and other working conditions of domestic farm workers in the United States, see "The New Braceros" 1977: 4-9.

11. Thus we find some Mexicans in the East Coast stream (see page 36).

12. The crew leader, like the labor contractor, is a middleman. Friedland and Nelkin (1971:6) considered the crew leader to be not only the person who recruits labor and contracts employers, as does a labor contractor, but also the person who maintains the crew as a social unit outside the work situation. Quite often a contractor, who in Florida only recruits workers on a daily basis, will become a crew leader in the North, where he manages all aspects of the crew.

13. Bauder *et al.* 1976:32-34. The number of workers is measured by wage items (a wage item is the employment of one worker for one employer during any part of the year). A seasonal worker is a worker who has done 25-149 days of farm wage work during a given year.

14. Bauder *et al.* 1976: Chapter II, Tables 2.1, 2.2 and 2.8-16. For the fourteen-state study area the following percentages for types of farm work were estimated: dairy farms, 40 percent; fruit and nut farms, 11 percent; cash grain and other field crops, 8 percent; tobacco farms, 1 percent; vegetable farms, 8 percent; poultry farms, 6 percent; livestock and general farms, 14 percent; miscellaneous farms, 9 percent; cotton farms, less than 1 percent; and nonfarm agricultural employers, 3 percent.

15. An important development in the education of migratory children is the agreement made by forty-seven states to prepare a Transfer Records Form for each child. These forms are computerized and when a migratory child enters a class, the most important information on the child is available within hours and a complete record on the child is available in a couple of days. The Migrant Data Bank is located in Arkansas, and terminals are operative throughout the country. Data on the child's identification, health, and achievements in school are provided (see Mattera 1971:51-57).

16. The study is structured around three themes: (1) the disorganized and unpredictable character of migratory farm worker life; (2) the adaption of the migratory worker in his daily life to the disorganized character of his existence; and (3) the extent to which the worker is trapped in the migratory farm labor system, in which external and internal factors contribute to impede change from within the system (Friedland and Nelkin 1971:1-2). Excerpts from the students' field diaries portray the grim lives of these workers. Anyone interested in the migratory farm labor problem must read this shocking account of migratory farm work in the East Coast stream.

17. It is not quite clear how the data for this study were gathered, but it appears that most of the information is based on personal testimony of workers in the fields. Whether or not this information is indicative of the overall situation is questionable.

3

UNEMPLOYMENT INSURANCE IN AGRICULTURE: RECENT POLICIES AND THE 1970 SURVEY

Our discussion of the socioeconomic situation of farm workers in the United States, and particularly of the problems confronting the migratory workers, leads to focusing on unemployment insurance in agriculture. Farm workers have traditionally been excluded from this type of social legislation, yet if it were extended to them — and especially to the migratory workers — it would surely give them some of the income security they so badly need.

Certain recent changes in the general attitude toward unemployment insurance and agriculture have been significant for these workers and have served to motivate a survey of farm workers and farm employers which was carried out to analyze the particular problems that would arise if unemployment insurance was extended to agriculture. Through this survey, very specific and detailed data could be collected on farm workers on the East Coast of the United States. Because of their specific character, these data have provided a unique opportunity for analyzing a variety of aspects of the farm workers' lives and work, and in particular that of the migratory farm workers.

To gain a better understanding of unemployment insurance and agriculture, we will first review the history of unemployment insurance in the United States,

Notes to this chapter may be found on pages 61-62.

the reasons why it was not extended to agriculture, the changing political and social climate *vis-à-vis* the poor after World War II, and the influence this had on the socioeconomic position of the farm workers. A description will be given of the action taken on agricultural unemployment insurance by the U.S. Congress in 1970 and of the fifteen-state survey that was taken to estimate the cost of extending such insurance to agriculture. In conclusion, recent legislation providing limited employment insurance coverage to farm workers will be reviewed.

1. WHY FARM WORKERS WERE EXCLUDED FROM UNEMPLOYMENT INSURANCE

The first programs in the United States offering protection to workers against loss of income due to involuntary unemployment were developed by the trade unions (Fritsch 1976:117-127). These early experiments were not very successful because the unemployment insurance programs were initiated during periods of unemployment, and the trade union income protection plans were not able to continue benefit payments when the periods of unemployment became extended. Furthermore, interest in these programs decreased rapidly when the economic situation improved. Companies also started to develop their own programs to insure their workers against loss of income during periods of unemployment. Basically, however, the company plans for income protection had to cope with the same problems as the trade union plans, namely, how to maintain benefit payments during longer periods of unemployment.

The company plans generally placed greater emphasis on maintaining fiscal solvency than did the union plans, either by reducing benefits or extending the initial pre-benefit waiting periods, but few were able to meet successfully the requirements of longer term unemployment. (Fritsch 1976:120)

The failures of the voluntary plans developed by the trade unions and companies led to an increased interest in compulsory plans organized by the government. Before 1930, because there was a widespread belief in the constant availability of jobs, an unemployed worker was looked upon as a person who lacked initiative to compete. During the Depression, however, the assumption that being jobless was the worker's fault could no longer be maintained. When the existing relief organizations became unable to carry the burden of massive unemployment, government proposals for unemployment insurance programs were introduced in the U.S. Congress and the state legislatures. But it was not until 1935 that the Social Security Act was passed and a system of unemployment insurance with a dual federal-state character was set up. Minimum requirements were established by the federal government, and each state was free to develop insurance programs that were best suited to conditions prevailing in the state. Because of this, the unemployment insurance systems of the various states were extremely diverse. Basically, the system set up at that time functions as follows. As provided for in the Federal Unemployment Tax Act, the unemployment insurance system assesses a federal tax on the payrolls of employers. This tax money is used to build up a reserve fund to finance benefit payments to eligible employees. Each employer who joins in the system pays a standard rate which is established by the state. After an initial period, experience ratings are used as the basis for determining an individual employer's rate: employers with irregular employment patterns pay a higher rate (up to a legal maximum), while employers whose workers experience little or no unemployment pay a lower rate, which may gradually drop to the minimum legal rate. The amount of the benefits an employee may receive if he or she becomes unemployed is determined by how long he or she has worked and the level of his or her earnings during a one-year period prior to filing the initial claim.[1] The federal government provides information on the programs in the various states.[2]

One of the groups of workers that was excluded from the unemployment insurance system was the farm workers.

Historically, the exclusion of farm workers from social legislation was based on the contention that, since employing units were small and scattered, the administrative and enforcement problems would be difficult. It was argued also that many small farmers had low and uncertain incomes and could not afford the cost of social insurance for their workers and that most farm workers have only a temporary attachment to any one employer or even, in many cases, to the agricultural work force. (*Manpower Report of the President* 1971:124)

It was further maintained that (1) inclusion of the agricultural workers in the unemployment insurance system would result in high cost rates because of the highly seasonal nature of agriculture work, and that (2) the benefits which were to be paid to farm workers might well exceed the contributions paid by the employers, so that the system would not be able to sustain itself.

It is obvious that such objections to including farm workers in an unemployment insurance system make no allowance whatsoever for the farm workers' needs or their opinions on the matter. This situation reflects the political position these workers are in: they comprise an uninfluential group of people that does not even have the right to organize into unions (see page 16). Agricultural employers, on the other hand, have traditionally been well organized and have become effective politically through representation by such organizations as the American Farm Bureau Federation. They maintain well-financed lobbies in Washington, D.C. and can influence public opinion to promote the kind of legislation that is favorable to the agricultural employer (Allen 1966:47-48; National Advisory Committee on Farm Labor 1967: 10; Monsen and Cannon 1965:96-133). As the records on farm legislation prove, these lobbies have been quite successful. Undoubtedly, the administration of social legislation in agriculture would be more complex than in other industries because the workers, due to the seasonal character of their work, have a more tenuous relationship with their employers. But if *any* group of workers needs a program like unemployment insurance, it is the farm workers. Compared to industrial workers, their employment situation is much more dependent on factors which are beyond their control: bad weather or a bad crop, for example, can considerably decrease the number of weeks they can work and, consequently, the amount they can earn.

2. THE CHANGING POLITICAL AND SOCIAL CLIMATE

During World War II there was very little unemployment in the United States, but after the war concern about why the nation's affluence was not being shared by all of its citizens began to grow. Myrdal's *An American Dilemma* (1944), Ferman, Kornbluh, and Haber's *Poverty in America* (1956), Harrington's *The Other America: Poverty in the United States* (1962), and Miller's *Rich Man, Poor Man* (1964), as well as many other books, brought the existence of a serious poverty problem in the United States to the attention of the general public. The flood of studies on poverty that was published by social scientists during the 1950s and 1960s featured urban poverty and racial problems, and little attention was given to problems affecting the farm workers (perhaps because they comprised a much smaller group than those affected by urban and racial problems). But there were journalists and filmmakers who tried (as they had during the Depression years) to bring the distressing plight of the farm workers — especially of the migratory farm workers — to the attention of the general public. Shotwell wrote her book, *The Harvesters* (1961),

Moore wrote *The Slaves We Rent* (1965), and Allen wrote *The Ground is our Table* (1966). The television documentary "Harvest of Shame" (1960)[3] also had a considerable impact on public awareness. A series of articles written by Wright in 1961 for the *New York World, Telegram, and Sun* created a national furor. Wright had shared the way of life of the migratory farm workers for several months and reported on their shameful conditions from his own personal experience (see Wright 1965).

It was not only the filmmakers and journalists who brought the dismal situation of the migratory farm workers to light: many individuals also tried, through private organizations, to have improvements made in the living and working conditions of these workers by publicizing the facts. For instance, The National Advisory Committee on Farm Labor, a nonprofit organization run by a group of volunteers, was founded to gather and spread information about the farm workers' living conditions and problems, about practices in farm labor, and about government policies. This Committee describes its purpose as follows: "Through public education on a nation-wide scale the Committee seeks to mobilize public opinion and to spark effective action by concerned groups and individuals."[4] Several other organizations are doing similar work: the Bishop's Committee on Migrants, a Roman Catholic social service agency, specializes in circulating information on migratory workers; the Migrant Ministry of the National Council of Churches, a Protestant organization which has been active since 1920, sends its representatives to the areas where migratory workers are concentrated in order to organize workshops in education, housekeeping, and home crafts, and to run out-patient clinics and sponsor child-care centers (Wright 1965:134).

How successful those organizations have been in their efforts to bring relief to migratory workers is not known, but it would appear (Friedland and Nelkin 1971:257) that auxiliary organizations and services (including government agencies) are sometimes too well represented in areas where there are only a few migratory farm workers and almost absent in areas where migratory workers gather. Coordinating the activities of the various organizations also seems to be a problem, because the organizations often have different interpretations of the nature of the migratory farm workers' problems and different strategies for solving them. Those who work directly with the migratory workers often become frustrated by their inability to make significant changes in the system of labor exploitation.

While it is impossible to measure the effect of the considerable number of private efforts to awaken the public conscience, it is clear that government interest in the problems of farm workers and in the special position of migratory farm workers has increased. In 1951 the President's Commission on Migratory Labor published its Report, entitled *Migratory Labor in American Agriculture*. This extensive study on the position of migratory farm workers included an important set of recommendations for improving their situation. In 1960 the Subcommittee on Migratory Labor of the U.S. Senate Committee on Labor and Public Welfare, which was created in 1959, published *The Migrant Farm Worker in America: Background Data on the Migrant Worker Situation in the United States Today* (1960),[5] which also provided an important survey of the problems of migratory farm workers. The government has also demonstrated its concern about the migratory farm workers by encouraging and subsidizing research on them: the Department of Agriculture, for instance, helped to finance a study by Larson and Sharp (1960) and commissioned Metzler to do his 1955 study. The Department of Health, Education, and Welfare wrote a report on children in migratory families for the Committee on Appropriations of the United States Senate (U.S. Congress, Senate, 1961), and it subsidized Marcson and Fasick's study on elementary summer schooling for migratory children (1964). President Lyndon B. Johnson also introduced legislation to help the poor as part of his plan for the "Great Society," and that legislation was later passed by Congress. Thus thanks to the change in the political and social climate during the 1950s and 1960s, and because of the new interest in human affairs, with its emphasis on the problems of the poor and on equal rights, the rights of the farm workers again attracted attention in government circles during this period, and some significant laws were enacted. Social security was extended to farm workers in 1951, and the minimum wage legislation passed in 1966 demonstrated that the administrative problems of dealing with this category of workers could be solved (Chapter 2, section 2). Nevertheless, the farm workers were still not covered by any system of unemployment insurance. Recommendations to include at least those agricultural employers who employed large numbers of farm workers were made several times, but were repeatedly rejected; the most recent unsuccessful proposal was made by the Nixon Administration in 1969, only a year before the unemployment insurance survey was carried out. In order to find out what has come of these recommendations, we will focus on the action taken in Congress on the 1969 proposal for extending unemployment insurance to agriculture, on the unemployment insurance amendments affecting interstate workers that were enacted in 1970, and on the fifteen-state unemployment insurance survey on which this investigation is based.

3. ACTION TAKEN BY CONGRESS: LEGISLATION AND A SURVEY

In 1969 the Nixon Administration proposed some amendments to Congress in order to change the laws on unemployment insurance; among them was a bill providing unemployment insurance coverage to certain farm workers. At the time, experience with and research on unemployment insurance coverage for farm workers in the United States was quite limited. It included only the following:

(1) In Hawaii, workers on large farms had been covered by unemployment insurance since 1959 (*Manpower Report of the President* 1971:125).

(2) In Puerto Rico, farm workers in the sugarcane industry had been covered by unemployment insurance (*Manpower Report of the President* 1971:125).

(3) In a few states (New York, for instance), unemployment insurance had been extended to agriculture on an optional basis (*Manpower Report of the President* 1971:125; Bauder and Bratton 1972:1).

(4) Studies had been made in four states — Arizona, Connecticut, Nebraska, and New York — in 1959 and 1960 on the costs and problems involved in providing unemployment insurance coverage to farm workers (*Manpower Report of the President* 1971:125; Bauder *et al.* 1976:20).

(5) Similar studies had been undertaken in Texas and California in 1964 and 1966 respectively, and such studies were also in progress in Washington and Minnesota (Bauder *et al.* 1976:20).

The amendments proposed by the Nixon Administration provided unemployment insurance coverage for farm workers who had worked for farm employers with four or more workers on their payroll for at least twenty weeks in a calendar year (*Manpower Report of the President* 1971:124). This was generally considered to be feasible from the administrative viewpoint, but a dispute arose over the cost of extending such a scheme to agriculture. The Senate supported a more restrictive amendment that would have only extended unemployment insurance to those farm workers who had worked for employers who had employed eight or more workers for at least twenty-six weeks in a calendar year. The House-Senate Conference Committee rejected this amendment, arguing that more information was needed on the effects of extending unemployment insurance to farm workers (*Manpower Report of the President* 1971:124).

Congress agreed with the Committee that more experience and research was needed on the impact of unemployment insurance on agriculture, and because of this the version of the Employment Security Amendments enacted in 1970 did not provide unemployment insurance coverage for farm workers. The question arises of whether it really was the lack of information on the proposal's financial feasibility that caused it to be rejected: it could well have been an example of effective lobbying by the organized farm employers who were to be taxed to finance the scheme. Be this as it may, in order to gather more information on unemployment insurance in agriculture, the amendments directed the Secretary of Labor to set up a research program to study the impact of extending unemployment insurance to agricultural workers (*Manpower Report of the President* 1971:124-125). The result was an extensive study on the impact of extending unemployment insurance to agriculture, in which fifteen states cooperated. The Unemployment Insurance Service, which is part of the Manpower Administration of the United States Department of Labor, and the Agricultural Experiment Stations of twelve universities worked together to carry out the project. Because several states were surveyed simultaneously, the government had an excellent opportunity to observe the effect that employment in different states would have on the benefits and costs of an unemployment insurance program for agricultural workers. In other words, the study was designed especially to measure the effect that the migratory farm worker would have on the benefits and costs of such a scheme, for it is the migratory rather than the nonmigratory farm worker who may be expected to be unemployed during a substantial part of the year. The research focusing on this effect was doubly opportune in view of the rules that the 1970 amendments had laid down on out-of-state employment, which will be described below.

While the Employment Security Amendments of 1970 once more prevented the extension of employment insurance to agricultural workers, they did include regulations providing important improvements for nonfarm workers working in more than one state. All states are now required to cooperate in implementing the payment of benefits to those workers who earned wages or were employed in two or more states and who present a valid claim for compensation. Before these regulations were established, several states had worked out plans for adding up wages earned in different states in order to pay benefits to eligible interstate workers, but not all the states had participated. Under the new regulations, which involve calculating the total wages and days of employment covered by the unemployment insurance program in any state, a worker who has not worked long enough or earned enough in one state to receive benefits may nonetheless qualify for benefits by combining earnings and days of employment in all the states he or she has worked in. Furthermore, if a worker is eligible for benefits on earnings and employment in one state, these benefits can be increased by adding the wages earned and days of employment in other states (U.S. Department of Labor, Manpower Administration Bureau of Employment Security, 1972: 3.18). In New York state, for instance, the benefits a worker can receive are calculated on the basis of a percentage of the average weekly earnings; in taking this average the worker can choose, out of his total period of employment, the twenty weeks in which he earned the most (Bauder and Bratton 1972:25). Another change brought about by the 1970 amendments is that workers are no longer required to be physically present in a given state in order to collect unemployment insurance benefits from it.[6] If the total of a worker's wages and days of employment is enough to entitle him or her to benefits, the paying state acts as an agent for the state that is liable for the benefits claimed. The money is then transferred from one state to another (U.S. Department of Labor, Manpower Administration Bureau of Employment Security 1972:3.17-18). Such measures encourage workers who are covered by unemployment insurance and become unemployed to move on and look for work in other states.

If unemployment insurance is extended to farm workers, it will be the migratory workers who will require special attention in order to properly estimate the cost of such a program. This is because their earnings and days of employment are spread over more than one state. It is thus particularly interesting to see how adding up earnings and days of employment in several states will affect these workers, and how it will influence the costs of extending unemployment insurance to agriculture.

4. AIMS AND RESULTS OF THE 1970 SURVEY

The possibility for a farm worker to combine employment and earnings in all the states worked in during a given year in order to qualify for benefits or to get more benefits is of course extremely important to migratory farm workers particularly, and it consequently played a key role in determining the objectives of the fifteen-state survey on the impact of extending unemployment insurance to agriculture. These objectives were:

(1) To estimate the number of hired farm workers in the Northeast and their demographic characteristics.
(2) To determine the labor force experience of these workers including their employment and unemployment experience, and duration of agricultural and nonagricultural work.
(3) To estimate the number of agricultural employers meeting alternative criteria for unemployment insurance coverage for their workers.
(4) To estimate the number of potential beneficiaries, their demographic, social, and vocational characteristics, including age and sex, and the amount, duration, and exhaustion of their benefits.
(5) To estimate contributions (payments) from employers and benefits to beneficiaries under alternative criteria for coverage.
(6) To estimate the effect of potential combined wage and interstate claims on claimant's eligibility, duration of benefits, weekly benefit amounts, and the benefit-cost rate. (Bauder *et al.* 1976: 22)

Data on the employers were gathered by mailing questionnaires. Information about the workers was collected through personal interviews with 12,666 workers in fourteen eastern states.[7]

The objectives of the survey clearly required that the data obtained on the workers should include detailed information on the type of work done, on labor-force experience (i.e., the number of weeks of unemployment), and on the earnings of the farm workers. The worker's questionnaire consequently focused on acquiring detailed information on a fifty-two-week period, starting with the week ending on 5 July 1969 and finishing with the week ending on 27 June 1970. For each week in this period, the worker's location (by state), occupation, earnings, and the nature of his or her employer's business were recorded. If the worker did not work during a certain week, the interviewer would ask the worker why he or she had no work; if the worker had received unemployment benefits for nonfarm work, the amount was recorded.

In addition to the detailed information which was gathered through the fifty-two week histories, data were collected on such personal characteristics of the workers as age, sex, ethnic group membership, etc. Furthermore, extensive information was gathered on certain socioeconomic characteristics, such as years of schooling and the worker's family situation (see Appendix A for the worker's questionnaire). The data requirements for analyzing the implications of extending unemployment insurance to agriculture were such that a wealth of data could be collected on the farm workers on the East Coast who, like most farm workers, have so often been bypassed by research and policy analyses.

The results of the survey showed that if it is assumed that all farm work would be covered by unemployment insurance, 75 percent of the farm worker population would have enough earnings and days of employment — agricultural and nonagricultural — to be entitled to receive benefits from the unemployment insurance system if they were to become involuntarily unemployed. The percentage of the worker population that would actually qualify to receive benefits — i.e., that had one or more weeks of unemployment and thus was entitled to compensation — was estimated to be 22 percent. The average payment to these beneficiaries was estimated to be $385. Using more restrictive criteria for coverage — such as, for instance, covering only those farm employers who employed four or more workers for twenty weeks or more, or had a payroll of $5,000 or more in any calender quarter — was estimated to reduce the proportion of workers that would be covered by unemployment insurance by 26 percent, and the number who would actually receive benefits by 11 percent. As was expected, if all farm employees were covered by unemployment insurance, a higher proportion of interstate migratory workers (39 percent) than nonmigratory workers (15 percent) was estimated to be entitled to receive benefits. Furthermore, estimates showed that among both migratory and nonmigratory workers, a higher proportion of workers who were members of ethnic minorities than of white workers would be entitled to receive benefits.

As to the cost of unemployment insurance covering all farm employment, the industry cost-rate for agriculture for the fourteen states was estimated to be 3 percent (this rate is the proportion that the benefits allocated to agricultural earnings would be of the taxable agricultural earnings, assuming that full coverage was extended to all agricultural employment; Bauder et al. 1976: 97, 105). Using the fifty-two-week period as the base period and assuming that the work histories were repetitive, the addition of full coverage for farm workers to the unemployment insurance system was estimated to raise the benefits to be paid to these workers from $4.3 million (which is the cost of covering only the nonfarm work done by farm workers) to $20.2 million (Bauder et al. 1976:105).

The results of the 1970 survey made it quite clear that the lack of data could no longer be used as an argument for postponing the extension of unemployment insurance to agricultural workers. Yet it was not until 1976 that legislation was finally enacted to extend unemployment insurance to some farm workers. The Federal Unemployment Amendments of 1976, that became effective on 1 January 1978, provided unemployment insurance coverage to an additional nine million workers, of which 7.7 million were municipal and county employees, 600,000 were state employees, and less than 500,000 were farm workers (Hickey 1978:14-17; and Elterich 1978b:18-24). As has been the case with all farm worker legislation, only a portion of the workers were covered. These amendments covered only about two fifths of all hired agricultural workers — namely, those who have worked for employers who had ten employees during a period of twenty weeks or more, or who paid $20,000 or more in cash wages in any calendar quarter (Hickey 1978:14). This means that only the workers who have worked on large farms will receive benefits. It was estimated (Elterich 1978a:23-33) that the workers who would actually benefit from the new unemployment insurance legislation would receive an average of $386 in benefits each year, while their earnings would average $2,843. Given this income level, one certainly wonders how these people stay alive. In this sense it is quite clear that the legislative action taken in response to the 1970 survey has been very disappointing: more general unemployment insurance coverage is desperately needed.

While the 1970 survey did not result in the extension of unemployment insurance to all farm workers, it certainly did gather a wealth of information on a category of workers that until recently has been treated scantily by social scientists. It is for this reason that the data collected in the 1970 unemployment insurance survey have been used as the major secondary data source in the analysis of the situation of the migratory workers in Chapters 4-7.[8]

If we place the socioeconomic data on farm workers on the East Coast of the United States in the wider context of research on labor problems in agriculture in general — research which usually limits itself to the economic problems related to the demand for and the supply of labor — it is quite clear that the particular combination of sociological and economic data used in this investigation of farm workers offers excellent possibilities for an interdisciplinary analysis. Such an analysis is furthermore motivated by the following:

(1) Although rural poverty is a recognized and increasingly serious social problem in the United States, the farm workers, who comprise an important part of this problem, have until recently been neglected.

(2) Most of the few studies that have focused on farm workers have dealt only with migratory farm workers, and even these studies are quite fragmentary: almost all of them are limited to either a small sample in a certain area or a small sample of an ethnic minority group (usually blacks).

(3) The high cost of collecting data on such an elusive group of workers, combined with the factors mentioned above, make further exploration of these secondary data not only scientifically relevant and significant, but also urgently necessary from the viewpoint of policy making. This is first of all because these

workers are leading utterly miserable lives, and policies to improve their plight must be implemented as soon as possible. It is also because the extent and type of data collected for the 1970 unemployment insurance survey offered a good opportunity for the kind of interdisciplinary research which is required for effective socioeconomic policy making.

NOTES

1. For a detailed description of unemployment insurance in the United States, see Haber and Murray 1966.

2. The United States Department of Labor provides information for each state separately on the types of employees and employers that are covered under the state law, the ways the programs are financed, the benefits that are payable and the conditions under which they are paid, and the administrative organization that runs each program. See the U.S. Department of Labor, Manpower Administration, Bureau of Employment Security, 1972.

3. This documentary (CBS Television 1960) was prepared by Edward R. Murrow in co-operation with Fred Friendly in 1960 for the news program "CBS Reports" (Wright 1965: 34).

4. This text is on the back page of *Farm Labor Organizing 1905-1967: a Brief History* (National Advisory Committee on Farm Labor 1967).

5. U.S. Congress, Senate, Committee on Labor and Public Welfare 1960. Since 1960 the Subcommittee on Migratory Labor has prepared regular reports on the migratory farm labor problem in the United States.

6. This is quite advantageous to the worker because some states may have more generous benefit systems than others.

7. The states which were surveyed included Maine, New Hampshire, Vermont, Massachusetts, Rhode Island, Connecticut, New York, New Jersey, Pennsylvania, Delaware, Maryland, West Virginia, Florida, Ohio, and Texas. The first twelve states were organized into the Northeast Region for the purpose of cooperative regional research within the framework of the Agricultural Experiment Station System. The study was conducted in conjunction with Regional Research Project NE-58 of the Northeast Agricultural Experiment Stations. Ohio, Florida, and Texas joined the Northeast Region because they were interested in extending unemployment insurance to agriculture.

The data were collected and analyzed by the University of Connecticut, Pennsylvania State University, the University of Delaware, Cornell University, the University of Massachusetts, the University of New Hampshire, the University of Vermont, Rutgers University, the University of Maryland, the University of Florida, Ohio State University, and Texas A. & M. University. The project was jointly funded by the participating Experiment Stations and the United States Department of Labor. The NE-58 Technical Committee and its Project Committee directed the study. The results of the survey are documented in Bauder *et al.* 1975 and Seaver *et al.* 1976.

8. It should perhaps be mentioned here that this investigation of the statistical data collected in the 1970 survey of agricultural employers and farm workers in fourteen eastern states was initiated only *after* the data had been collected for the quite limited purpose of studying the impact of extending unemployment insurance to agriculture. For this reason the data served as a secondary source and put certain limitations on the analysis.

4

MOBILITY OF THE MIGRATORY FARM WORKER

1. TRAVELING TO FIND WORK

The most dominant feature of migratory farm worker life is the need to travel to remain employed. The migratory farm worker goes wherever there is a demand for workers to care for the crops: to plant, to weed, and to harvest. Several writers have vividly described this yearly movement of men, women, and children who follow the crops as they grow, ripen, and finally are picked. One wrote:

They begin their seasonal journeys in late January or early February with south Florida citrus crops, then move from field to field, through tomatoes and potatoes in Florida; corn, snap beans, and cucumbers in the Carolinas; berries and fruits in Virginia and Maryland; then perhaps vegetable crops again in Delaware, New Jersey, and New York. Many follow the crops into northern New England and Canada, where, in late November and early December, they help bring in another potato harvest. (Wright 1965: from the Preface)

Working their way from the South to the North and back again, migratory farm workers travel through the East Coast states, taking on whatever work they can find:

Notes to this chapter may be found on pages 96-98.

...a giant river of southern Negro families...pours out of Florida. Up the eastern seaboard it flows through the Carolinas, a branch of it going off to Virginia's Shenandoah Valley. The main stream ferries the James River and toils up the eastern shore of the Chesapeake. The fruit and vegetable farms of Pennsylvania, New Jersey, and New York recruit thousands of these Negro families, and a few of them go all the way to Maine to pick up potatoes in Aroostook County. (Shotwell 1961:29-30)

The Report of the President's Commission on Migratory Labor described the travels of the migratory farm workers as follows:

Migratory farm laborers move restlessly over the face of the land, but they neither belong to the land nor does the land belong to them. They pass through community after community, but they neither claim the community as home nor does the community claim them. (*Migratory Labor in American Agriculture* 1951:3)

Traveling to find work is the feature of the migratory farm workers' lives which most typifies and distinguishes them. In the course of a season, the workers earn their living in not one or two states, but in several states — and perhaps in more than one place in some of these states. Descriptions such as these make it quite clear that the annual movements of these workers must have a disruptive effect on their families: among other things, traveling interrupts the migratory children's schooling. The literature on these workers also indicates that relationships exist between the mobility of the migratory workers and certain other personal and socioeconomic characteristics which typify them (section 1.3 of this chapter). Before analyzing the data, the mobility of the workers and the relationships between their mobility and their socioeconomic characteristics will be examined on the basis of that literature.

1.1. *Migration during the Depression Years*

The lives and work of the migratory farm workers have been documented by journalists and photographers, as well as by government agencies. Until about twenty-five years ago, however, social scientists paid almost no attention to the plight of these workers. One exception among them was Nels Anderson, who wrote a monograph on the hobo (1923) and a study on migration during the Depression years (1940). Although Anderson's work dealt with all the migratory workers and not the migratory farm workers in particular, what he said was important because his approach was clearly sociological and emphasized the relationships between the workers' characteristics and their geographic mobility. The most important relationship described by Anderson was the influence of family size on mobility.

During the Depression unemployment was widespread in the United States, and many people started to travel to find work. In September 1933 the Federal Emergency Relief Administration (FERA) created the Transient Relief Program to lend assistance to the overburdened relief programs that had been set up by the states. The Transient Relief Program provided help to transients by opening centers along the migration routes throughout the United States. By registering the "people on the move" in these centers, valuable information on the transients was collected in the two-year period during which this federal program was in effect. Studies based on the data gathered at the relief centers were published by the Division of Social Research of the Works Progress Administration (W.P.A.) and appeared in the Division's series of research monographs.[1]

The most significant feature of Anderson's work on migratory workers was his collation and analysis of the results of the W.P.A. monographs and various other relief studies. These provided an overall picture of the migratory movements during the Depression years and of the relationship between mobility and the workers' family compositions. Anderson observed the following about this relationship:

Single transients move on short notice and travel faster and farther with less effort; the single transient also needs to carry very little. When a man moves his wife and children, he faces the necessity of looking ahead and settling on a destination before starting. Family migrants travel with more caution. (Anderson 1940:104)

The typical migrant family is small. Families of two persons comprised 35 percent of the total, whereas for the nation two-person families comprised 25 percent of all families. Three-person families were 25 percent for the migrants compared with 23 percent for the families of the nation. Four-person families were 17 percent for the migrants and 19 percent for the nation, while families of five persons or more comprised 23 percent for the migrant group but were 33 percent for the nation. It appears that the families with four children or more are too much burdened to venture on the road. (Anderson 1940:105-106)

One of the W.P.A. studies came to the following conclusion about geographic mobility and the size of the family:

Logically, the presence of children and other dependents should tend to restrict the mobility of families under adverse conditions. And, indeed, a comparison between the size of migrant families and families in the resident relief and general population reveals that size of family was one of the selective factors in depression migration. (Webb and Brown 1938:96)

Outdated as these studies may be, they are nonetheless important because they relate the mobility of these migratory workers to other characteristics. The conclusion that the unattached migrants were more mobile than migrants who traveled with a family[2] is particularly interesting in comparison to the conclusions on mobility and worker characteristics at the end of this chapter.

1.2. Migratory Workers on the East Coast

Before reviewing the research dealing specifically with the mobility of migratory farm workers, a short survey should be given of the studies that have been done on migratory farm workers in the eastern part of the United States. None of these put much emphasis on the degree of mobility of these workers, and most of them are quite general: they take a sample of migratory farm workers, usually the blacks, and inventory the workers' characteristics. (Metzler's work[3] and that of Motheral, Thomas, Larson, and Sharp[4] are examples of this type of research.) Besides these fact-finding studies, there are others which focus on a given aspect of migratory farm worker life. The education of migratory children is the most popular subject: quite an extensive comparative investigation has been done on educating migratory children in a county in Florida, Virginia, Texas, and Illinois (Greene 1954); another study has described educating black migratory farm workers and their children in farm labor camps in New York state (Sharp and Larson 1960). A large section of a report on a sample of southern Illinois strawberry pickers has also dealt with the education of migratory children (Brooks and Hilgendorf 1960).[5] An examination of elementary summer schooling for migratory children in New Jersey (Marcson and Fasick 1964) is quite significant because of its description of the social factors affecting the elementary school performance of migratory children and its special emphasis on black children.

Other aspects of migratory farm worker life, such as the socioeconomic impact that migratory workers have on the communities they live in while they are working (Persh 1953[6]) and the crew leader system (Shostack 1964 and Friedland 1967[7]), have also been studied.

One of the most thorough examinations of the lives and work of the migratory workers on the East Coast was made by several social scientists at the Industrial and Labor Relations School of Cornell University. Within this framework, students shared the life and work of black migratory farm workers as participant observers and recorded the day-to-day experiences of the workers (see also pages 45-46). Several studies have been published on the basis of these records. One of them (Friedland 1967) explored the migratory labor stream as a channel of geographic and occupational mobility, using information on workers who had dropped out of the stream and intended to settle in the North. Another documented labor wastage on New York farms and the attitudes of migratory farm workers toward work (Friedland 1969). Also included among these publications is a study using the concept of marginality to analyze reactions of migratory farm worker crews to living in isolated camps on the margin of a larger society (Nelkin 1969). Another study, entitled *On the Season* (1970), dealt with three aspects of the migratory labor system — employment practices, the uncertainties of the life style in camps, and the fact that migratory farm workers are ignored — and pointed out that by housing the workers in isolated camps, their presence is made hardly noticeable. This low profile is maintained by the agricultural employers, but the workers, for their part, also avoid outsiders and any kind of disturbing incident that might call attention to their group.

The Cornell group's research includes an examination of the social boundaries of the migratory labor system, the motives for and consequences of entering the migratory stream, the way the recruitment system works, and the relationships between agricultural employers, crew leaders, and workers in the migratory labor system (Stewart 1968). The most comprehensive study done by the group is a vivid and perceptive description of the farm labor camps (Friedland and Nelkin 1971) showing how disorganized and unpredictable the life of the migratory worker is, how the worker adapts to the disorganized character of his existence, and the extent to which the worker is trapped in the migratory farm labor system.

While these studies are very valuable in themselves, they contain little information on the mobility of the workers — the distances they cover, the frequency of their movements, and the places they stop — and on possible relationships between mobility and the workers' characteristics. There are some scattered observations, occasional remarks, and a few hints, but there is no comprehensive analysis of the influence that the characteristics typifying the workers may have on how much they travel.

1.3. Mobility and Worker Characteristics

Most of the research cited above deals either with migratory farm workers in a certain area or with a certain category of migratory farm workers. Some mention is made of the workers' migratory movements, the states in which the workers were employed over a twelve-month period, and the kinds of crops they dealt with. Metzler, for instance, is one of the few authors who indicated the number of movements during a one-year period: he reported that practically none of the black migratory workers in his sample moved in the nomadic fashion observed in the West Coast stream.[8] His impression of mobility on the East Coast is quite different from the descriptions (mentioned above) of continuous movement in this migratory stream (Shotwell 1961:29-30; Wright 1965: Preface; quoted on page 63). Larson and Sharp (1960: 35), in their two samples, observed even less mobility between states than Metzler found.[9] The discrepancies between the journalistic descriptions of migration on the East Coast and the movements observed by social scientists such as Metzler, Larson, and Sharp are indeed substantial, and are certainly interesting in light of the conclusions about mobility that are drawn in this investigation.

While migratory movements and employment patterns on the one hand, and migratory movements and earnings on the other, have been given some attention,[10] very little has been done to relate the observed variations in migratory movements to the personal and socioeconomic characteristics of the workers. The only characteristic that has been related to mobility is the education of migratory children. When the parents are "on the season," keeping their children in school becomes a problem because they have to travel. Special summer schools for migratory children do exist in the North, but there are not enough of them; even if there were, it would still be difficult for the parents to decide to send their children to school, rather than having them work in the fields to supplement the family income. The result is that migratory children often fall behind the other schoolchildren, and this frequently makes it difficult for them, when they grow up, to break out of the farm labor stream and find better employment. As education seems to be an effective means of escaping from the migratory farm workers' very low position on the occupational ladder, schooling has been the main subject of much of the research done on migratory farm workers in the past twenty-five years. The influence that educating migratory children has on their parents' mobility has also been treated (Metzler 1955:17, 69), and observations showed that, in general, families with school-aged children did not leave their home bases in Florida later in the spring, or return to them earlier in the fall, to keep their children in school in Florida. On the other hand, the migratory farm workers with school-age children did move less often than other migratory farm workers. The relationship between the presence of school-age children in the family and the degree of mobility has unfortunately not been explored further. In a study done in New York on schooling for migratory farm workers and their children, it appeared that having school-age children did have an effect on the migration pattern:

About 5 percent of the children either remained in the home locality after their parents left or returned early in the fall to avoid loss of school time. It seems probable that, in other cases, the movement of either the entire family or the mother is scheduled so as not to interfere with the schooling of the children. (Sharp and Larson 1960:9)

Other writers have observed a similar relationship between the childrens' education and the mobility of their parents.[11] The New York education study reported that 89 percent of the children surveyed traveled with their families during the entire period of following the crops (from 1 September 1956 to August-September 1957; Sharp and Larson 1960:9). An investigation dealing specifically with the educational opportunities of migratory children (Greene 1954:109-123) indicated that migration seriously interfered with these opportunities, and that parents with more education were more consistent about keeping their children in school; no mention was made, however, of workers' characteristics that might influence their mobility. A study of migratory farm workers in New Jersey (Marcson and Fasick 1964:3) showed that a distinction can be made between migratory farm workers who (a) stay at a job for only a short period and travel thousands of miles to work in many states, and those who (b) live in one place for six to nine months of the year and move to another place to do farm work for the rest of the year. The majority of the migratory farm workers in the New Jersey study were contract workers who followed the latter mobility pattern. Although the differences between the patterns were made quite clear, no relationship was mentioned between them and the workers' characteristics.

In the Cornell study of migratory farm workers who had dropped out of the migratory stream permanently (Friedland 1967), it was pointed out that a small number of the migratory farm workers deliberately used the stream to move to the North and find employment in the urban industrial labor market, but that they were often deterred from leaving the stream by fear, uncertainty, and the long, cold winters. As to the worker characteristics that could be related to mobility, it appeared that the young male workers with no family ties were the ones who did more than just talk: they actually tried to stop migrating and to find some other kind of work (Friedland 1967:42-46).

Mobility has been described as the psychological as well as the concrete freedom of movement or freedom of choice which a person has, or thinks he has, within the constraints of the migratory farm labor system (Stewart 1968: 128). On the basis of this approach, a mobility construct can be developed which may be seen as a mediator between structure and process. Geographic mobility is an important component of this mobility construct, as are both the migratory farm worker's family responsibilities and his or her education. In developing a mobility index based on this construct (Stewart 1968:126-127), an attempt was made to distinguish between two types of migratory farm workers: one type has a more dependent attitude, knows less about the migratory system, and seeks less information; the other type is more independent, knows more about the system, seeks security through the manipulation of his own abilities within the system, and relies less on others. The index that is constructed is arbitrary, as Stewart said in discussing the ways in which it worked differently for women. She concluded: "Although the relationships which this construct enables us to observe are quite strong, the construct itself actually raises as many questions as it provides answers." (1968: 152) Nevertheless, the ideas it is based on are of particular importance to this investigation. The emphasis on the fact that the migratory farm worker needs to be geographically mobile in order to maximize his alternatives in the migratory farm labor stream, and the recognition of the role that family responsibility play in the migratory farm worker's freedom of movement, are especially relevant to the relationships between geographic mobility and worker characteristics.

Another Cornell study (Friedland and Nelkin 1971) has shown that educating children can cause a conflict for migratory parents. On the one hand, the parents value education and know it is the only way to keep their children out of the migratory farm labor stream; on the other, they know that if the children go to school, they cannot supplement the family income "...and they are a constraint on the necessary mobility of their parents." (1971:253)

As this overview of the research shows, contrasting observations have been made on the degree of mobility of migratory farm workers in the East Coast migratory stream. Undoubtedly, the basic reason for migratory workers to move is to earn a living. Taking this as a basis, the studies make clear that certain workers are more mobile than others, but almost nothing is said about what distinguishes more mobile workers from less mobile ones. If policies and programs aimed at helping the migratory farm workers are to be formulated, policy makers *must* know how mobile the various groups of migratory workers are, because it will be considerably easier to arrange education, training, health facilities, and housing for workers who move once or twice during a season, than for those who are continually on the move.

During the Depression the significance of the relationship between mobility and the compositions of the workers' families was recognized by researchers (section 1.1 of this chapter). Unattached migrants were observed to be more mobile than migrants who moved with a family, and the disruptive effect of migratory movements in the East Coast stream, especially on the education of children, was described. However, the influence of the workers' characteristics on mobility were hardly dealt with (except *vis-à-vis* education [pages 66 and 68-69], but the researchers who wrote about this clearly disagreed with each other). The analysis presented on the following pages is intended to fill this gap in our understanding of migratory farm worker life.

2. THE DEGREE OF MOBILITY IN THE EAST COAST MIGRATORY STREAM

2.1. *The Sample*

Statistical data that were collected for the 1970 unemployment insurance survey of agricultural employers and workers in fifteen states in the United States[12] comprise the data base for the analysis in this section and the following chapters. Fourteen of the states that were surveyed are located in the eastern part of the United States; as we are dealing only with the East Coast migratory labor stream, the survey data from outside that area — that is, from Texas — has been excluded from the analysis. No interviews could be made in Virginia, North Carolina, South Carolina, and Georgia because these states did not participate in the survey. However, workers interviewed in any of the fourteen states in the survey may have worked for some time during the survey period (see page 74) in one of these states, and in this sense all of the states on the East Coast have been included.

Since a listing of the farm worker population was not available, the workers had to be reached through their employers. The United States' Social Security program's reports provided the basic listing of the agricultural employer population in the surveyed states. Under this program, employers are required to file reports on the earnings of all employees who have earned at least $150 or have worked for at least twenty days during a given year.[13] A stratified random sample with optimum allocation was drawn from the agricultural employer population[14] in the fourteen eastern states. A random sample of workers was then taken from a stratified subsample of the employer sample. All employers with eight or more hired workers were included, and a random sample was drawn from the employers with seven or less hired workers. On the day the interviewer made his visit, a randomly selected percentage of the workers (but never less than two workers) was interviewed if the farm had eight or more workers. If the farm had seven or less workers, all of the workers were interviewed.[15]

This complicated sampling technique can be described as two-stage stratified random sampling which, given the lack of a listing of the worker population, was considered to be a valid technique for estimating population characteristics. The size of the total payroll was used as the stratifying characteristic for the employer sample in order to obtain a better estimate of the population characteristics that were sought, since the size of an employer's payroll is closely related to the major item to be estimated – that is, the employer's contribution towards an unemployment insurance fund.[16] As to the workers' sample, it was assumed that all workers in an unbiased sample of employers would constitute an unbiased sample of all workers (Bauder *et al.* 1976:26, 178-184). Using this method, a sample of 12,666 farm workers was drawn in the fourteen states in the survey.

It was estimated that this sample would effectively represent the almost 242,000 agricultural workers in these states. In 1970 the total hired farm labor force (i.e., those aged fourteen years or older who have done some kind of farm work for cash wages during the year) in the United States was estimated to be about 2.5 million (U.S. Department of Agriculture, Economic Research Service 1970:1). In the same year the civilian labor force was 82.7 million,[17] of which only a small portion (3 percent) was agricultural workers.

This fourteen-state sample of 12,666 farm workers in the East Coast migratory stream will be used throughout this investigation. A question we must ask ourselves is whether that sample is truly representative. Obviously, the best way to get the most representative sample would be to draw at random from a complete listing of all workers, but for lack of such a listing another solution had to be found. By using the Social Security listing of employers, the selected worker sample may have been slightly biased because employers who paid less than $150 in wages during the year were excluded from the lists. Thus workers employed for only a few days by employers who hired no other workers during that year had no chance of being included in the sample. Unemployed workers also could not be included. On the other hand, by conducting interviews with the workers during the periods of peak employment and at the place of employment, the numbers and kinds of workers that could be interviewed were maximized, because even the most casual — and most elusive — worker would be quite likely to be on the job. It is very probable that given these circumstances, the sample provides a very reasonable representation of the farm worker population in the fourteen states.[18]

Out of this sample, 3,785 workers were classified as "interstate migratory farm workers" and defined as workers who had left home for one night or more to do temporary work in another state during the twelve-month period preceding the interview. The analysis in this chapter deals only with these 3,785 migratory workers, who constitute 29 percent of all workers in the sample. Those farm workers who remained in one state but left their home overnight to do temporary work in another county were called "intrastate migratory farm workers." This category of workers was very small (slightly more than one hundred persons), constituting 1 percent of the farm workers in the sample. As this investigation of the workers' mobility deals only with those migratory workers who move *between* states, the intrastate migratory workers were grouped with the nonmigratory workers. This grouping raises the question of the significance for migratory workers of crossing a state line: it is "being migratory," and not whether one moves between states or between counties, that is relevant for these people. Furthermore, some states are so large that the intrastate migratory workers may cover greater distances than interstate migratory workers. Nonetheless, there are two important reasons for focusing on the interstate migratory workers and disregarding the small number of intrastate migratory workers in the sample. First of all, the survey did not compile information on the number of counties in which each intrastate migratory worker was employed (see the Questionnaire in Appendix A); it only indicated that the intrastate migratory worker had been away from home overnight for a certain period during the year and had worked in another county. For the interstate migratory farm workers, however, the state in which the worker resided during each week of a fifty-two-week period was recorded so that the degree of interstate mobility among these workers could be measured. The second reason for disregarding the intrastate migratory workers is that this investigation, like the survey, is policy oriented.

Because most of the social legislation and policies in the United States are enacted and implemented at the state level, either by the state government or by the federal government working through the state, it is the state, and not the county, that determines what social benefits are available. Furthermore, the benefits available in each state may differ, and as a result a migratory worker's place of residence may determine the kind of benefits he or she is entitled to receive. It is therefore important for both the worker and the government to know which state is considered to be the worker's resident state. Clearly, from the viewpoint of policy, intrastate movements are less important.

Just as a few intrastate migratory workers were grouped among the nonmigratory farm workers, so have a number of workers (around 12 percent of the 3,785 interstate migratory workers) who migrated both between states and within states been included among the migratory workers. This was done because of the survey's orientation towards policy making for interstate migration. For the same reason, and for lack of complete information (as with the intrastate migratory workers), the intrastate movements of these workers were not further analyzed.

Migratory farm workers, as well as other farm workers, are usually considered to be poorly educated people who are members of ethnic minorities. This image corresponds with information provided by the sample of 3,785 interstate migratory farm workers: their median number of years of education was seven, and 40 percent of them were black, 31 percent were Puerto Rican, 15 percent were Mexican, and 3 percent were in other ethnic groups; only 11 percent were white. Two other aspects were also quite distinct in the sample. First of all, the workers were quite young, their median age being 29.1 years. Secondly, slightly more than 15 percent of the workers in the sample were women, which indicates that since World War II, the number of female migratory farm workers has increased.

2.2. Analysis of the Migratory Patterns

During a fifty-two week period that began with the week ending on 5 July 1969 and lasted through the week ending on 27 June 1970, detailed information was collected for each week on the work situation of the farm workers in the sample. A Questionnaire (see Appendix A) was used to record the state in which the workers worked, what jobs they did, and how much pay they received during the fifty-two-week survey period. This week-by-week information made it possible to trace the interstate movements of these workers throughout the year.

Figure 4.1. *The Location of Migratory Farm Workers during Each Week from 5 July 1969 to 27 June 1970*

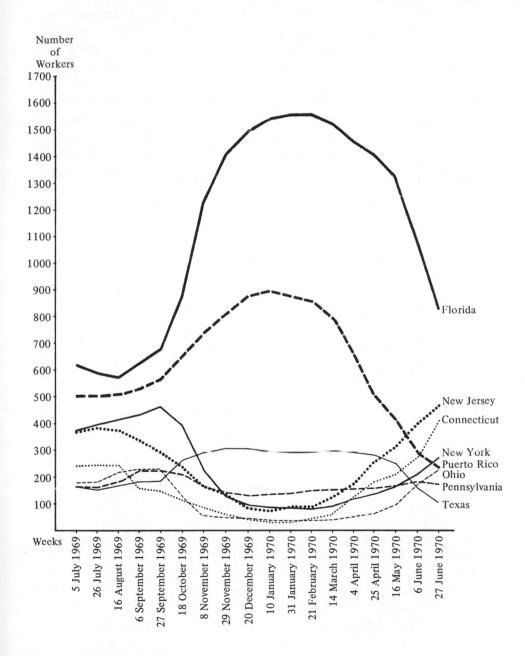

Figure 4.1 shows the locations of the 3,785 migratory farm workers during the entire fifty-two-week period. Clearly Florida, Puerto Rico, and Texas were the states where most of the migratory workers spent the winter: 72 percent of the 3,785 migratory farm workers stayed in these states, while only 27 percent were in the other states.[19] Florida was the state in which the largest percentage of migratory farm workers — 41 percent — stayed during the winter; Puerto Rico followed with 23 percent; then Texas with 8 percent (2 percent of the workers resided in Georgia, but Georgia has not been included in Figure 4.1). During the rest of the year the workers generally moved to the other states. Some of the states where the migratory farm workers stayed in the summer also had significant numbers of migratory farm workers staying over in the winter: the largest group was found in Pennsylvania, where 4 percent of the migratory farm workers spent some time during the winter months (see Figure 4.1); 2 percent were in New Jersey and 2 percent were in New York. One percent of the workers or less, or none at all, spent some time during the winter in each of the other states in the survey. Thus Florida, Puerto Rico, and Texas are certainly the states which serve as home base areas for the migratory farm workers in the East Coast stream. This would suggest that each of the ethnic groups in this stream has a home base area of its own. In fact the survey revealed that, of the 41 percent of migratory workers who lived in Florida for several weeks in the winter, 70 percent were black; of the 8 percent of migratory workers who lived in Texas for some time during the winter, 95 percent were Mexican; and of the 23 percent of migratory workers who lived in Puerto Rico for some time in the winter, 99 percent were Puerto Rican.

The locations of the migratory farm workers are very different during the peak employment period in the summer. As Figure 4.1 shows, during the week ending on 16 August 1969, the number of migratory farm workers in Florida dropped to its lowest: only 572 of them were there. While this is 15 percent of all migratory workers, it is *less than half* of the number of migratory farm workers who stayed in Florida in the winter. But as the figure shows, this 15 percent indicates that Florida is also the state where the largest number of migratory farm workers reside in the summer, when the number of available jobs is much less than from January to May. This suggests that there is a high turnover among the migratory workers — that is, that many of the people who had resided in Florida during the full fifty-two-week survey period had only quite recently joined the migratory stream (or, in some cases, rejoined it after doing other work).

During the same week in August, 13 percent of the workers were in Puerto Rico and 4 percent were in Texas. Thus the survey showed that the following

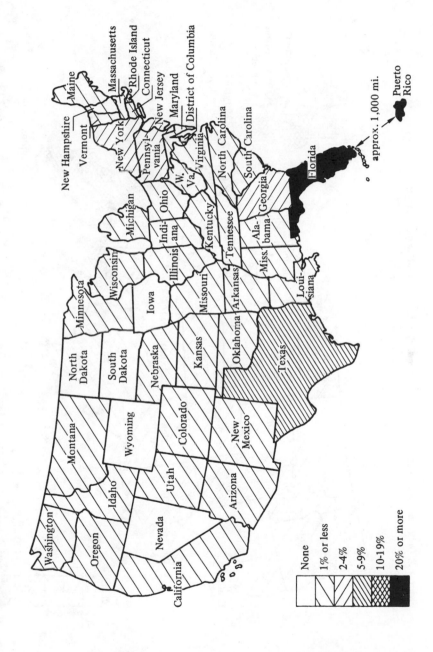

Figure 4.2. *The Location of Migratory Farm Workers during the Week Ending on 31 January 1970*

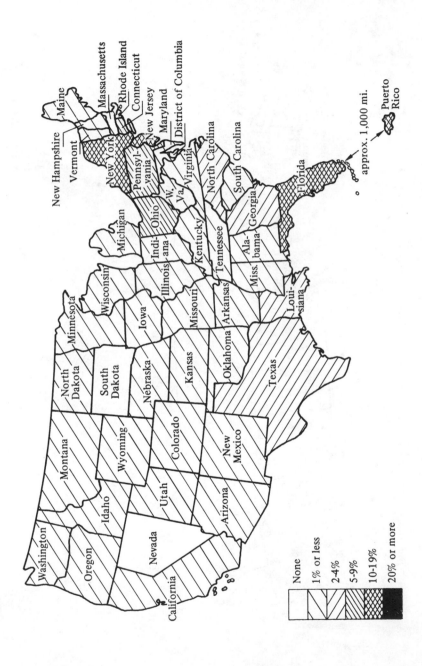

Figure 4.3. The Location of Migratory Farm Workers during the Week Ending on 16 August 1969

None
1% or less
2-4%
5-9%
10-19%
20% or more

percentages of workers were present in the following receiving states in the North:

New York	11 percent	Ohio	6 percent
New Jersey	10 percent	Pennsylvania	5 percent
Connecticut	7 percent	Michigan	3 percent

Only 2 percent or less of the migratory workers were in other states during this period.

Figures 4.2 and 4.3 illustrate the migratory farm workers' mobility by showing the locations of these workers in the fourteen states during two different weeks (one in summer and one in winter) of the fifty-two-week survey period. Figure 4.2 indicates where the workers were during the week ending on 31 January 1970; Figure 4.3 indicates the same for the week ending on 16 August 1969. Together, the two figures show that at both of these two specific times, the migratory farm workers were spread over many states. Even though the survey dealt only with workers interviewed in fourteen East Coast states, the data showed that the migratory workers resided in not only these fourteen states but in all of the East Coast states, including the states that did not participate in the survey (Virginia, Georgia, North Carolina, and South Carolina). Moreover, there were migratory workers in most of the other states in the United States as well, as Figure 4.3 shows. Thus the general impression that the migratory farm worker is a long-distance traveler who moves from state to state appears to be accurate.

Migratory farm workers do travel from state to state, but they do not cover such great distances as Figure 4.3 would suggest. The survey showed that most of the migratory workers who left their homes for at least one night to do temporary work in another state in fact worked in only a small number of states during that period (see Table 4.1).

This more limited mobility is demonstrated by the fact that 52 percent of the migratory workers in the sample worked in a maximum of two states during the fifty-two-week period, while 12 percent worked in four or more states, and only 4 percent worked in five or more states. This leads to the conclusion that the majority of the migratory farm workers travel much less, in the sense of moving from state to state to find work, during a year than was assumed; only a small minority moves more or less continually to a number of states. This conclusion contradicts some of the journalistic descriptions of migratory farm workers (pages 63-64), but coincides with observations made by social scientists.

Table 4.1. *Number of States Worked in by Migratory Farm Workers*

Number of states worked in[a]	*Migratory farm workers*	
	Number	*%*
1[b]	805	21
2	1,177	31
3	1,334	36
4	309	8
5 or more	152	4
Total	3,777	100

Undefined: 8

[a] The number of states in which the migratory workers worked was recorded during a fifty-two-week period beginning with the week ending on 5 July 1969 and lasting through the week ending on 27 June 1970. A state was counted twice if a worker had returned to it after working in another state.

[b] Migratory farm workers were defined as farm workers who, during the twelve-month period previous to the date of their interview, left their homes for one night or more to do temporary work in another state (see page 73). As all the migratory farm workers could of course not be interviewed on the same day, the twelve-month period previous to the interview varied, while the fifty-two-week period was fixed and was therefore the same for every worker. Those migratory farm workers who were interviewed at the end of the interview period, and whose "twelve-month period previous to being interviewed" could therefore not cover all fifty-two weeks, provided information that fully covered the fixed fifty-two-week period and included the week ending on 5 July 1969. Question 11 of the Questionnaire (see Appendix A) provided the main criteria for distinguishing between workers who were migratory and those who were not. The actual mobility of the worker was analyzed on the basis of the fixed fifty-two weeks. This procedure may have resulted in defining some of the people who worked in more than one state during the fifty-two-week period as nonmigratory workers, while others who did not work in another state during the fifty-two-week period may have been defined as migratory farm workers on the basis of question 11. For instance, those who worked for the same company in two states, or those who moved to a residence in another state during the fifty-two-week period and thus lived in more than one state during the survey period, were not included with the migratory workers (question 11). On the other hand, some of the workers who considered themselves to be interstate migratory workers may not have worked in another state during the fifty-two-week period, but they did work in at least two states during the twelve months preceding their interview. The migratory workers who did not work in another state during the fifty-two-week period were very frequently workers who had joined the stream recently. The data suggest a considerable turnover in migratory farm work (see page 76).

Metzler's study of a sample of black migratory farm workers in Florida revealed that 50 percent of these workers worked in one state outside Florida, 35 percent worked in two states outside Florida, and 15 percent worked in three of more states outside Florida (1955:26).[20] Larson and Sharp's New York study indicated even less mobility in one of its samples (1960:35; see note 9 of this chapter), but the data were not entirely comparable and both studies were limited to black migratory farm workers.

A more meaningful comparison can be obtained by examining the data on the number of states in which members of each ethnic group in migratory farm work worked during the fifty-two-week period. These are presented in Table 4.2.

Table 4.2. *Ethnic Group Membership and Number of States Worked in*

Ethnic group membership	Number of states worked in				Total	
	1	*2*	*3*	*4 or more*		
	%	%	%	%	%	*(N)*
White	28	32	31	9	100	(416)
Black	25	34	32	9	100	(1,507)
Puerto Rican	17	33	40	10	100	(1,183)
Mexican	14	24	36	26	100	(550)
Other[a]	29	16	36	19	100	(108)
Total	21	31	36	12	100	(3,764)

Undefined: 21
$X^2 = 190.6$ 12 df.   sign. at .05
Phi = 0.22

[a] The category labeled "other" included the workers who could not be classified in one of the four ethnic categories. Most of the workers (58 percent) in this category were in New York, and the results indicated that they were mostly from Jamaica and the Bahamas. There were also a few Philippinos and Canadians. It is therefore not unlikely that most of the workers in the "other" category in the fourteen-state sample were from the West Indies.

The table shows that 59 percent of the black migratory workers in the sample were employed in a maximum of two states during the fifty-two-week period; 32 percent worked in three states and 9 percent worked in four or more states. These findings are quite similar to percentages given in the Florida and New York studies (Metzler 1955:26; Larson and Sharp 1960:35; see also notes 8 and 9 of this chapter). Although there is a time gap of thirteen to fifteen years between the unemployment insurance survey and the Florida and New York studies, and although the fifty-two-week period in the survey does not in all cases coincide with the twelve months preceding each interview, the degree of interstate mobility among black migratory farm workers was almost the same in all three sources.

Table 4.2 also shows that the white, black, and Puerto Rican migratory farm workers were more or less equally mobile, while the Mexicans in particular, and to some extent the workers in the category labeled "other," moved more: 26 percent of the Mexican migratory farm workers worked in four or more states and 38 percent worked in a maximum of two states. This means that of the various ethnic groups in this sample, the Mexicans were the most mobile; this may in part be due to the fact that most (but not all) Mexicans come from a home base area in Texas, which is a great distance from the East Coast. It seems likely that migratory workers who have to travel such a distance to reach the East Coast would pick up jobs in other states while traveling.

To further explore the migratory farm workers' patterns of migration, information on the number of *different* states in which the workers were employed during the fifty-two-week period was analyzed. This was done to find out whether the workers who were employed in three states actually were in three different states (e.g., Florida, Virginia, and New York) during the fifty-two-week period, rather than following the low mobility pattern of workers like the New Jersey migratory farm workers (described in Marcson and Fasick 1964; see page 69), who live in one place for six to nine months of the year and then move to another place for the rest of the year. Table 4.3 shows the number of different states in which members of the ethnic groups in migratory farm work were employed during the fifty-two-week period.

Table 4.3. *Ethnic Group Membership and the Number of Different States Worked in*

Ethnic group membership	Number of states worked in				Total	
	1	*2*	*3*	*4 or more*		
	%	%	%	%	%	*(N)*
White	28	59	10	3	100	(416)
Black	24	60	13	3	100	(1,507)
Puerto Rican	17	67	14	2	100	(1,183)
Mexican	14	45	27	14	100	(550)
Other	29	52	17	2	100	(108)
Total	21	60	15	4	100	(3,764)

Undefined: 21
X^2 = 274.7   12 df.   sign. at .05
Phi = 0.27

A comparison of Tables 4.3 and 4.2 shows that many of the workers who, in Table 4.2, are listed as having worked in three states, are listed as having worked in two states in Table 4.3. In Table 4.2, 36 percent (1,332 workers) of all migratory workers in the sample worked in three states, but in Table 4.3 only 15 percent (575 workers) worked in three *different* states. This means that more than half of the workers who worked in three states very likely followed the less mobile pattern, leaving their home base state to work in one other state and then returning to their home state (going from, say, Florida to New York to Florida or from Puerto Rico to New Jersey to Puerto Rico). Only 19 percent of the migratory workers worked in three or more different states, and only 4 percent worked in four or more different states. As in Table 4.2, the degree of mobility among the whites, blacks, and Puerto Ricans was nearly the same, while the Mexican workers were considerably more mobile: 41 percent worked in three or more different states and 14 percent worked in four or more different states.

Before looking into whether there is a relationship between the degree of interstate mobility and the various worker characteristics, the question of whether the migratory farm workers prefer their migratory existence to other ways of life should be dealt with. Information on the workers' attitudes was collected during the survey by asking the interstate migratory farm workers whether they would have liked to spend the entire year in the state where they were interviewed, *if* they could have earned a steady income there.[21] Whether a worker is a member of an ethnic group may have an influence on his or her desire to remain in the state where the interview took place, and for this reason the answers to this question, which are shown in Table 4.4, were tabulated according to ethnic group membership.

Table 4.4. *Ethnic Group Membership and the Desire to Stay in the State where Interviewed*

Ethnic group membership	Desire to stay in state where interviewed		Total	
	yes	*no*		
	%	%	%	*(N)*
White	67	33	100	(276)
Black	73	27	100	(1,366)
Puerto Rican	62	38	100	(1,099)
Mexican	64	36	100	(463)
Other	85	15	100	(104)
Total	68	32	100	(3,308)

Undefined: 477
$X^2 = 53.7$ 4 df.   sign. at .05
Phi = 0.13

Sixty-eight percent of all the migratory farm workers would have preferred to spend the entire year in the state where they were interviewed, *if* they could have earned a steady income there. Unfortunately, the question that was posed to the workers was not very clearly formulated, and it is therefore possible that migratory farm workers who did not want to spend the entire year in the state where they were interviewed would nonetheless have preferred to stop migrating, or that they would have preferred to spend the entire year in a state other than the one in which they were interviewed. The Puerto Ricans and Mexicans showed less interest than both the workers in the "other" category and the black workers in spending the entire year in the state where they were interviewed; the white workers were in between. It is very likely that the Puerto Ricans and Mexicans felt more strongly than the others about returning to their winter communities because they wanted to be able to live with people who speak their language and have the same cultural background (very few of these people live in the states where the interviews took place).

It was mentioned above that workers in the category labeled "other" generally wanted to stay in the state where they were interviewed. In New York the majority of workers in the "other" category were Jamaican or Bahamian; since most of the workers in this category were interviewed in New York, it is safe to assume that quite a few of these workers were from the British West Indies. The data suggested that most of these foreign workers would have liked to settle in the United States.

Except for the workers in the "other" category, the black workers had the highest percentage of migratory farm workers who would have preferred to stay in the state where they were interviewed if they could have earned a steady income. This raises the question of whether such attitudes reflect the migratory worker's "dream" of moving to the North:

A grandiose dream of the interstate migratory agricultural worker, born and reared in a tar-paper shanty in the backwoods Deep South, is that his first trip up the road, way up north, on the season, will be his last. He has heard tell, perhaps from friends or relatives who've made the trip — or trips — before, maybe from a fellow stoop laborer with whom he worked side by side in a bean patch, that he'll find a pot of gold at the end of his rainbow and there'll be no bossman to take his share off the top. He's heard, too, that everybody lives big "up north" where the big cities are and that "they" don't allow cheating on wages. He's been told that he would get paid for every hour he worked up the road in the north — sometimes even at overtime rates. The "gov'ment" takes care of everyone who needs help, as long as they need it, but most of the time you can make it easily enough on your own. (Wright 1965:82-83)

This dream seldom comes true, and the question is: do black migratory farm workers really have such a strong desire to settle in the North? To answer this question, a comparison was made between those black migratory workers who were interviewed in Florida (the home base state for many black migratory workers) and those interviewed in the northern states. The question posed during the interview was: "Would you stay in [the state of interview] the year-round if you could earn a steady income here?" Ninety percent of the black migratory farm workers interviewed in Florida (482 workers) indicated that they would have liked to stay in Florida; 66 percent of the black workers in the ten northern states in the survey[22] (723 workers) would have liked to stay in the state where interviewed. These percentages do not correspond with the impression that the black migratory farm workers have only one wish, which is to settle in the North. They bear out findings affirming that the South is becoming increasingly attractive to black people (Campbell, Johnson, and Stangler 1974:514-528).

Considering the question of whether the migratory farm workers would prefer to continue to travel in order to find work clearly shows that, although the data were not conclusive (due to the lack of clarity in the question used in the interviews), more than two thirds of the migratory farm workers in the sample certainly would have preferred to stop traveling and settle down in one of the fourteen states in the survey. Furthermore, it is possible that the one third of the migratory farm workers who did not want to stay all year-round in the state where they were interviewed nonetheless preferred to stop migrating, but wanted to settle in some other state.

3. WORKER CHARACTERISTICS AND THE DEGREE OF INTERSTATE MOBILITY

Although several writers have reported that the degree of mobility among migratory farm workers varies (section 1 of this chapter), very little has been said about the relationship between the degree of mobility and the socioeconomic characteristics of the workers. The studies that deal with mobility treat it as the independent variable (pages 68-71). To gain a better understanding of the relationship between mobility and the workers' characteristics, interstate mobility must be taken as the dependent variable, because from a policy viewpoint, it is important to find out whether certain characteristics of migratory farm workers act to constrain or stimulate interstate mobility. An understanding of these relationships is essential to developing programs which can benefit the migratory farm workers.

The descriptions of the migrations which took place during the Depression indicated that migratory *families* were more cautious in their movements — and therefore less mobile — than *unattached* migratory workers (pages 64-66). In more recent research on migratory farm workers on the East Coast, conflicting statements have been made about the influence of school-age children on the migratory patterns of their parents (pages 68-69). As this research comprises the only available information, it will be used as a starting point for analyzing the data.

First, let us examine the relationship between the presence or absence of the family while the worker is migrating (called "family travel status") and the degree of interstate mobility. This is presented in Table 4.5.

Table 4.5. *Family Travel Status and the Number of States Worked in*

Family travel status	Number of states worked in				Total	
	1	2	3	4 or more		
	%	%	%	%	%	(N)
All family members traveled with respondent	17	30	36	17	100	(648)
Some family members traveled with respondent	18	31	38	13	100	(582)
No family members traveled with respondent	24	30	35	11	100	(2,001)
Not applicable (no family)	14	38	38	10	100	(205)
Total	21	30	36	13	100	(3,436)

Undefined: 349
$X^2 = 29.6$ 9 df.   sign. at .05
Phi = 0.09

Table 4.5 shows that family travel status does not make any great difference in interstate mobility. The presence or absence of the family affected the worker's interstate mobility only to a small degree. This certainly conflicts with observations made during the Depression, which suggested that unattached migratory workers are more mobile than workers who travel with their families. In fact, as the category in Table 4.5 with the highest degree of interstate mobility (the fourth column) shows, the workers whose family members did not travel with them and the workers who had no families comprised, in comparison to the other two worker categories, the smallest percentage (11 percent and 10 percent respectively) of the workers listed in that column. However, the workers who traveled with all their family members had, compared to the other family travel status categories, the highest percentage (17 percent) of workers in the category with the highest interstate mobility.

Because, among Puerto Rican workers, there are frequently large numbers of contract workers who have left their families at home (Marcson and Fasick 1964:18), and because Mexican workers are known for taking their entire families with them (U.S. Congress, Senate, Committee on Labor and Public Welfare 1960:7), it was expected that there would be differences in family travel status based on membership in one of these two ethnic groups. Table 4.6 presents the family travel status of the workers according to ethnic group membership. (Because the category labeled "some of the family members travel with respondent" was rather vague, only the two extreme categories — "all family members travel with respondent" and "no family members travel with respondent" — have been listed.)

Table 4.6. *Ethnic Group Membership and Family Travel Status*

Ethnic group membership	Family travel status			
	All family members traveled with respondent	No family members traveled with respondent	Total	
	%	%	%	(N)
White	34	66	100	(235)
Black	25	75	100	(1,074)
Puerto Rican	3	97	100	(888)
Mexican	78	22	100	(347)
Other	7	93	100	(95)
Total	25	75	100	(2,639)

Undefined: 359
Excluded: "Some traveled" = 582; "Not applicable" = 205
$X^2 = 781.0$ 4 df.   sign. at .05
Phi = 0.55

Table 4.6 shows that there was a striking difference between the various ethnic groups as far as their decisions to travel with or without their families are concerned. Most Puerto Ricans left their families at home, as did the workers in the "other" category. The great majority of Mexican workers brought their families with them, while a larger percentage of white workers than blacks, Puerto Ricans, and those labeled "other"[23] took all their family members with them.

Once the family has decided to move, its presence did not appear to be a constraint on the migratory farm worker's interstate mobility. On the other hand, many migratory farm workers did leave their families at home: almost two thirds of the workers in Table 4.5 traveled without any of their family members, and most of the migratory workers in each ethnic group, except the Mexicans, left their families behind, as Table 4.6 shows. The differences in the mobility of the various ethnic groups and the differences in family travel status suggested that the relationship between the migratory farm worker's mobility and the family travel status should be explored further within each ethnic group. Because the Mexican workers were the only group that showed significant results for this relationship, only their results are presented: see Table 4.7.

Table 4.7. *Family Travel Status and the Number of States in which Mexican Migratory Farm Workers Worked*

Family travel status	Number of states worked in				Total	
	1	*2*	*3*	*4 or more*	*%*	*(N)*
	%	*%*	*%*	*%*		
All family members traveled with respondent	11	25	40	24	100	(269)
No family members traveled with respondent	35	23	17	25	100	(78)
Total	16	24	35	25	100	(347)

$X^2 = 30.7$ 3 df.   sign. at .05
Phi = 0.30

These results do not support suggestions that if a family accompanies a migratory worker, it acts as a constraint on the worker's movements. Compared to the Mexican workers who left their families at home, the Mexican workers who traveled with all their family members comprised about the same percentage of workers in the most mobile group in the table (listed under "4 or more states"), a much higher percentage in the second most mobile group (listed under "3 states"), and a much lower percentage in the least mobile group (listed under "1 state").

The data in Tables 4.5, 4.6, and 4.7 can only lead to one conclusion: once the family is on the road, its presence definitely does not restrict the migratory farm worker's interstate mobility.[24] Nonetheless, almost two thirds (62 percent) of all the migratory workers with families left them behind, as did about 72 percent of the non-Mexican migratory farm workers with families. The complications of traveling with a family did not result in less mobility among workers who traveled with their families as compared to those who traveled without them.

Instead, most of the migratory farm workers chose to have their families stay at home.[25] Only the Mexican migratory worker proved to be a typically "family-migratory" farm worker.

Another aspect of the mobility of migratory farm workers that has received some attention in the literature (see pages 68-70) is the relationship between the degree of mobility and the presence of school-age children in the family, which is presented in Table 4.8. Because any investigation of whether school-age children restrict the migratory farm worker's mobility must focus on the migratory workers who travel with all of their children, those workers who left some of their children behind in the home base area, or who had no children, were not included. The table compares the mobility of workers with school-age children to that of workers with non-school-age children.

Table 4.8. *The Presence of School-age or Non-school-age Children and Number of States Worked in*[a]

Presence of children	Number of states worked in				Total	
	1	2	3	4 or more		
	%	%	%	%	%	(N)
School-age	16	33	33	18	100	(314)
Non-school-age	20	23	42	15	100	(137)
Total	17	30	36	17	100	(451)

$X^2 = 6.6$ 3 df.   not sign.
Phi = 0.12

[a] This table includes only those migratory farm workers who traveled with all of their family members and who had school-age or non-school-age children. Children aged six to sixteen years were considered to be school-age children.

Table 4.8 shows that differences between the interstate mobility of workers who traveled with school-age children and those who traveled with non-school-age children were not significant. The workers with school-age children comprised a slightly larger percentage of the category with the highest mobility (listed "4 or more states") than the workers with non-school-age children. But in the category with the second highest mobility (listed under "3 states"), the workers with non-school-age children comprised the largest percentage. Taking the workers with school-age children and the workers with non-school-age children separately, and combining those workers from each of these two categories who have worked in three states, or in four or more states, we find that the workers who have worked in three states, or in four or more states, comprise 51 percent of the workers with school-age children and 57 percent of the workers with non-school-age children. As the difference in percentages is quite small, we must conclude that Table 4.8 does not suggest that school-age children limit the interstate mobility of their parents.

Since ethnic group membership has been shown to be an influential factor in the interstate mobility of migratory farm workers, the relationship between the presence of school-age or non-school-age children and interstate mobility was also investigated within each ethnic group.[26] Whites, blacks, and Mexicans showed about the same percentages as those in Table 4.8: the workers who traveled with school-age children comprised, compared to those with non-school-age children, a slightly higher percentage of the category with the greatest mobility (listed under "4 or more states") and a lower percentage of the category with the second greatest mobility (listed under "3 states"). The number of Puerto Rican workers (twenty) and of workers listed in the "other" category (eleven) was too small to be significant. Thus the assumption that school-age children limit the migratory movements of their parents is not borne out by the data.[27]

Restricting their migratory movements in order to allow their school-age children to attend school without interruption is not the only means migratory parents have to ensure that their children are in school continually. Other possibilities are leaving the children at the home base (with their mother or with a relative) so that they can attend the same school all year-round, or having the family stay as long as possible in the home base area and limiting migratory movements to the school vacations. As was shown in Table 4.6, the majority of the migratory farm workers in the survey left their families behind. In order to find out whether school-age children were left behind more often than non-school-age children, Table 4.9 compares the percentage of families with school-age children with the percentage of families with non-school-age children and lists the families who stayed behind separately from those who traveled with the workers. This presentation shows that the presence of school-age children in a migratory farm worker's family had no effect on the worker's decision to travel with or without his or her family members. When the same relationship was studied within each of the ethnic groups, only small differences were found, as far as the presence of school-age or non-school-age children is concerned, in the percentages for "all family members travel..." and "no family members travel...."[28]

Yet another way in which migratory parents may ensure that their children attend school continually is (as suggested in Larson and Sharp 1960) to schedule

Table 4.9. *The Presence of School-age or Non-school-age Children and Family Travel Status*[a]

Presence of children	Family travel status			
	All family members traveled with respondent	No family members traveled with respondent	Total	
	%	%	%	(N)
School-age	29	71	100	(1,087)
Non-school-age	30	70	100	(460)
Total	29	71	100	(1,547)

$X^2 = 0.1$ 1 df.   not sign.
Phi = 0.04

[a] Only those migratory farm workers who had children and who had traveled with all family members, or had left all their family members behind, are included.

their movements so that they leave the home base later in the spring and return to it earlier in the fall. Unfortunately, such a travel pattern could only be investigated in six states[29] in the fourteen-state survey area, where a more extensive questionnaire was used. Information on the workers' permanent addresses was only obtained in these states. This information could be used to count the number of weeks each worker spent in his or her home base state. Table 4.10 presents the relationship between the presence of school-age or non-school-age children and the number of weeks spent in the home base state, for those workers who traveled with all members of their families and were interviewed in one of the six states.

Table 4.10. *The Presence of School-age or Non-school-age Children and Weeks Spent in the Home Base State, for Workers in Six States Who Traveled with their Families*

Presence of children	Weeks in home base state				Total	
	0-19 weeks	20-29 weeks	30-39 weeks	40 or more weeks	%	(N)
	%	%	%	%		
School-age	44	9	26	21	100	(267)
Non-school-age	51	5	25	19	100	(111)
Total	46	8	26	20	100	(378)

$X^2 = 2.4$ 3 df.   not sign.
Phi = 0.08

Table 4.10 shows that, as far as the number of weeks spent at the home base is concerned, the workers with school-age children differed very little from workers with non-school-age children. The column with the least weeks in the home base state (listed under "0-19 weeks") had a lower percentage of families with school-age children (although it was still rather high: 44 percent) than with non-school-age children. The three columns with more weeks in the home base state had only slightly higher percentages of families with school-age children. However, the results did not indicate that workers with school-age children clearly stayed longer in their home base state than workers with non-school-age children.

The data presented in Tables 4.8, 4.9, and 4.10 strongly suggest that having school-age children does not limit the workers' migratory movements. This finding contradicts the assumption that school-age children restrict their parents' movements (Larson and Sharp 1960:9), but bears out observations to the contrary (Metzler 1955:17). Of course the question still remains of whether migratory farm workers are truly interested in their children's education. The data gathered in the 1970 survey provided no information on this point, but the attitudes of migratory parents towards educating their children have been investigated. One study reported that 80 percent of the migratory parents would have liked to have their children finish high school (Greene 1954:73) and found that the more years of schooling the parents had, the more weeks their children were enrolled in school and the greater the chance was that all children in the family were enrolled in school (Greene 1954:11). Another study showed that although migratory parents claimed to appreciate the importance of education, few were really concerned about keeping their children in school. "The lack of interest of many migrant parents in the education of the children is complemented by the pride they take in the financial contributions their children can make to their families by working in the fields." (Marcson and Fasick 1964: 240) A more recent study reported that migratory workers did value education for their children, but that the realities of their economic needs were in constant conflict with the desire to have their children educated (Friedland and Nelkin 1971:252-253). This is indeed confirmed by the analysis presented here.

4. MOBILITY REAPPRAISED

The mobility of the migratory farm workers, and the relationships between mobility and the workers' characteristics, have proved to be surprisingly different from what was generally assumed, as the following conclusions show.

(1) Although migratory farm workers in the East Coast stream are thought to be continually moving from state to state, the data and analysis presented here clearly indicate that this is not the case. The majority of the migratory workers in the sample moved to a certain state, worked there for a fairly extended period of time, and returned to the home base state. Only 12 percent of the migratory workers in the sample worked in four or more states. Thus it appears that the image that migratory farm workers have in the United States of constantly traveling from state to state is maintained and enforced by the presence, during certain periods of each year, of only very small groups of migratory farm workers in almost all of the states. Clearly, the large majority of the East Coast migratory farm workers do not fit this description because they are considerably less mobile.

(2) In Chapter 2, the Federal-State Farm Labor Services, which function as intermediaries in bringing together the agricultural employers and the available workers, and the Annual Worker Plan, which works out the scheduling for farm workers and employers each season, were described. The findings on the migratory workers' interstate mobility would seem to indicate that the Annual Worker Plan has to some extent been effective in accomplishing its aims, at least as far as planning interstate migratory movements is concerned, for the migratory workers in the sample moved to relatively few states. These findings suggest that the Annual Worker Plan may have succeeded, in the course of the years up to 1970 (when the survey was made), in improving its coordinating activities over the years, for while the number and duration of jobs available to migratory farm workers has decreased since World War II, the interstate mobility of, for instance, the black workers during 1970 was almost the same as it was found to be in 1955 (page 81). During this period the agricultural production process has continued to become more specialized and mechanized, and has generally reduced the need for migratory farm workers.

A good example of how rapidly mechanization can develop, and how it can change employment patterns and replace workers, is provided by the role the mechanical grape picker played in New York. This harvesting machine was introduced in New York during the 1967 harvest season. Three years later, it was estimated that 75 to 80 percent of New York grapes were harvested mechanically. The earliest mechanical harvesters replaced seventeen to thirty hand pickers (Shepardson, Markwandt, Millier, and Rehkugler 1970:3-5), but the most efficient ones replaced sixty-two to ninety-five pickers (Jordan and Dominick 1968).

It has been suggested that mechanization has aggravated problems in seasonal labor (U.S. Department of Labor 1959:68; Shotwell 1961:194) because it has created a need for more workers during increasingly shorter periods of time — the reason being that while mechanization has been very effective for certain crops, it has been only partially successful for others. Thus many workers are employed for short periods to work on those crops on which machines can only be used during part or parts of the growing and harvesting process. This results in very tight scheduling in farm work and makes it difficult for the migratory farm worker to follow the cycle of the crops and find enough work during the season. The data analysis does not, however, bear out the assumption that because of increased mechanization, migratory farm workers have to travel more to find work,[30] as is illustrated by the black workers mentioned above (page 81). In fact the Annual Worker Plan, through its coordinating activities, may well have neutralized the effects of mechanization on the duration of farm jobs by improving planning and scheduling, which would mean that during 1970, the farm workers did not have to travel more in order to remain employed. The low interstate mobility of migratory farm workers would bear out this possibility. Eighty-one percent of the workers were employed in a maximum of two different states during a fifty-two-week period, while only 12 percent worked in four or more states, and only 4 percent worked in five or more states.

As stated above, most of the migratory farm workers in the East Coast stream leave their home base to work in one other state — usually for an extended period of time — and then return to their home base. Thus it is not just the Puerto Rican and British West Indian contract workers, but the *majority* of the migratory workers, who follow this pattern. This fact is extremely significant for policy making in the sense that it should make it easier to plan for employment, transportation, and housing for migratory workers and schooling for their children, because only two states, rather than several, would be involved. Close cooperation between the agencies dealing with migratory workers in two states where the periods of high demand for farm labor are complementary, e.g., Florida and New York, could greatly improve the migratory farm workers' living and working conditions. Such cooperation between agencies should be aimed at tackling the problems that are of concern to the migratory workers, and at bringing them the benefits they need, instead of dealing exclusively with arrangements that benefit the agricultural employers, such as planning when the workers may leave Florida and ensuring that enough workers are available when they are needed. If the plight of the migratory farm workers is to be improved, the problems they have must be given full attention during the annual planning sessions.

(3) Analyzing the relationship between the workers' characteristics and the degree of interstate mobility has revealed that ethnic group membership is an important differentiating factor among the migratory workers.[31] Of all the ethnic groups in migratory farm work, the Mexicans traveled the most between states. Studying the effects of the presence of the worker's family on the degree of interstate mobility revealed that almost two thirds of the migratory workers in the sample left their families at the home base. Eighty-five percent of the Puerto Ricans traveled without their families, and very few white families were found on the road. However, the Mexican farm workers were an important exception: they may be characterized as "family-migratory" workers, for only 17 percent traveled without their families. After the Mexicans, the largest category of workers who traveled with their families were the blacks. In absolute numbers the black families almost equal the Mexican families, which means that the problems of migratory families in the East Coast migratory stream are to a great extent the problems of the Mexican and black families.

The divergent patterns of migration among the workers in the East Coast stream again emphasize the fact that, in studying farm labor, one must always bear in mind the importance of ethnic group membership. The data and analysis presented here prove that generalizations based on journalistic observations and/or research on only one ethnic group do *not* hold true for all migratory workers; moreover, they can be extremely misleading for policy makers.

This analysis also provides no evidence that workers who travel without their families move more between states than those who take all their family members with them. Furthermore, there is no evidence supporting the assumption that school-age children influence the migratory patterns of their parents, or that migratory farm workers with school-age children stay longer in their home base state than those with non-school-age children. The number of families with school-age children was not higher among the workers who traveled without their families than among those who traveled with their families.

(4) The data on mobility also suggest that once the family is on the road, the need to earn money overrules whatever aspirations the migratory farm workers may have to educate their children. Hopes and reality conflict on this point, and reality usually wins, as the following excerpt from a field diary illustrates:

I asked Ann what she wanted her three youngest children to be, and she said that she hoped the boy would be a doctor and the girls, teachers. A little later in the conversation I phrased my question a little differently: "What do you think they will be?" Her answer was quite matter of fact — "Cherry pickers." (Friedland and Nelkin 1971:253)

As the large majority of migratory farm workers travel without their families, it is the responsibility of the home base states to provide an appropriate education for the migratory workers' children and to ensure that these children attend school as regularly as other children. Even more important, it is certainly obvious that the very first thing that should be done is to increase farm labor wages to such a level that the migratory parents can earn enough money to support a family without having their children help them in the fields.

NOTES

1. The most important studies are Monograph III, *The Transient Unemployed* (Webb 1935): Monograph VII, *The Migratory-Casual Worker* (Webb 1937); and Monograph XVII, *Migrant Families* (Webb and Brown 1938).

2. Webb and Brown 1938: XVIII. It should be kept in mind that these studies used data that were collected at the centers where relief was distributed to all the people who were on the move, regardless of whether they were farm or nonfarm workers. These centers were located on the main migratory routes in the cities and not in the rural areas, hence migratory farm workers may have been underrepresented.

3. Metzler (1955) studied a sample of black migratory farm workers in the Belle Glade area of Florida. He described the number and timing of their moves, the sex, age, education, and family characteristics of the workers, their employment during the year, their earnings, their wage rates, and the types of work they did.

4. Motheral, Thomas, and Larson (1954) and later Larson and Sharp (1960) studied a sample of black migratory farm workers in farm labor camps in New York and concentrated on the situation in that state. Their studies provided a considerable amount of information on such characteristics of the workers as age, sex, family composition, education and working history during the year studied, and earnings.

5. The migratory workers dealt with in this study were actually part of the Midwest stream.

6. Persh (1953) studied the relationship between the migratory farm worker and the community and analyzed the effects of the presence of migratory farm workers on health, welfare, and medical services, and on law enforcement and education. He also examined the reaction of the community to these effects.

7. Shostack (1964) studied the various kinds of leadership among crew leaders. He distinguished two types — the impersonal and the family-oriented leader (Weber) — and described the different leadership styles of the two. Friedland (1967) studied the crew leader system by applying general sociological concepts of leadership style, social structure, and social organization.

8. Metzler found that half of the workers in his sample worked in one state outside Florida, just over a third in two states, and 15 percent worked in three or more states outside Florida (1955:25-27). He also found that a small number of these workers worked in

two or more locations in the same state and that almost all the workers who moved within a state also moved between states.

9. In their June 1957 sample, Larson and Sharp found that slightly more than two thirds of the migratory workers worked in two states, 26 percent worked in three states, and 4 percent worked in four or five states (1960:35). Their midseason 1957 sample showed that 54 percent worked in two states, 33 percent in three, and 11 percent worked in four or five states.

10. Metzler (1955:2, 69) reported that greater mobility resulted in more days of employment and higher earnings. Brooks and Hilgendorf (1960:47, 58) suggested that there was a positive relationship between mobility and the amount of farm work the workers can get. Also, the workers who moved more often earned more by doing farm work than the workers who moved less.

11. Brooks and Hilgendorf (1960:97-98) reported that: "The greater the amount of mobility during school terms, the more interference there will be with schooling. The shorter the period of time a family remains or expects to remain in a community, the less likely it is that the children will be sent to school. It may well be that this tendency is partly caused by a greater reluctance of parents who value education highly to migrate in search of work during school terms."

12. See Chapter 3, note 7, and Bauder et al. 1976.

13. Not included on the Social Security listings are those employers who hired individual workers for twenty days or less or paid less than $150 in wages during one year. See Bauder et al. 1976:29.

14. Among the agricultural employers were both farm employers and agricultural nonfarm employers (such as custom operators, labor contractors, and processors).

15. All the interviews were made during the peak period of agricultural employment (July through October) in 1970, and all of them took place on the farms. In Florida the workers were interviewed from October 1970 through January 1971. Precautions were taken to avoid interviewing a worker twice. The workers were paid for the time taken by the interview.

16. See Chapter 3 for a description of unemployment insurance in the United States.

17. Economic Report of the President 1971:222, Table C-2. The civilian labor force includes all workers aged sixteen years or older.

18. To check the representative validity of the sample, an attempt was made (after consultation with Dr. P.J. McCarthy and Dr. J.D. Francis, both of Cornell University) to apply one of the random subsample replication (RSSR) techniques (see Costner 1972: Chapter 4). Unfortunately, the cost of this method turned out to be prohibitive.

19. The state of residence of 1 percent of the workers was unknown.

20. In Metzler's study as well, a state was counted twice if a worker returned to it after having worked in another state.

21. See the questionnaire in Appendix A. Unfortunately, no direct question was asked about the desire to stop migrating. Interpreting the answers to the question used in the questionnaire was complicated by the phrases "state where interviewed" and "if a steady income could be earned."

22. These were Massachusetts, Connecticut, Maine, New Hampshire, Rhode Island, Vermont, New Jersey, New York, Ohio, and Pennsylvania.

23. If all the workers who had family members with them (which would include the category labeled "some family members travel with respondent") were considered, the following percentages would be obtained for "No family members travel with respondent":

whites, 57 percent; blacks, 60 percent; Puerto Ricans, 85 percent; Mexicans, 17 percent; "others", 82 percent.

24. The presence of the family may, however, influence the duration of the worker's absence from the home base. See pages 90-91 for a discussion of this point with reference to school-age children.

25. In their comparison of migratory farm workers in 1953 and in 1957, Larson and Sharp (1960:21) observed that in 1957, fewer dependents were accompanying the workers.

26. Because they were not significant and in order to maintain readability, the results are not presented.

27. Small children in migratory families could also have created difficulties for their parents. To explore this further, the relationship between the presence of small children (i.e., between families in which the parents traveled with pre-school-aged children only) and the interstate mobility of the workers was analyzed. No significant results were obtained.

28. The greatest differences in percentages were found among the whites. Fifty-three percent (N = 72) of the white migratory workers with school-age children had no family members who traveled with them. Of the white migratory workers with non-school-age children, 63 percent (N = 41) had no family members who traveled with them. This suggests that the presence of school-age children was actually an advantage in doing migratory farm work.

29. The six states were Florida, New Hampshire, New York, Ohio, Pennsylvania, and Vermont. 8,046 workers, or two thirds of the total sample of 12,666, were interviewed in these states.

30. We should bear in mind that these migratory farm workers may have fewer days of actual employment per year than they did fifteen years ago.

31. The workers' characteristics discussed in this chapter included the presence of family members while traveling, ethnic group membership, and the presence of school-age children. The influence of other worker characteristics (i.e., education, age, and crew membership) on the degree of interstate mobility were also explored, but no significant results were obtained.

5

DIFFERENCES IN THE EARNINGS OF
MIGRATORY FARM WORKERS

Most of the migratory farm workers leave their homes and travel northwards in order to earn money (although some do this for other reasons; see page 37). Advertisements in the workers' home towns, in the newspapers, and on the radio promise them work, and they hear rumors about making good money harvesting up North. Once they are on the road, however, their high hopes are soon replaced by disillusionment:

He heard about Pole, a migrant labor crew leader in Selma, Alabama, who was recruiting a crew to go north. He [the crew leader] would be coming through the county on the way to Florida to do the early summer harvest of the citrus crops. Lonnie had no money and regarded the chance to travel with the crew as an opportunity. Encouraged by several people who told him he could make some money, he joined the crew and went with them to Florida. There he began to have regrets; but because he had no money to pay his return fare, his decision could not be reversed. (Friedland and Nelkin 1971:20)

The women were talking about how they weren't going to come back next year. They came up this year on the promise that they would make money. Emma told how she heard a radio advertisement in Belle Glade about coming north with Frank. The broadcast promised a real good time, lots of money, lots of fun. She really thought she would be doing well to come. (Friedland and Nelkin 1971:21-22)

Notes to this chapter may be found on pages 127-129.

A group of Florida boys complained about how they had been recruited. A man came by and told them he was bringing people up to work in a small town just outside New York City. He told them the wages on the job were very good. There was a labor shortage in New York and the crop was ready, but there weren't enough people to pick it. Wages were going up for they needed men badly. When they heard they were going to be near New York City, they hopped on the bus and then found they were stuck way out in the woods, several hundred miles from the city. (Friedland 1971:22)

As the season progresses, the workers' expectations about earnings begin to diminish:

When people first came to the camp they said, "Well, I at least want to make enough money to get out of debt." Since then it seems to be, "I want to get enough to get a 'man' [a bottle of wine]." (Friedland 1971:188)

The family from Selma was saving to buy a used car with the money earned picking. Their goal was $350.00. They didn't realize they would have to get insurance for the car, which would also cost them quite a bit. In any case, by midseason they no longer talked about it, and seemed to have forgotten completely about getting a car. (Friedland 1971:188)

Obviously, the migratory farm workers described above expected too much, but the question is: are such workers exceptional cases, or are the earnings of all migratory farm workers really so low? In order to answer this question, this chapter will examine the annual earnings of the individual worker, and in particular the differences in earnings among the workers.

While there are indications that quite substantial differences in earnings do exist,[1] little is known about the nature of and reasons for the differences. To find out more about this, we will first review the research which has been done on the earnings of farm workers in the United States; thereafter, the methodology used in analyzing these earnings differences will be explained. Regression analysis will then be used to study the factors influencing the differences. Two models will be developed: one for the migratory workers and one for the nonmigratory farm workers. The migratory model and its statistical results will be presented first. Then, to put the earnings of the migratory farm workers in the proper perspective, they will be compared to those of the workers who are occupationally closest to them — the nonmigratory farm workers. This will be done by analyzing a separate, nonmigratory model. Because the migratory workers' way of life is quite different from that of the nonmigratory farm workers (see Chapter 1, section 2), this comparison should reveal some significant differences.

1. DIVERSE FACTORS AFFECTING EARNINGS

Farm workers are among the lowest paid workers in the United States (page 15). Statistical data on the farm worker earnings have been collected by various government agencies, through the decennial censuses of population, and by other means,[2] and we can conclude from these that the general level of farm earnings is low and unemployment is substantial. These statistical data do, however, have their limitations. Because of the different ways in which the samples are taken and the worker categories are defined, the statistics are often not comparable.[3] Furthermore, while they give information on earnings, on the number of days spent doing farm work, and on a few characteristics of the workers, the categories of workers are too vaguely defined and the number of worker characteristics reported on is too limited to allow us to gain any real insight into the complicated question of differences in the earnings of farm workers.

More descriptive studies on farm workers (mostly dealing with migratory farm workers; see Chapter 2) have gathered information on the earnings of specific sections of the farm worker population and offer a few suggestions as to why such great differences exist. For example, a study on a group of black migratory farm workers described the annual and daily earnings from all wage work over a period of twelve months (Larson and Sharp 1960: 41-44). In 1957, when this group was studied, men were observed to earn considerably more than women. It was concluded that this was because the women had worked fewer days during the year and had lower average earnings per day. It should have been obvious that this would be the case, for the sample used in this study included women who worked as farm wage workers during only part of the year.

A report on migratory workers in the mid-continent stream computed the average daily and yearly earnings of various categories of workers (Metzler and Sargent 1960:33-37) and showed that earnings vary widely: one in twelve male heads of households earned more than $2,000 yearly and one in ten earned less than $500. The variations in daily earnings recorded in Texas were thought to be indicative of the steady improvement in the economic position of the Spanish-American workers, who are increasingly able to get better paid jobs in farm labor. Such workers avoid work on vegetable crops since it pays less than cultivating or picking cotton; this is because work in the cotton fields is considered to be a step above stoop labor. Similarly, workers who can drive trucks or tractors earn considerably more than those who work in the fields.

A study of black migratory farm workers in the East Coast stream (Metzler

1955:38-55; 65-69) also reported on earnings by year, by day, by state, by crop, and by sex. It showed that experience in migratory farm work, interstate mobility, the sex of the worker, and the combination of farm and nonfarm work had differentiating effects on the earnings of these black migratory farm workers.

All these studies provide more information than the statistical reports on the lives and work of the migratory farm workers, but they all have the disadvantage of making no clear distinction between the various types of workers who do migratory farm work. For instance, if students and housewives are not excluded from calculations of average annual earnings, the statistics obtained will be misleading because these individuals usually do farm wage work for relatively short periods of time (and their earnings are often supplementary to other earnings or income); thus including their earnings in the calculations lowers the average of yearly earnings for migratory farm workers. Another major shortcoming of these studies is the lack of insight into how the various factors influencing earnings operate simultaneously and whether certain factors have a stronger influence than others.

A recent study on unemployment and annual farm earnings (Holt 1976:65-78) pointed out the problems presented by the different types of workers in the farm labor force and analyzed annual farm worker earnings quite accurately by excluding workers under sixteen years of age and workers whose participation in the labor force was low (part-year and part-time workers).[4] Because this study was restricted to full-time workers only,[5] the full-time workers with two or more weeks of unemployment could be compared to those who had no unemployment.[6] This comparison showed that the annual earnings of 68 percent of all the full-time workers in the study who had two or more weeks of unemployment amounted to less than $3,000.[7] It was argued that unemployment was very probably a significant factor in making the percentage of workers with annual earnings under $3,000 so high. Following this argument, the next observation in the study is quite surprising: 26 percent of the workers without unemployment had earnings of less than $3,000. Thus unemployment cannot be taken as the causal factor in this case. It was then argued that the low earnings in this category of full-time workers can only be explained by relatively few hours of work per week, or low hourly wage rates, or both. The conclusion was:

The low earnings problem among agricultural workers appears to stem chiefly from low labor force participation among some workers and low earnings among others. Unemployment plays a significant but not preponderant role in the problem. (Holt 1976:78)

The above emphasizes the importance of distinguishing between the various kinds of workers in farm labor when analyzing earnings. The main point of the study is this: it is not only unemployment that causes low earnings in farm work; other factors, such as fewer hours of actual work and low wage rates, also have depressing effects on farm earnings. Although this study did not explore the effect of unemployment in comparison to other factors influencing farm worker earnings, it definitely indicated that certain factors other than unemployment may be important causes of low earnings in farm work and of earnings differences.

Another factor which could be significant in analyzing farm worker earnings is membership in an ethnic group, as was suggested in an article on minority workers in New York state (Bauder 1973:16-19) in which white farm workers proved to have earned more during the year than black, Puerto Rican, and Mexican workers.

Another — seemingly obvious — reason for the differences in farm worker earnings could be the differences in wage rates in different regions. The United States is a large country, and the wage rates in certain states are higher than in others. In fact, in January-June 1970 the average hourly wage for pre-harvest and harvest work on the tomato crop was $1.65-$1.75 in California, $1.30 in Florida, $1.30 in South Carolina, and $1.25-$1.50 in Texas (Wilson 1972:26). There could also be considerable differences in wage rates in a region as large and diversified as the East Coast. However, both studies on the earnings of migratory farm workers in this region (Metzler 1955 and Holt 1976) showed that differences in earnings cannot be explained by differing wage rates. The mid-Atlantic states and Connecticut had roughly the same labor market for migratory workers (Holt 1976:68), and the piece rates paid in the East Coast states in 1955 were surprisingly uniform (most of the work done in these states was — and is — paid on a piece-rate basis). Variations throughout the East Coast were generally no greater than the local variations (Metzler 1955:49). It was concluded that "...[the fact] that rates for a particular operation are at this uniform level probably attests to the fact that the Atlantic Coast from Florida to New York has come to be a single labor market." (Metzler 1955:49) This of course does not preclude considerable variations in earnings resulting from the different types of harvest and other agricultural jobs.[8]

The previous pages have shown that very little is known about why there are such considerable differences in the earnings of individual migratory farm workers. To find the causes, the rest of this chapter will focus on characteristics of the workers which appear to have an effect — either positive or negative — on earnings. It should be borne in mind, however, that lack of knowledge about these differences is only one reason for focusing on them. The main reason is that if effective policies aimed at benefiting these workers are to be formulated and implemented, a better understanding of the configuration of factors influencing the earnings of the individual worker must be gained.

2. THE EARNINGS FUNCTION: METHODOLOGY

The wages earned doing farm work are the only source of annual earnings for some farm workers; other workers combine farm work and nonfarm work; others, such as students and housewives, do farm work only temporarily in order to supplement other earnings or income.

In this analysis, workers in the sample who did farm work only temporarily will be excluded because they form a separate category, and their inclusion in the analysis would distort the average of the annual earnings of farm wage workers. Such workers very probably do not depend solely on farm earnings to pay their living expenses, and moreover, their social status is not determined by this work. We will therefore deal with only those farm workers who depended on hired farm work, or a combination of hired farm and nonfarm work, to earn a living.[9] The workers who depended on a combination of hired farm and nonfarm work will be included because it is quite common among migratory farm workers to do farm work in the North and nonfarm work while living at the home base in the South; quite a number of Puerto Rican migratory farm workers, for example, do construction work in their home-base area (Bauder 1976b:109).

By restricting the earnings analysis to farm workers who did hired farm work only, or a combination of hired farm and hired nonfarm work, during the year, a sample was obtained of 9,061 workers whose earnings were known.[10] For a sample as large as this, the costs of studying earnings by using regression analysis are very high; a 25 percent random subsample was therefore taken from the original sample and was used in analyzing the earnings of the farm workers on the East Coast.

Since the late 1950s, economists have been using earnings functions as a tool for analyzing differences in earnings (see, for instance, Adams 1958:390-398; Morgan *et al.* 1962; Hirsch and Segelhorst 1965:392-399; Rees and Shultz 1970). In the field of the economics of education in particular, earnings functions are used to isolate the effect of education on earnings. In these functions, the earnings of an individual (or a group of individuals[11]) are related to age (x_1), the level of schooling (x_2), sex (x_3), and a number of other characteristics (x_i).

$$E \text{ (earnings)} = f(x_1, x_2, x_3, ..., x_i)$$

The regression coefficients of the independent variables x_i represent the effect of these variables on the dependent variable E. The algebraic relationship between the dependent and independent variables is assumed to be linear. A great variety of independent variables is used in research which aims to explain differences in earnings. Besides the common explanatory variables, age and education (see Hirsch and Segelhorst 1965:392-399; Weiss 1970:150-159; Rees and Shultz 1970; Griliches and Mason 1972:74-103), such explanatory variables as race, marital status, region and residence, family background, and sex are also used.[12] The first section of this chapter showed that such variables as the type of farm work, sex, interstate mobility, and ethnic group membership could also influence the earnings of farm workers.

For such nonquantitative variables as sex, race, and marital status, the concept of "dummy" variables (Wonnacott and Wonnacott 1970:68-73; Johnston 1972:176-186) will be used. This concept enables the inclusion of nonquantitative variables in an earnings function. A dummy variable has only two potential values, one or zero. For example, if the model is:

$$E = a + bx_1 + cx_2$$

where x_1 is education and x_2 is the sex of the worker,

then if $x_2 = 1$, the worker is male;
and if $x_2 = 0$, the worker is female.

The single equation is now equivalent to the following two equations:

$$E = a + bx_1 + c \quad \text{for male workers}$$
$$E = a + bx_1 \quad \text{for female workers}$$

where c is the estimated effect of sex on earnings.

What happens, in effect, is that instead of developing a separate model for men and for women, the sex variable is brought into the regression so that the same slope b is imposed for both men and women. This is a restriction, but it may be less of a disadvantage in our particular case, in which considerably fewer women (6 percent among the migratory workers) than men are involved, than developing a separate model for women would be, because that would result in an unreliable estimate of the slope due to the small number of observations. It is therefore more reasonable to pool all the data to estimate one slope coefficient (b). The function simply shifts for $x_2 = 1$, leaving the slope b the same; thus it is assumed that education has the same effect on the earnings of men as it has on the earnings of women.

Dummy variables have been used in many studies. In a study on education in Kenya (Thias and Carnoy 1972:27-62), they were used for such socioeconomic variables as the father's literacy, membership in a tribal group, occupation, and the type of school attended. An examination of the effect of education on the earnings of blacks and whites (Weiss 1970:150-159) used marital status, veteran status, and whether the work was located in or outside a metropolitan area as dummy variables. A description of an urban labor market (Rees and Shultz 1970) used race, schooling, marital status, and sex.

Regression analysis is a powerful statistical tool for showing both the simultaneous effect of the various socioeconomic variables on earnings and the relative effect of each independent variable. These features of regression analysis make it an appropriate instrument for gaining more insight into the factors influencing the earnings of the individual farm worker, and it will therefore be used to investigate the earnings of the migratory and nonmigratory farm workers in our sample. Dummy variables will be included in the functions so that the effect of nonquantitative variables on earnings can also be studied.

3. THE MIGRATORY FARM WORKER MODEL

A number of factors influence the earnings of migratory farm workers, but the average level of farm worker earnings (which, as mentioned above, is very low) is determined by the amount of money the employers are able and willing to spend on farm labor. In Chapter 2 (pages 37-39), and in the first section of this chapter, we saw that agricultural employers work together in deciding upon the wage rates and working conditions that are to be offered to the migratory farm workers. As a result, the workers are confronted with rather uniform wage rates for the various farming activities on the East Coast (see Metzler 1955; Holt 1976). The workers have no control over the levels of these wages, nor can they control many other outside factors — such as the weather, the demand for farm labor, etc. — but these nonetheless determine in large part the general level of their earnings. Despite the uniformity of wage rates and the workers' incapacity to control outside factors, there seem to be considerable differences between the earnings of the individual farm workers (pages 101-102). An analysis of the differences in earnings among individual farm workers will allow us to find out which farm workers earn more, which earn less, and what the causes of the differences may be. A better understanding of the factors associated with earnings differences among farm workers should be of key importance to policy makers who are concerned with improving the lot of these workers.

In this section the migratory farm workers' earnings will be related to other characteristics of the workers by constructing an equation in which earnings E is a function of other characteristics which are likely to have an effect on earnings. The characteristics to be used in the regression analysis will be chosen by taking the available earnings studies and research on migratory farm workers as a basis. Earnings will be defined as all earnings received for hired work during the fifty-two-week survey period. Bonuses and extra pay received at the end of a harvest season or at the end of the year will be included, but such fringe benefits as housing, meals, and transportation will not.[13]

A general study of the factors that determine an individual's earnings noted that:

Age, sex, race, native ability, social class background, place of residence, branch of employment, occupation and on-the-job training are other important determinants of personal earnings. But apart from age, none of them are as powerful in their influence on earnings as the numbers of years of schooling completed. (Blaug 1972:23)

Although we are concerned here with a special occupational category in that it is situated at the very bottom of the occupational ladder, the variables which usually have a considerable effect on earnings, such as age and education, may be expected to influence the earnings of migratory farm workers. For instance, one may expect migratory farm workers with more years of schooling to earn more than migratory farm workers who have spent fewer years in school; one may also expect the older migratory farm workers to be likely to earn more (at least up to a certain age) than the younger workers, because age increases experience and older workers are more familliar with the ins and outs of migratory farm work than younger workers.

The previous chapters showed that irregular employment is inherent in migratory farm worker life. Studies on the employment and earnings of migratory farm workers always make a point of indicating the number of days or weeks of unemployment each migratory farm worker has (see, for instance, Larson and Sharp 1960:35-41; Metzler 1955:30-38; and Holt 1976:65-78). Migratory farm workers have no income if they have no work, and weeks of unemployment therefore have a substantial effect on their annual earnings. In recent years, the impact of unemployment on the workers' earnings has probably been increased by mechanization, which has reduced the need for seasonal workers and altered patterns in the demand for farm labor, so that continuous employment of farm workers during the season has become less and less feasible. A good illustration of this is provided by harvesting in Michigan (Sturt 1970:4). Farm workers used to come to Michigan in May and June of each year to harvest strawberries and asparagus; they would move on to harvest cherries and cucumbers, and then harvested tomatoes and apples. In 1970, however, most of the tart cherries and cucumbers were harvested mechanically, and the continuity in the farm workers' employment was disrupted. It may be that, because of the disruptive effect of mechanization, migratory workers either have to travel more to find work, or wait out longer periods of unemployment (Shotwell 1961:194); however, this investigation provided no evidence that migratory farm workers traveled more in 1969-70 than they did fifteen years earlier (see pages 79-81). Because no comparative data exist on longer periods of unemployment, we have no way of knowing whether increased mechanization has lengthened the migratory farm workers' period of unemployment. As to finding out the number of days or weeks the worker is employed during a given year, the data collected in the 1970 unemployment insurance survey have their limitations, as only the effect that the number of weeks worked during the fifty-two-week period had on the workers' annual earnings can be investigated through the earnings function. It is very probable that the more weeks the worker is employed, the higher his earnings will be.

So far age, education, and the number of weeks of work have been mentioned as variables which affect earnings; to these we must add membership in an ethnic group, which, as the studies on earnings indicate, also affects earnings. Most of the research on racial discrimination and its effects on earnings focuses on the differences between whites and nonwhites in the United States. In a study of occupational structure in the United States, it was observed that blacks are not given equal job opportunities and are also paid less for the same job than whites.

Differentials in occupational opportunities are not the ultimate economic disadvantage of nonwhite Americans. Nonwhites also tend to receive less income than whites in comparable occupational positions. (Blau and Duncan 1967:212-213)

Other research on racial discrimination supports these findings. An earlier study (Siegel 1965), in which the differentials in average earnings between whites and nonwhites were investigated within major occupational categories at various educational levels by using data from the 1960 census of the population, revealed that the "cost" of being a black is around $1,000 a year. This "cost" was attributed to racial differences in mean earnings if the effects of such factors as the region (e.g., South or the North), the major occupational category, and the level of education on earnings were accounted for (Siegel 1965:41-57).[14]

A study on the effect of education on the earnings of blacks and whites (Weiss 1970:150-159) revealed that the lower earnings of blacks in certain age categories could not be completely explained by lower achievements in school. The blacks' mean earnings were estimated by using the same qualifications and characteristics as were used for whites; they turned out to be less than the actual mean of white earnings for all four age groups. The conclusion was: "The difference between the 'predicted' black and actual white averages is due to discrimination and to racial differences in variables not included in this study." (Weiss 1970:155)[15]

Besides the studies focusing on comparing the differences in the earnings of black and white workers,[16] there are a few studies which examine the differences in earnings between several ethnic categories. An important contribution to gaining a better understanding of the relative socioeconomic positions of the various ethnic minority groups in the United States is Schmid and Nobbe's article on nonwhites (1965:909-922), which dealt with considerably more than the differences between blacks and whites. Differences in the socioeconomic status of the various ethnic groups were measured by taking education, occupation, and income as three interrelated indicators of socioeconomic status. The 1959 data on income and the 1940, 1950, and 1960 data on education and occupation were used. It was shown that in terms of incomes, the white male population ranks first, followed by the Japanese, the Chinese, the Philippinos, the blacks, and finally the American Indians, who are at the bottom of the social ladder. Although the Japanese and Chinese outranked the whites in occupational status, and the Japanese outranked the whites in education, the whites still ranked first in income. "Apparently, members of nonwhite minorities are paid less for the same services than are members of the white majority." (Schmid and Nobbe 1965:918) This article also provided some significant information on Puerto Ricans and other individuals with Spanish surnames (1965:921, fn.), who are usually classified as whites by the Bureau of the Census,despite the fact that they form distinctive ethnic groups in the United States.[17] Using data collected in the southwestern United States, it was found that Puerto Ricans and others with Spanish surnames rank lower than whites, Japanese, Chinese, and Philippinos on all three measures of socioeconomic status. Although they rank slightly lower than blacks and Indians on education, they rank higher than these two groups on occupation and income.

Another study that went farther than simply exploring the traditional white-nonwhite dichotomy is Rees and Shultz's book (1970) on the Chicago labor market. It indicated that three different kinds of discrimination lower the earnings of nonwhites and Latin Americans:

The first is discrimination in the amount and quality of schooling they have received. The second is the smaller likelihood of their finding steady employment in a particular occupation for given levels of education. The third is the receipt of lower earnings per hour within an occupation for given education. (1970:163)

Adjusting for age, years of schooling, seniority, and experience, and using earnings per hour of work as the dependent variable, the third kind of discrimination and the part of the first kind that refers to the quality of schooling were measured. The differences in earnings between whites on the one hand, and nonwhites and Latin Americans on the other hand, were estimated and showed negative coefficients for nonwhites and Latin Americans ranging from 3 to 13 percent as a percentage of the mean earnings in the occupations studied. These findings strongly suggested that there was discrimination against nonwhites and Latin Americans (Rees and Shultz 1970:161-166).

Having considered these two relevant earnings studies, both of which explore differences between several ethnic categories, let us return to what has been written about farm worker earnings. As it is well known that a wide variety of ethnic groups does farm work, it is surprising that so little research has been done on the differences in earnings between these groups, the more so because observations have been made to the effect that ethnic group membership could be a factor in determining differences in earnings among farm workers (Padfield and Martin 1965:154-169; see also Bauder 1973:16-19). This may be because the earnings of the migratory farm workers were known to be so low that it did not seem possible that there could be any significant range in the differences among the individual workers' earnings. It may also have been because earnings have generally been approached from the viewpoint of wage rates — i.e., the amounts the employers have to pay — rather than the viewpoint of income — i.e., the amount the workers have to live on. The analysis of mobility in Chapter 4 revealed that ethnic group membership plays an important role in the workers' mobility. In order to study the impact of ethnic group membership on the farm workers' earnings, the four ethnic categories — whites, blacks, Puerto Ricans, and Mexicans — used in the analysis of mobility will serve as dummy variables in the earnings function.

Another variable that has received considerable attention in earnings studies, and also in some studies on migratory farm workers, is the sex of the worker. Within certain occupations, "differences in pay based on sex are in general larger than those based on color or origin." (Rees and Shultz 1970:167) It goes without saying that the women received the lower pay. A study on income differences in Yugoslavia showed that given a certain level of education and experience, and a certain type of work and industry, women earned considerably less than men (Thomas 1973:208-211). The amount of research on this and other forms of discrimination against women is rapidly increasing.[18]

Up to the Depression and during the resultant social upheaval, migratory farm work was done mainly by unattached men; but with the increasing popularization of the automobile, which made it possible for families to travel together, women and children became part of the migratory farm work force (Anderson 1940:58-60). In fact, 6 percent of the workers in the 25 percent subsample (described in the previous section) were women (this figure excludes women who combined farm work and housekeeping). Divisions of labor according to sex, in which some jobs are considered to be inappropriate for women, have also been observed: for example, unloading a truck filled with bags of potatoes is considered to be a man's job, while grading and scaling potatoes is women's work (Friedland and Nelkin 1971:33, 88, 90). As it is not unlikely that the wages paid for lighter (that is, women's) work are lower, the sex of a worker will be included in the earnings function as a dummy variable.

Skilled as well as unskilled workers are found among farm workers, just as they are found in any other category of workers. The term "unskilled worker" usually refers to a manual worker or a worker who does work requiring very little specialized training or experience. Although the work of a farm laborer is generally not considered to require any particular skills, there is quite a variety of more or less specialized jobs in farm work. Some workers operate mechanical harvesters and others specialize in greenhouse or nursery work. It is very likely that the more specialized farm workers earn more than farm workers who only weed or pick beans. To account for these differences, the farm workers will be divided into occupational categories according to the work they have done during the year. Those workers who worked all year-round as unskilled farm laborers, and those who combined unskilled farm work with unskilled nonfarm work (including work in a private household), will be considered to be unskilled laborers.[19] All other workers will be considered skilled in some way and will be grouped together. Although this variable cannot be very precise, it may give some indication of the relationship between occupational skills in farm work and the level of an individual worker's earnings, and may provide insight into the structure of farm worker earnings.

We will also examine family background and the role it may play in the workers' earnings. The family background of an individual is usually considered to be an important factor in determining the kind of education and training the worker will acquire, and it appears to affect one's choice of occupation and thus one's earnings. There is no consensus about the magnitude of this effect on earnings (Bowles 1972:219-251; Becker 1972:252-255). While the direct effect of schooling on earnings may have been overestimated, the direct effect of family background has been thought to be underestimated (Bowles 1972:219-222). With the help of the earnings function we will examine whether, within a small segment of the occupational structure, social background has an influence on earnings. In collecting the data for the 1970 unemployment insurance survey, the workers were asked what their fathers' occupation was when they were in their teens. The answers to this question will be used as an approximation of family background. A distinction will be made between the fathers who had worked only as farm workers and those who had also had occupations other than that of hired farm worker. We will assume that, for an individual in his or her teens, having a father who has done hired farm work only limits educational and/or occupational opportunities more than having a father who has had jobs other than that of hired farm worker. This is because farm workers receive very low wages and live and work in rural areas where the opportunities for education and vocational training are very limited. We will further assume that this is reflected in individual earnings.

The previous chapters have shown that mobility is the feature of the migratory farm worker life that is most characteristic. We have also seen that job insecurity is prevalent. Another feature of migratory farm work is the possibility of having the family members travel with the migratory worker and work together to increase family earnings. Although children under sixteen years of age are prohibited by law from doing farm labor — at least when school is in session (see page 17) — child labor is a well-known phenomenon in American agriculture. The children usually are not employed independently from their parents, but they do help their parents — e.g., by filling the baskets and buckets during the harvest — and may contribute considerably to the family's earnings (Marcson and Fasick 1964:8-9; 235-236; Friedland and Nelkin 1971: 246-247). It is therefore likely that migratory farm workers who travel with their families will have higher earnings than those who leave their families behind or are unattached.

A number of variables that may influence farm worker earnings have been mentioned: age, education, weeks of work, ethnic group membership, sex, skills, family background, and family travel status. Other variables which are known to have a differentiating effect on farm worker earnings cannot be included in the earnings function because no data on them are available. One such variable is the effect of the type of crop on earnings, i.e., the effect of the low wages paid for picking beans, for example, as compared to the higher wages for picking up potatoes (Metzler 1955:42-43). Another is the number of days or hours of work done, which is the most accurate measurement of the amount of time a worker has worked. Instead of using this unit of measurement, a rather crude unit — the number of weeks of work — had to be used to estimate the time the worker was employed during the year. This means that although there may be a substantial variation in the number of hours and days worked per week in farm labor (Holt 1976:73), the function only measures the number of weeks worked.

Using our 25 percent subsample of interstate migratory farm workers, we will make a regression analysis of the influence which the variables mentioned above had on the earnings of this category of workers from July 1969 to June 1970. The earnings function is as follows:

$$E = a + b_1 A + b_2 A^2 + b_3 C_1 + b_4 C_2 + b_5 W + b_6 R_1 + b_7 R_2 + b_8 R_3 + b_9 R_4 + b_{10} S + b_{11} J + b_{12} \Gamma + b_{13} T$$

where:

E = earnings, from July 1969 through June 1970 (the dependent variable).

a = the constant.

$b_{i(i=1,...,13)}$ = the coefficients.

A = the age of the migratory farm worker.

A^2 = age squared.[20]

C_1 = a dummy variable for education: migratory farm workers with 9-12 years of schooling have a one; others have a zero.

C_2 = a dummy variable for education: migratory farm workers with 13 years of schooling or more have a one; others have a zero.

0-8 years of schooling function as a base for C_1 and C_2.

W   = the number of weeks during which the migratory farm worker has been employed in the fifty-two-week period.

R_1 -R_4 are dummy variables for ethnic group membership.

   R_1 = 1 represents the black migratory farm workers; others have a zero.

   R_2 = 1 represents the Puerto Rican migratory farm workers; others have a zero.

   R_3 = 1 represents the Mexican migratory farm workers; others have a zero.

   R_4 = 1 represents migratory farm workers who are not white, black, Puerto Rican or Mexican. They may be Bahamian, Philippino, Canadian, or Indian; others have a zero.

   The whites are used as a base for R_1 -R_4.

S   = a dummy variable for sex: a male migratory farm worker has a one; a female migratory farm worker has a zero.

J   = a dummy variable for occupational skills: all migratory farm workers who have done work that requires certain skills during the fifty-two-week period have a one; those who have done unskilled work only have a zero. Nonspecialized farm work done throughout the year, or a combination of nonspecialized farm with unskilled nonfarm work (including work in a private household), is considered to be unskilled labor. A worker employed in any other occupation during the fifty-two-week period is considered to have some skill.

F   = a dummy variable for the main type of employment of the worker's father while the migratory farm worker was in his or her teens: migratory farm workers whose fathers were hired farm workers during that period have a one; others have a zero.

T   = a dummy variable for travel status of the family: a migratory farm worker who traveled with all members of his family has a one; others have a zero.

The results of the regression analysis of migratory farm workers are presented in Table 5.1.

The model explains 43 percent of the variation in the earnings of the migratory farm workers. This is quite a satisfactory explanatory power for a regression analysis based on individual observations; an explanatory power of over 50 percent is considered to be high and rather exceptional for individual observations (Chiswick and Mincer 1972:38).[21]

Table 5.1. *Migratory Farm Worker Earnings: Regression Coefficients of Explanatory Variables*

Variable		Coefficient	F-value
A	(age)	43.5	2.9
A^2	(age squared)	-0.6	3.1
C_1	(9-12 years of education)	256.5	3.7
C_2	(13+ years of education)	1304.7	8.4
W	(weeks of work)	82.1	278.1
R_1	(black)	-357.5	2.7
R_2	(Puerto Rican)	-763.5	10.8
R_3	(Mexican)	-942.1	13.1
R_4	(other, excl. whites)	-832.7	3.7
S	(sex: male)	1097.4	18.9
J	(occupational skills)	118.4	.8[a]
F	(job of father: hired farm worker)	-173.3	2.1[a]
T	(all family members traveled with worker)	477.4	8.8

Constant: -1438.6

R^2 (adj.) = .43

F = 36.1

Number of observations: 595

Mean earnings: $3,493

Standard dev.: $1,826

[a] Not significant at .05 level.

The range of differences in earnings within a category of workers which is one of the lowest paid in the United States is shown to be very great indeed. As was expected, the regression analysis reveals that the number of weeks of employment is an important variable. The coefficients of the quantitative variables can be interpreted as an increase (or as a decrease, depending on the sign) in dollars earned per year for each unit increase in the variable. For example, every additional week of employment increases yearly earnings by an average of about $82.

Analysis of the two age variables, which are also quantitative variables, shows that older workers earned more on the average than younger workers, but the older the workers became, the greater the chance was that the increases in earnings would taper off, as variables A (age) and A^2 (age squared) indicate. Age is usually considered to be a proxy variable for experience (see, for instance, Blaug 1972:29), and more experience generally increases earnings. To investigate the effect of experience in farm work on the earnings of migratory farm workers, A and A^2 were replaced by the variables "years of experience in farm work" and "experience squared."[22] The results indicate that these variables had an insignificant effect on earnings: an increase in years of experience in farm work did not increase a worker's earnings. This illustrates the special character of migratory farm work: anyone with a pair of hands and a strong body can do the job; the experience that older workers have does not increase their earnings. An explanation for the higher earnings of older migratory farm workers may be that they are more familiar with the ins and outs of migrating.

The interpretations of the nonquantitative (dummy) variables differ slightly from those of the quantitative variables. For example, the regression coefficient of variable S (sex) should be interpreted as follows: being a male migratory farm worker results in average annual earnings that are almost $1,100 more than those of the female workers. Thus the cost of being a woman is very high in migratory farm work. (It should be noted once again that the annual earnings of the migratory workers are very low: in 1970, annual mean earnings were only $3,495 per year; see Table 5.1.) The question arises of whether this is a reflection of (1) direct discrimination against women – i.e., that women are paid less than men for the same work; or (2) more indirect discrimination – i.e., that women have access to a limited number of jobs because they are expected to do the lighter work and are paid accordingly; or (3) that women are paid less because they are held responsible for caring for the children, cooking, and other household chores and consequently spend fewer hours working in the fields than men. The studies on migratory farm workers give some clues about the last two possibilities: one pointed out that it is very likely that the relatively low level of wage rates for, e.g., picking beans, is related to the fact that many women and children do this kind of work (Metzler 1955:2, 38-48); another mentioned that not all farm work is considered to be suitable for women (Friedland and Nelkin 1971; see page 111). Furthermore, because taking care of the children and doing other household chores takes time, the women may do relatively few hours of farm work. Even when they are in the fields, they have been observed to spend considerable time watching the children and conversing (Friedland and Nelkin 1971:184). Whatever the explanations for these low earnings may be, the earnings function clearly shows that in migratory farm work, whether the worker is a man or a woman has a strong impact on yearly earnings.

The education variables, C_1 and C_2, show that even in a category of workers in which manual labor is predominant, the number of years of schooling influences earnings considerably. Workers with thirteen years or more of education earned an average of $1,300 more per year than workers with up to eight years of schooling.

One very surprising finding that has emerged from this analysis of earnings is that ethnic group membership has a great influence on the migratory farm workers' earnings. Variables R_1, R_2, R_3, and R_4 (ethnic group membership) show that the differences in earnings among the various ethnic groups in migratory farm work are substantial. The Mexican migratory farm workers were in the worst position as far as earnings are concerned, earning an average of almost $950 less during the fifty-two-week survey period than the white migratory farm workers. The migratory farm workers in the category labeled "other" and the Puerto Ricans were slightly better off than the Mexicans; the blacks were closest to the whites in their earnings. The position of the blacks may reflect the fact that they have been more aggressive than Mexicans and Puerto Ricans in demanding the same rights as the whites. The equal rights movement has focused on the blacks and may to some extent have also affected the black migratory farm workers' earnings. The results of this analysis could also be formulated as follows: when white and black migratory farm workers are compared, we find discrimination against the blacks; but when Puerto Ricans and Mexicans are compared to whites, we find that they are much more the victims of discrimination.

Migratory farm work allows the worker to travel with his or her entire family and thus to increase the family's earnings by having the family members work. The regression analysis gives a significant result for variable T ("all family members travel with worker"), which indicates that on the average, the workers who traveled with all of their family members earned more than other workers. This finding qualifies earlier studies on migratory farm workers, in which the simple fact of having a family — in other words, of being responsible for supporting a family — was thought to be a factor that would increase a worker's earnings. For instance, it has been observed that male heads of black migratory families had more employment and earned more than other workers (Metzler 1955:31-39), and that married men did their work more quickly than single men (Friedland and Nelkin 1971:183-185). A migratory farm worker described the responsibility of a married man as:

When you have a family, you gotta work. If you got bellies to feed, you don't have a choice. When you're single and nobody depends on you, then you can do what you want, because all you need is money enough to feed yourself. (Friedland and Nelkin 1971:184)

As was stated above, the regression analysis shows that workers who brought their families with them "on the season" earned more than other workers. To test the effect that being married may have on earnings, variable T was replaced by a dummy variable for marital status. Workers who were married had a one; others a zero. The results show that being married did *not* result in significantly higher earnings. In the instances where married men were observed to work faster than single men (Friedland and Nelkin 1971), it was clear from the context that these married men had their families with them. Thus the results of the regression analysis suggest that the characteristic of having the family travel with the worker provides a more accurate indication of the effect on earnings than the characteristic of being married. Using the first characteristic has the additional advantage that the migratory farm worker families with only one parent are adequately dealt with in the earnings function.

The regression analysis indicates that the social background of the migratory farm worker did not have a significant effect on the worker's earnings. Variable F (the job of the worker's father during the worker's teens) shows that workers whose fathers were hired farm workers when the workers were young earned less than other workers on the average, but the difference was not significant.

The worker's ability to do work requiring certain skills or (specialized) training did have a positive, but not significant, effect on earnings, as is shown by variable J (occupational skills). The expectation that migratory workers who were employed in more skilled jobs during the year (24 percent) would have higher average earnings than the migratory workers who did unskilled work was not borne out. The fact that migratory workers did not receive higher wages for more skilled work is one of the most surprising and exceptional features of this occupational category (see also Chapter 7, section 3).

In Chapter 4 we saw that the degree of interstate mobility among migratory farm workers varied. We have also seen that a sample of black migratory farm workers in Florida (Metzler 1955) showed higher yearly earnings for workers who were employed in three or more states than for those who worked in only one or two states. The more mobile workers had more days of employment and their earnings were consequently higher. The same applied to workers who combined farm and nonfarm work (Metzler 1955:48-55, 69). In an earlier run of the earnings function (which is not presented here), a variable for interstate mobility and a variable for the combination of farm and nonfarm work were included, but both proved not to be significant and thus did not contribute to explaining the differences in migratory farm worker earnings.

4. THE NONMIGRATORY FARM WORKER MODEL

Having examined the earnings function for migratory farm workers, let us develop an earnings function for nonmigratory farm workers to find out how the two categories compare. In the nonmigratory model, as in the migratory model, the 25 percent subsample (page 104) will be used.[23] The differences between the socioeconomic positions of the migratory and nonmigratory workers are well illustrated by some of the variables which were analyzed in the migratory model.

Variables	Nonmigratory farm workers (N = 1,429)	Migratory farm workers (N = 595)
Mean weeks of employment	49.0 weeks	43.7 weeks
Years of farm work for the employer on whose worksite the worker was interviewed	7.8 years	3.1 years
Those working in skilled occupations during the fifty-two-week period	35 percent	24 percent
Those with thirteen years or more of schooling	10 percent	2 percent
Those with nine to twelve years of schooling	50 percent	33 percent

The nonmigratory farm worker enjoys more job security than the migratory farm worker in the sense that he or she has more weeks of employment each year and works longer for the same employer. Also, the nonmigratory worker is more viable socially because he or she is more often employed in skilled occupations and has more education (although the mean age of nonmigratory farm workers in this sample was 38.5 years, compared to 35.6 years for migratory farm workers).

Most of the variables used in the migratory model will also be used in the nonmigratory model, i.e., age, education, weeks of work, ethnic group membership, sex, skills (defined by grouping of occupations), and the occupation of the father while the worker was in his teens. Only the "family travel status" variable will be excluded, as it does not apply to nonmigratory farm workers. In its place, the marital status of the worker will be used as the family variable, although it did not prove to be significant in the migratory model. The variable for the number of years a worker was employed by the same employer, which was excluded from the migratory model because it proved not to be significant, will also be used in the nonmigratory model. It is probable that workers who work for the same employer for a number of years are appreciated and paid more than temporary workers, and that they are more experienced in the work they do. It is therefore not unlikely that the longer a worker stays with the same employer, the higher the earnings will be.

Ethnic group membership is included in both earnings functions, but not in the same way. In the migratory model the blacks, Puerto Ricans, Mexicans, and those labeled "other" were used as dummy variables; each category had a value of one, while the whites were used as the base and had a value of zero. This would not be appropriate to the nonmigratory model because of the small number (6 percent) of Puerto Ricans, Mexicans, and others, while 77 percent of the migratory workers were white and 16 percent were black. In the nonmigratory model only the black workers will be given a value of one; the whites, together with the few Puerto Ricans, Mexicans, and others, will be taken as the base. The reasons for using a slightly different base for the ethnic group membership variable will be described further when the results of the nonmigratory earnings function are analyzed.

The nonmigratory earnings function, which comprises the variables described above, is as follows:

$$E = a + b_1 A + b_2 A^2 + b_3 C_1 + b_4 C_2 + b_5 W + b_6 R + b_7 S + b_8 J + b_9 F + b_{10} P + b_{11} M$$

where:

E = earnings from July 1969 through June 1970 (the dependent variable).

a = the constant.

$b_{i(i=1,...,11)}$ = the coefficients.

A = age of the nonmigratory farm worker.

A^2 = age squared (see note 20 of this chapter).

C_1 = a dummy variable for education: nonmigratory farm workers with 9-12 years of schooling have a one; others have a zero.

C_2 = a dummy variable for education: nonmigratory farm workers with 13 years of schooling or more have a one; others have a zero.

     0-8 years of schooling functions as a base for C_1 and C_2.

W = the number of weeks during which the nonmigratory farm worker has
       been employed in the fifty-two-week period.
R = a dummy variable for ethnic group membership: black nonmigratory
       farm workers have a one; others have a zero.
S = a dummy variable for sex: a male nonmigratory farm worker has a
       one; a female nonmigratory farm worker has a zero.
J = a dummy variable for occupational skills: all nonmigratory farm
       workers who have done work that requires certain skills during the
       fifty-two-week period have a one; those who have done unskilled
       work only have a zero. Nonspecialized farm work done throughout
       the year, or a combination of nonspecialized farm with unskilled non-
       farm work (including work in a private household), is considered to be
       unskilled labor. A worker employed in any other occupation during
       the fifty-two-week period is considered to have some skill.
F = a dummy variable for the main type of employment of the worker's
       father while the nonmigratory farm worker was in his or her teens:
       nonmigratory farm workers whose fathers were hired farm workers
       during that period have a one; others have a zero.
P = the number of years a nonmigratory farm worker has done farm wage
       work for the employer on whose worksite he or she was interviewed.
M = a dummy variable for the worker's marital status: married non-
       migratory farm workers have a one; others have a zero.

The results of the regression analysis of nonmigratory farm workers are presented in Table 5.2 (on page 122).

The model for nonmigratory farm workers explains 39 percent of the variation in earnings, which is a little less than the explanatory power of the migratory model but is still satisfactory (see page 114).

As was expected, the results show that the variables which usually differ-
entiate workers' earnings also influenced the earnings of the nonmigratory farm
workers. The number of weeks of work is a highly significant variable: every
additional week of employment increased the yearly earnings by almost $83.
This increase was nearly the same for the migratory farm workers ($82).

Older nonmigratory workers earned considerably more than younger nonmigratory workers: the average increase in earnings per year was $268, while it was
only $44 for migratory workers. Thus age is a far less important factor in the mi-
gratory workers' earnings than in the nonmigratory workers' earnings. For older

Table 5.2. *Nonmigratory Farm Worker Earnings: Regression Coefficients of Explanatory Variables*

Variable		Coefficient	F-value
A	(age)	267.7	121.5
A^2	(age squared)	-3.0	114.1
C_1	(9-12 years of education)	779.0	30.5
C_2	(13+ years of education)	2193.9	94.2
W	(weeks of work)	82.9	130.0
R	(black)	-357.1	4.5
S	(sex: male)	1483.4	83.5
J	(occupational skills)	1150.1	81.3
F	(job of father: hired farm worker)	-230.9	2.3[a]
P	(years of employment with employer where interviewed)	25.3	10.9
M	(married)	778.7	31.2

Constant: -7316.0
R^2(adj.) = .39
$F = 83.2$
Number of observations: 1,429
Mean earnings: $4,786
Standard dev.: $2,817

[a] Not significant at .05 level.

nonmigratory workers, however, the increments became smaller more rapidly than for older migratory workers (for nonmigratory workers $A^2 = -3.0$, while for migratory workers $A^2 = -0.6$). The fact that, as the nonmigratory farm workers grew older, their earnings rose sharply and then leveled off sharply, reinforces findings on regular hired labor in New York (Cunningham 1969) showing that the payment levels of the youngest workers were low, but increased very sharply as the worker grew older; after the age of thirty to thirty-four years, they decreased quickly and continued to decline as the worker aged. The New York study concluded that the younger workers, who were the best paid and most capable, left their jobs in agriculture for nonfarm jobs, so that the less capable workers, who have fewer years of schooling and are probably less productive, were left behind in the agricultural work force (Cunningham 1969:19-20). The lower curve for the migratory farm workers' earnings would seem to indicate that there are not that many well-paid young migratory workers in farm work who are able to leave the migratory stream: migratory farm workers are usually less educated than nonmigratory workers, and their prospects of finding well-paid nonfarm jobs are not very good. Age does not seem to be so important for the migratory worker: the earnings levels for the various age groups were more similar among the migratory workers than among the nonmigratory workers.

As in the migratory model, age was substituted for experience, and the quadratic term of age was substituted for the quadratic term of experience. The nonmigratory model, unlike the migratory model, shows significant results for the experience variable: in it, age acted as a proxy variable for experience, but in the migratory model it did not. We may conclude that experience plays the same role in nonmigratory farm worker earnings as it does in the earnings of other workers (Blaug 1972:29). This means that the differences between the migratory and nonmigratory workers are substantial and that the position of the nonmigratory workers may in fact be more closely related to that of the nonfarm (industrial) workers than to that of migratory farm workers who do the same kind of jobs.

The male nonmigratory farm workers in the 25 percent subsample used in the earnings function earned an average of close to $1,500 more than the female nonmigratory farm workers; the male migratory farm workers earned an average of $1,100 more than the female migratory workers. Again, it should be kept in mind that in the samples of both migratory and nonmigratory farm workers, only those female workers who had done no housekeeping, and were fully dependent on farm work or nonfarm work during the fifty-two-week survey period, were included. This underscores the inequality of opportunities for women as compared to men in farm work.

As the two education variables, C_1 and C_2, show, education increased the earnings of nonmigratory farm workers more than the earnings of migratory farm workers. A nonmigratory farm worker with nine to twelve years of schooling earned an average of $779 more per year than the less educated nonmigratory worker, while a migratory farm worker with the same amount of schooling earned an average of only $257 more per year than a less educated migratory worker. For workers with thirteen years of schooling or more, the differences were even larger: a nonmigratory worker earned an average of $2,194 per year, while a migratory worker earned an average of $1,305 more per year.

The earnings function for migratory workers reveals substantial differences in the earnings of the various ethnic groups, but the nonmigratory function presents quite a different picture: black nonmigratory farm workers earned an average of $357 less than the average for all other ethnic groups combined. Their average was almost the same as the average for black migratory workers, but the base was slightly different. In the migratory function, in which four dummy variables were used for ethnic group membership and whites were used as a base, all four variables had significant results. But in the nonmigratory model, in which the number of Puerto Ricans, Mexicans, and workers labeled "other" is quite small, no significant results are found for these three ethnic groups. Therefore only the black workers are included in the final model. It is worth noting that the results which were not significant yielded positive regression coefficients for Puerto Ricans and Mexicans; this corroborates observations made in New York that Puerto Rican and Mexican nonmigratory farm workers have relatively high median earnings.[24]

Married nonmigratory farm workers earned an average of $779 more than nonmigratory farm workers who were unattached (i.e., who were no longer or had never been married). Marital status did not prove to be significant for migratory workers.

Nonmigratory workers who had worked for the same employer for longer periods of time earned more than workers with shorter periods of employment, but the average increase in earnings per year of employment, only $25, was quite small. The number of years of employment did not prove to be significant for migratory workers.

The highly significant results for variable J (occupatonal skills) in the nonmigratory function reveal a substantial difference between migratory and nonmigratory workers. Workers who were employed in occupations in farm or nonfarm labor requiring no special training, or in work in a private household, during the fifty-two-week period earned considerably less — $1,150 on the average — than workers who only did work requiring specific skills or specializations.

The only variable which did not significantly influence the earnings of either migratory or nonmigratory farm workers (i.e., was not significant at the .05 level) is the father's occupation while the worker was in his or her teens. This finding runs counter to the contention that the direct effect of family background on earnings has been underestimated (Bowles 1972:219-222; see also page 112). In both cases, the regression coefficients were negative, but the results would not allow the conclusion that a farm worker's social background (determined by the father's occupation during the worker's teens) has an effect on earnings.

5. CONCLUSIONS: UNEQUAL OPPORTUNITIES IN FARM WORK

The two earnings functions reveal some striking differences that clearly illustrate how desperate the socioeconomic position of migratory farm workers is. The variables that were not significant in the migratory model but were significant in the nonmigratory model attest to the impersonal and unpromising nature of migratory farm work. As far as earnings are concerned, the migratory workers have no prospect of being able to "move up in the world" by gaining experience, working more years for the same employer, or acquiring skills: such efforts do not pay off. All that the agricultural system in the United States asks of these workers is strong muscles and a good pair of hands. Their occupational opportunities are much more restricted than those of the nonmigratory and nonfarm workers.

Nonmigratory farm workers are in a position similar to that of nonfarm workers. The relationships they showed between worker characteristics and earnings are comparable to those of industrial workers: work experience, skills, and marriage had a positive effect on their earnings. For the migratory farm workers even marriage, which in earnings studies generally corresponds with higher earnings because the head of a household is assumed to be responsible for supporting more people and thus to need to earn more (page 117), did not have a significant effect on earnings.

The migratory farm workers' degree of dependence is clearly illustrated by the nature of the variables affecting their earnings — age, sex, education, ethnic group membership, weeks of work per year, and whether the family members traveled with the worker. The first four (except education to some extent) are beyond the workers' control. Even if these could be controlled, they would yield only small increases, for the characteristics which, among the nonmigratory (and generally among nonfarm) workers, are related to increases in earnings — such as age, more years of education, and being a male — offered considerably smaller monetary rewards to the migratory farm workers. Thus the only options the migratory farm worker seems to have to increase earnings is to work more weeks, to work faster, or to bring the family along; but the living and working conditions of migratory workers make these options very difficult to realize.

It is surprising to find that at such a low level of earnings, the average differences between the earnings of women and men are very substantial. This can only lead to the conclusion that women who do farm work have very unequal opportunities compared to men. Thus in agriculture, as in other industries, women are discriminated against purely on the basis of their sex.

Among the most striking findings of the earnings analysis are the *differences* in the degrees of discrimination against the various ethnic minority groups in the migratory sample. Although this category of workers is at the bottom of the occupational and prestige ladder and its mean earnings are barely above the poverty level, very substantial differences in earnings related to ethnic group membership have been exposed. This suggests that workers who are members of ethnic minorities are given less hours or days of work during each week, or get only the most poorly paid jobs.

As to the possible links in migratory farm work between certain ethnic groups and poorly paid jobs, studies made in Florida showed that blacks and Texas Mexicans generally harvest vegetables, and Puerto Ricans and Caribbean workers cut sugarcane and work on vegetable and citrus crops; the pay for all these jobs is low. Domestic whites, on the other hand, plant and work in packing houses, which pays much better (State of Florida Legislative Council... 1963:12). The situation in nonmigratory farm work is quite different: Puerto Ricans and Mexicans are not discriminated against as far as their earnings are concerned (pages 123-124). It seems that once they are in a structural setting in which they can prove themselves and perform like any other workers, they may no longer experience discrimination, at least not in earnings. This, however, does not apply to black workers, as the model for nonmigratory farm workers shows. The cost of being a black is about the same for the migratory worker as it is for the non-migratory worker.

The fact that the socioeconomic position of the migratory farm worker is much worse than that of the nonmigratory farm worker leads to the following question: what type of worker — what type of individual — joins the migratory stream, and what type stays at home? The following chapter will focus on a comparison of these two types.

NOTES

1. Married men have been observed to work faster and earn more than single workers (Friedland and Nelkin 1971:183-186). Blacks working for the same employer as Puerto Rican contract workers had lower wage rates than the Puerto Ricans (Wright 1965:95-96). Substantial differences in earnings were also indicated by Metzler and Sargent (1960:33-37).

2. (1) The Economic Research Service of the U.S. Department of Agriculture publishes data collected by the Bureau of the Census (U.S. Department of Commerce) as a supplement to the regular Current Population Survey (CPS).
(2) The quinquennial censuses of agriculture make farm labor job counts by obtaining information from employers or places of employment through establishment surveys.
(3) Data on farm workers are produced by the Statistical Reporting Service (SRS) of the U.S. Department of Agriculture.
(4) Information on seasonal hired workers is published by the U.S. Training and Employment Service (USTES) of the U.S. Department of Labor.
(5) The Bureau of Labor Statistics (BLS) of the U.S. Department of Labor publishes monthly reports, including estimates of the size and composition of the agricultural work force of all employees whose major activity is farm work.

3. For instance, the BLS's monthly reports give information on individuals whose major activity is farm work. The Economic Research Service publishes data on the workers who do some farm work for wages during the year. USTES provides data on seasonal hired workers only. Most of the statistical reports define casual workers as those who do less than twenty-five days of farm wage work during a year, and noncasual workers as those who do twenty-five days or more of farm wage work during a year. The noncasual workers are divided into three categories: (1) seasonal workers, i.e., persons who do 25-149 days of farm wage work during a year; (2) regular workers, i.e., persons who do 150-249 days of farm wage work during a year; and (3) year-round workers, i.e., persons who do 250 days or more of farm wage work during a year. The quinquennial censuses of agriculture use slightly different definitions in the studies they publish: "seasonal workers" are workers who are employed on *one* farm for less than 150 days during a year, and "regular workers" are those who are employed on *one* farm for 150 days or more during a year.

4. Holt (1976:69-73) considered the workers who were employed or potentially available for employment to be part of the labor force. Only those non-working weeks during which the worker was sick, injured, or in school were considered to be periods when the worker was not "potentially available."

5. Holt (1976:72) defined a full-time worker as any agricultural worker sixteen years of age or older who was in the labor force for forty-five weeks or more and earned an average of $20 a week or more.

6. Holt (1976:72) selected two weeks (rather than one) as the "threshold level" because one week of unemployment was not compensable in some states in his study area. Thus, workers in his study who were listed as not having been unemployed may in fact have been unemployed for one week.

7. The poverty level, or the weighted average threshold at the low-income level, was $3,164 for farm families in 1970 (U.S. Department of Commerce, Bureau of the Census, 1970a:19-20).

8. Earnings are affected by variations in yields, by the weather, by conditions in the fields, and of course by the type of worker employed. They also vary per crop (as mentioned above): for example, Metzler (1955:39-43) found that the wages for picking beans were much lower than the wages for harvesting potatoes.

9. To be on the safe side, workers who spent one week or more in school, housekeeping, retirement, or self-employment during the fifty-two-week survey period were excluded from the earnings analysis. Workers whose earnings were partly or entirely unknown were also excluded.

10. Of the sample of 12,666 migratory and nonmigratory farm workers, 3,302 spent at least one week in school, housekeeping, retirement, or self-employment. The earnings of 303 of the remaining 9,364 were unknown or missing. It should be kept in mind that the data on earnings were based on the workers' recollection of their earnings during the fifty-two-week survey period. This raises the question of how well the workers were able to remember what they had earned over such a long period. In a part of the survey area (Florida), the workers' information on their earnings was compared with the employers' information, and this showed that the workers were inclined to report higher earnings than what they actually had. They apparently forgot the bad days of low earnings and remembered only the better days. This implies that the farm workers' yearly earnings are even lower than what was indicated by the survey.

11. Grouped data have the disadvantage that when they are averaged, an important part of the variations in earnings is taken out before the dependent variable enters the regression. This was not a problem in the regression analysis presented here.

12. See Rees and Shultz (1970) and Weiss (1970:150-159) for the use of race; Weiss also used marital status. Hanoch (1967:310-329) used region and residence and Bowles (1972: 219-251) used family background. Rees and Shultz (1970) also used sex as an independent variable.

13. The studies on migratory farm workers provide very little information on fringe benefits. Friedland and Nelkin (1971:3-15, 35-50) suggested that migratory farm workers quite often have to pay rent when they live in a camp and are also charged for their meals. Transportation to the North, and to and from work, is usually provided free of charge.

14. According to Johnson and Sell (1976: 183-190), the "cost of being black" increased between 1959 and 1969.

15. The independent variables used were achievement, age, marital status, veteran status, and the number of weeks worked. The dependent variable was annual earnings in 1959.

16. In such statistical counts as the censuses of population, nonblack ethnic minority groups (Mexican Americans, Chinese, Japanese, and nonblack Puerto Ricans) are usually in the white category. This means that in making comparisons, one is really comparing the blacks with all the other categories.

17. The 1970 *United States Census of Population* gave more information on individuals of Spanish heritage than previous censuses.

18. For an overview of the problem of discrimination against women in earnings in the western industrialized countries see OECD 1979: Chapter III.

19. The 1970 Census of Population Occupation Classification was used. The codes for the occupations which were considered to be unskilled are: 740-796, 822-824, and 980-986.

20. A quadratic variable for age is included in the model in order to approximate the reality of age-income profiles for farm workers. Other studies have shown that the earnings of older workers do not continue to increase, but taper off at a certain point; in manual work particularly, where physical strength counts the most, older workers face a decrease in earnings after a certain age.

21. See Appendix C (pages 200-202) for a much higher explanatory power of the model using log earnings and log weeks.

22. Unfortunately, the survey data did not provide information on how long the migratory farm workers had been migratory. Because of this, the number of years a migratory farm worker had been doing farm work for wages was used as a definition of "experience."

23. Workers who spent one week or more in school, housekeeping, retirement, or self-employment during the fifty-two-week survey period, and workers whose earnings were partially or totally unknown, were excluded from the subsample.

24. Bauder (1973:16-19) assumed that the Puerto Ricans' and Mexicans' relatively high annual earnings resulted from working on farms where relatively high wages were paid, such as nurseries and farms that grow horticultural specialties. No information was given on how these minority workers came to be concentrated on these specialized farms. The 1970 census of the population (U.S. Department of Commerce, Bureau of the Census, 1970: Table 94) also showed the median earnings of male farm laborers and farm foremen of Spanish heritage to be relatively high ($3,075 per year) compared to the median earnings of all other male farm laborers and farm foremen ($2,597), of white male farm laborers and farm foremen ($2,874), and of black male workers in the same category ($1,868).

6

MIGRATORY AND NONMIGRATORY FARM WORKERS: A COMPARISON

The earnings analysis has shown that various factors which affect the earnings of migratory farm workers have different effects on the earnings of nonmigratory farm workers. This would indicate that these two categories of workers are much more dissimilar than they have generally been thought to be, although they do the same kind of work. It may also indicate that there is a relationship between some or all of these factors and migrancy.

This chapter will take the worker's migratory status as the dependent variable, and it will investigate the relationship between various socio-economic factors and this variable in order to find out what types of farm workers join the migratory stream, and how they compare to the workers who stay at home. This may lead to certain generalizations about the character-istics that are associated with migrancy. Suggestions about the factors that may be expected to influence migratory status will be gathered from the literature on occupational opportunities and occupational choices in the United States, from studies on migratory farm workers, and from the analyses in Chapters 4 and 5. The relationships between these socioeconomic factors and migratory status will be analyzed by taking migratory status as the dependent variable (section 2).

Notes to this chapter may be found on page 161.

1. OCCUPATIONAL OPPORTUNITIES AND THE MIGRATORY FARM WORKER

The occupation of farm worker enjoys very little prestige in the United States: "Popular stereotypes characterize most hired agricultural workers either as migrants and members of one or another ethnic or racial minority group, or as white winos." (Bauder 1973:16) A study on occupational prestige in the United States between 1925 and 1963 showed that the farm worker is close to the bottom of the prestige ladder, but no distinction was made between the farm worker with a regular job – the nonmigratory worker – and the migratory worker. The sharecroppers who owned no livestock or equipment and did not manage a farm were distinguished from the farmhand and were ranked even lower (Hodge et al. 1966:325). We can safely assume that the migratory farm worker, had he been distinguished separately, would be ranked as low as the sharecropper and perhaps even lower.

An in-depth analysis of the occupational structure in the United States concluded that: "Equality of opportunity is an ideal in the United States, not an accomplished fact." (Blau and Duncan 1967:207) Part of this analysis focused on the occupational achievements of blacks as compared with whites; by controlling for differences in educational levels, social origins, and first jobs, it revealed that in 1967, the occupational chances of blacks were still inferior to those of whites (1967:209) and that blacks were discriminated against in terms of occupational opportunities. "It is the cumulative effect of the handicaps Negroes encounter at every step in their lives that produces the serious inequalities of opportunities under which they suffer." (1967:238) Since we are concerned here with one of the lowest-ranking occupations in the United States, these findings are very relevant, for they indicate that the least desirable jobs are held by workers who suffer the most from unequal job opportunities – that is, the blacks.[1] Comparing migratory to nonmigratory farm work has shown that migratory work has the most unpleasant features: uncertainty about earnings, lack of remuneration for experience and skills, the need to travel in rickety buses and trucks, and dismal living and working conditions. Since the members of ethnic minority groups seem to have the more unpleasant jobs and since these jobs are predominant in migratory farm work, we can assume that there is a link between ethnic group membership and being migratory.

Chapters 4 and 5 showed that an analysis of the significance of ethnic group membership must go beyond the black-white dichotomy and consider other ethnic groups as well, for considerable differences were revealed both in the interstate mobility and the yearly earnings of the blacks, Puerto Ricans, and

Mexicans. Therefore, when looking for specific characteristics of migratory farm workers as compared to nonmigratory farm workers, a distinction should be made between these four ethnic groups.

Migratory farm work has repeatedly been described as dirty, irregular, monotonous work that requires no skills. A good pair of hands and a strong back is all one needs, but workers with quick fingers can move faster and workers with strong bodies can work longer. Migratory farm work is one of the few kinds of labor in the occupational structure in which the worker's education and training is not an important factor, although it has some influence. Considering how unpleasant the migratory farm workers' lives and work are, and how low the earnings are, it is reasonable to assume that people who do this type of work have very little education and few occupational skills. The earnings analysis in Chapter 5 showed that more years of education resulted in higher earnings for migratory and nonmigratory farm workers, although the migratory workers' increases in earnings were much smaller. It may be that the level of education is a characteristic which distinguishes the migratory from the nonmigratory farm worker. Having an occupation in farm work requiring certain skills or training was also found to have a significant positive effect on the earnings of nonmigratory farm workers, but was not significant for the earnings of migratory farm workers. From this it was concluded (page 124) that for the migratory farm worker, doing farm jobs that involve more skills or training than ordinary farm work has no effect on earnings, while it does increase the nonmigratory farm worker's earnings. To get a clearer impression of the role played by skills or specialization, the more or less skilled occupations in farm work will be examined to determine whether a relationship exists between skills and the nonmigratory status of the worker.

In studies on occupational achievement and occupational choice, the job of a worker's father proved to be a factor which influences the worker's occupational opportunities. The father's job seems to play a role not only in the formal education a child receives, but also in the outlook a youngster develops about occupational possibilities and about his or her own choice of occupation (see, for instance, Ginzberg et al. 1951; Dyer 1958; Slocum 1967; Sewell and Shah 1968; Taylor 1968; Haller and Woelfel 1972).

An analysis of the occupational choices of young people in lower-income groups suggested that "...one of the major limitations facing the lower income group is their modest level of expectation with respect to their occupational choice." (Ginzberg et al. 1951:154) The process of determining occupational choices in the lower income groups was characterized as "passive and stunted." (1951:155)

It has also been observed that in semi-skilled and unskilled occupations particularly, the family may have a restrictive effect on the occupational opportunities of their children:

> Research shows that the most important single persuasive influence of occupational choosers are their families. Yet, given the changes in occupational structures in the urbanized societies, many families, particularly those in the semiskilled and unskilled occupations, have a limited perspective of opportunities in future occupations. Accordingly, their range of influence is limiting to the aspirant. (Taylor 1968:215)

The data do not permit an in-depth study of how migratory and nonmigratory farm workers choose their occupations, but do enable us to investigate whether there are any significant differences between migratory and nonmigratory farm workers in terms of the kinds of jobs their fathers had when the workers were in their teens. In the earnings analysis (Chapter 5), it was assumed that having a father who was a hired farm worker would have a more restrictive effect on the worker's earnings than having a father who had some other occupation. The earnings function showed a negative (but not significant) result for this assumption, for both the migratory and the nonmigratory farm worker whose father was a hired farm worker. Here, it will be assumed that workers whose fathers were hired farm workers are more limited in their occupational choices and more likely to find themselves in the unpleasant and insecure job of migratory farm worker.

A number of the characteristics that may lead a worker to do migratory farm work have been mentioned: membership in an ethnic minority group, the lack of education or specific occupational skills, and the job of the worker's father. All these characteristics involve circumstances that the migratory worker can do almost nothing about, which indicates that the worker does this type of work because there are no other choices. However, migratory workers may also have more positive reasons for doing this work — that is, they may do it by choice, assuming that it will offer certain attractive opportunities. The young farm worker from the South may consider migratory farm work to some extent attractive because it offers a chance to leave the South, where job opportunities in farm work have been declining, and look for work in the North. It has been observed that young workers in particular try (but usually do not manage) to move out of the migratory farm labor stream and settle in the North (Friedland 1967:42-46); observations have also shown that black migratory farm workers on the East Coast are rather young (Metzler 1955:11; Larson and Sharp 1960: 18-21). High birth rates, the lack of job opportunities, and mergers of many small, marginal farms have forced young black workers from the South to move and search for work elsewhere. Under these circumstances, migratory farm work can be a stepping-stone for the young black from the South (U.S. Congress, Senate, Committee on Labor and Public Welfare 1960:8). Conversely, migratory farm work is much less attractive for older workers: it is exhausting and may become too demanding physically, and the traveling and substandard living and working conditions are harder on the older workers. Also, the family circumstances may change; for example, several members of the family may find local employment, so that the older workers no longer have to migrate to earn a living (Metzler and Sargent 1960:2).

Given the differing circumstances for younger and older workers, an investigation of whether there are more young and less older workers among migratory farm workers, as compared to nonmigratory farm workers, may further clarify the characteristics which are associated with migrancy.

An interesting statement has been made about the relationship between the size of the family and the decision to join the migratory farm labor stream:

There is some evidence that adolescents are to be found in the farm wage labor force, not simply because they were born into migrant families and migrant parents cannot make enough to support whole families, but because parents who were not earning enough at other jobs to support their families entered the migrant stream precisely in order for their adolescent children to bring in income. The parents may be able to earn no more than previously; but family income may be increased during the period in which there are older children to support if the parents enter a line of work in which they can find employment for their children as well as themselves. (Marcson and Fasick 1964:235)

The large size of many migratory families has also been commented upon:

Apparently size of family is associated with the need to migrate. When the family becomes too large for the earnings of one worker to support all its members, the household head looks for work that will permit other members to contribute to the family income. (Metzler and Sargent 1960:2)

Thus migratory farm work may be attractive to certain workers in the years of their lives during which they have large families to support. (Of course, having their families with them in no way diminishes the hardships encountered while they are "on the season.") Given these circumstances, we may assume that comparing family sizes among migratory and nonmigratory farm workers will indicate whether family size is related to migrancy.

Another feature of the migratory farm workers' family life which has received quite some attention is the high percentage of broken marriages and fatherless families. Although one study found only a few broken marriages in its migratory farm worker sample, it turned out that almost all heads of these broken families were women, and the proportion of unattached workers who had experienced broken marriages was quite high (Brooks and Hilgendorf 1960:33-34). A sample of black migratory farm workers in Florida also showed a high proportion of families in which women were heads of the household (Metzler 1955:11). The incidence of fatherless families among black migratory farm workers has been mentioned as the most significant factor producing the relatively high percentage of broken homes in this category of workers (Greene 1954:50). A study on the stability of black migratory farm worker families revealed that many marriages among migratory workers were quite enduring, but that it was the father who was missing in the unstable families (Marcson and Fasick 1964:49, 51). Also, "the predominant pattern of family relations consists of temporary liaisons established for convenience during the season." (Friedland and Nelkin 1971: 122) Investigating the frequency of broken marriages among migratory and non-migratory farm workers will indicate whether broken marriages are associated with being migratory.

As we have seen, migratory farm work may have some appeal for some workers, while for others it is the only option because there are no other jobs. Taking migrancy as the dependent variable, the next section will examine the relationship between this variable and the worker characteristics which were found (in this and the previous chapters) to typify migratory farmers or to distinguish them from other (farm) workers.

2. MIGRATORY STATUS AND FARM WORKER CHARACTERISTICS

The sample taken for the 1970 unemployment insurance survey (see Bauder *et al.* 1976) will be used as the data base for analyzing the worker characteristics that may be associated with the migratory status of the farm workers. As Chapters 4 and 5 showed that ethnic group membership is highly significant for the mobility and earnings of these workers, our analysis of the characteristics that distinguish migratory from nonmigratory farm workers will begin with the ethnicity variable. We will not limit the analysis to the black-white dichotomy, as is often done in this type of research, but will distinguish the Puerto Ricans and the Mexicans as well.

2.1. *Ethnic Group Membership and Migratory Status*

In the earnings analysis (Chapter 5), a 25 percent subsample of the farm workers was used (this was done to reduce research costs). Here, the original sample of 12,666 migratory and nonmigratory workers will be used but, because of the great variety of workers in the farm labor force, some of the more marginal categories will be excluded. Thus this analysis will deal with workers who depended on farm work only, or on a combination of hired farm and nonfarm work, to make their living, and who consequently derived their social status mainly from their position as hired workers. Workers who were students, housewives, retired, or self-employed and used migratory farm work to earn some extra money will not be included[2] (this group comprised 3,302 persons). The ethnic category labeled "other" will also be excluded because it is not possible, in such a mixed category, to distinguish the characteristics that are significant for each ethnic group. (The "other" category comprised only 122 workers and included white Canadians, black Jamaicans, Indians, and Philippinos.) This leaves a sample of 9,242 workers, of whom 2,900 were migratory and 6,304 were nonmigratory. (The migratory status of 38 workers was not known.)

First, the relationship between ethnic group membership and migratory status will be analyzed: see Table 6.1.

Table 6.1. *Ethnic Group Membership and Migratory Status*

Ethnic group membership	*Migratory status*		*Total*	
	Migratory %	*Nonmigratory* %	%	*(N)*
White	5	95	100	(5,028)
Black, Puerto Rican, or Mexican	63	37	100	(4,176)
Total	32	68	100	(9,204)

Undefined = 38
$X^2 = 3,527.0$ 1 df.   Sign. at .05
Phi = 0.62

Table 6.1 clearly shows that the chance for a white farm worker in the sample of becoming part of the migratory stream was quite small, while for members of ethnic groups which are minorities in the United States — blacks, Puerto Ricans and Mexicans — this was quite different: almost two thirds of the farm workers in these groups were migratory farm workers. Examining the three ethnic minority groups separately, we find that 52 percent of the black farm workers were migratory and 48 percent were nonmigratory; 75 percent of the Puerto Rican farm workers were migratory and 25 percent were nonmigratory; 86 percent of the Mexicans were migratory and 14 percent were nonmigratory. Thus in general, workers who do farm work and are also members of an ethnic minority group have a good chance of being migratory; this is especially the case for Puerto Rican and Mexican workers.

To further explore the options which the four ethnic groups have in farm work, the kind of work they do will be investigated. As mentioned above, some farm workers depend on farm work only to earn their income, while others combine farm with nonfarm work. The latter type of worker must have some skill or specialization that makes him or her more able to find employment other than farm work: in other words, he or she has more and more diverse occupational opportunities. Table 6.2 presents the relationship between the migratory farm workers' ethnic group membership and the type of work done; it reveals that while almost two thirds of the workers in ethnic minority groups depended on hired farm work only, less than one half of the white workers depended on hired farm work only.

Table 6.2. *Migratory Farm Workers: Ethnic Group Membership and Types of Work Done*

Ethnic group membership	*Type of migratory farm work*			
	Hired farm work only	*Hired farm and nonfarm work*	*Total*	
	%	%	%	*(N)*
White	45	55	100	(266)
Black, Puerto Rican, Mexican	63	37	100	(2,634)
Total	61	39	100	(2,900)

Undefined = 10
$X^2 = 30.34$ 1 df.   Sign. at .05
Phi = 0.10

We have assumed that those workers who are most often the victims of unequal job opportunities — i.e., members of minority groups — have the least desirable jobs (page 131). The findings in Tables 6.1 and 6.2 bear out this assumption. Farm workers in ethnic minority groups had a two-to-one chance (Table 6.1) of being in the insecure and unpleasant position of the migratory worker. The vast majority of the white farm workers were, on the other hand, nonmigratory. The weak position of the workers in ethnic minority groups, as compared to white workers, is further illustrated by Table 6.2, which shows that in migratory farm work, it was the ethnic group members who more often than not did farm work only and thus were extremely limited in their occupational opportunities. This makes them very vulnerable to unemployment, among other things.

2.2. Education, Occupational Skills, and Migratory Status

The first part of this section aims to find out what the probability is that, given a certain level of education, a farm worker will be migratory. This will be done by examining the relationship between education and migratory status. As it may be assumed that the younger workers have more years of schooling than the older workers, this relationship will be investigated separately for a younger (aged 25-34 years) and for an older (aged 45-54 years) category of workers.

Because the educational opportunities for women are not equal to those for men, the sex of the worker may act as an intervening variable in this relationship. As most of the workers interviewed in the sample were men, this part of the analysis is limited to male farm workers; in this way we are able to control for the possible effect of sex on the relationship between education and migratory status.[3] The male workers in the two age cohorts comprise 3,051 of the workers in the sample. Table 6.3 shows the relationship between education and migratory status for male farm workers within the two age cohorts.

The table shows that the fewer years of schooling a worker had, the greater the chance was of being migratory in both age cohorts. It also bears out the assumption that younger farm workers have more years of schooling than older workers: 56 percent of the 1,759 workers aged 25-34 years had nine years of schooling or more, and 33 percent of the 1,246 workers aged 45-54 years had nine years of schooling or more.

Section 2.1 shows that the farm workers who were members of ethnic minority groups are more apt to be migratory than white farm workers. This section indicates that fewer years of schooling is associated with being migratory. As the educational opportunities for the various ethnic groups in the United States are unequal, it is quite likely that being a member of an ethnic minority group and a relatively low level of education are associated with each other. This leads to the assumption that workers in ethnic minority groups are migratory farm workers because of their lack of schooling. To test this assump-

Table 6.3. *Education and Migratory Status of Male Farm Workers Aged 25-34 Years and 45-54 Years*

Education	Migratory status Age cohort 25-34 years			Migratory status Age cohort 45-54 years		
	Migratory	Nonmi-gratory	Total	Migratory	Nonmi-ratory	Total
	%	%	%	%	%	(N)
0-4 years	65	35	100 (186)	53	47	100 (334)
5-8 years	47	53	100 (580)	27	73	100 (506)
9-12 years	29	71	100 (868)	20	80	100 (336)
13$^+$ years	12	88	100 (125)	13	87	100 (70)
Total	37	63	100 (1,759)	31	69	100 (1,246)

Undefined = 19
X^2 = 146.3   3 df.   Sign. at .05
Phi = .29

Undefined = 27
X^2 = 110.6   3 df.   Sign. at .05
Phi = .30

tion, the relationship between education and migratory status will be considered within each of the four ethnic groups in the sample. Tables 6.4 and 6.5 present this relationship for male farm workers in the two age cohorts (25-34 years and 45-54 years) used above.

The results for both age cohorts confirm what Table 6.1 already indicated: the white farm workers in the sample had only a small probability of being migratory, while it was much more probable that members of ethnic minority groups would be migratory. Puerto Ricans and Mexicans were again shown to be predominantly migratory, while the blacks were more evenly represented among migratory and nonmigratory workers. Tables 6.4. and 6.5 show that among the Puerto Ricans and Mexicans, education had almost no influence on migratory status. The blacks aged 45-54, however, showed a significant result: for them, *more* years of schooling *was* associated with being migratory. (The black workers aged 25-34 years also had a higher percentage of migratory workers with nine years of schooling or more than with eight years or less, but the difference is not significant.[4])

Table 6.3 implies that there is a simple relationship between education and migratory status: the fewer the years of education, the greater the probability

Table 6.4. *Education and Migratory Status of Male Farm Workers Aged 25-34 Years in Four Ethnic Groups*

Education	White			Black			Puerto Rican			Mexican		
						Ethnic group membership and migratory status						
	Mi-gratory %	Non-migratory %	Total % (N)	Mi-gratory %	Non-migratory %	Total % (N)	Mi-gratory %	Non-migratory %	Total % (N)	Mi-gratory %	Non-migratory %	Total % (N)
8 years or less	11	89	100 (234)	58	42	100 (199)	74	26	100 (273)	85	15	100 (60)
9 years or more	5	95	100 (633)	67	33	100 (274)	66	34	100 (74)	67	33	100 (12)
Total	6	94	100 (867)	62	38	100 (473)	72	28	100 (347)	82	18	100 (72)
Undefined = 19	$X^2 = 11.5$ 1 df. Sign. at .05 Phi = 0.11			$X^2 = 1.7$ 1 df. Phi = 0.06			$X^2 = 1.7$ 1 df. Phi = 0.07			$X^2 = 2.3$ 1 df. Phi = 0.18		

Table 6.5. Education and Migratory Status of Male Farm Workers Aged 45-54 Years in Four Ethnic Groups

Education	White			Black			Puerto Rican			Mexican		
	Mi-gratory %	Non-migratory %	Total % (N)	Mi-gratory %	Non-migratory %	Total % (N)	Mi-gratory %	Non-migratory %	Total % (N)	Mi-gratory %	Non-migratory %	Total % (N)
8 years or less	10	90	100 (359)	44	56	100 (280)	77	23	100 (160)	78	22	100 (41)
9 years or more	7	93	100 (313)	56	44	100 (80)	70	30	100 (10)	100	-	100 (3)
Total	8	92	100 (672)	47	53	100 (360)	76	24	100 (170)	80	20	100 (44)
	$X^2 = 1.6$ 1 df. Phi = 0.05			$X^2 = 3.8$ 1 df. Sign. at .05 Phi = 0.10			$X^2 = 0.2$ 1 df. Phi = 0.03			$X^2 = 0.8$ 1 df. Phi = 0.13		

Ethnic group membership and migratory status

Undefined = 27

that a farm worker is migratory. Tables 6.4 and 6.5 show, however, that it is not education, but ethnic group membership, that is associated with the migratory status of the farm worker. It was only among the older blacks in the sample that education had a significant influence on migratory status, but this influence is the reverse of what is implied by Table 6.3.

The second part of this section aims to find out what the probability is that, given certain occupational skills, a farm worker will be migratory. The occupational groupings used in the earnings analysis in Chapter 5 (see note 19) will be used here. Unskilled workers will be defined as those workers who, during the fifty-two-week period, worked as farm laborers or combined nonspecialized farm work with unskilled nonfarm work, or with work in a private household. Workers who did more specialized work (e.g., work in a greenhouse or at a nursery) will be considered to have some skill. The relationship between having an occupational skill and migratory status will be worked out for male farm workers in the age cohorts used in studying the relationship between education and migratory status: see Table 6.6.

Table 6.6. *Occupational Skills and Migratory Status of Male Farm Workers Aged 25-34 Years and 45-54 Years*

Occupations	Migratory status Age cohort 25-34 years			Migratory status Age cohort 45-54 years		
	Migratory	Nonmigratory	Total	Migratory	Nonmigratory	Total
	%	%	% (N)	%	%	% (N)
Unskilled	42	58	100 (1,147)	36	64	100 (928)
Some skill	30	70	100 (620)	20	80	100 (341)
Total	38	62	100 (1,767)	32	68	100 (1,269)

Undefined = 11   Undefined = 4
X^2 = 22.4 X^2 = 27.1
1 df.   Sign. at .05   1 df.   Sign. at .05
Phi = 0.11   Phi = 0.15

Table 6.6 shows that workers who did unskilled work were more likely to be migratory than workers who had jobs requiring some skill; this was the case in both age cohorts. Sixty-five percent (1,147) of the workers in the sample aged 25-34 years were unskilled, and 73 percent (928) of the workers aged 45-54 years were unskilled.

Because ethnic group membership may complicate the relationship between occupational skills and migratory status, as it did with education, Tables 6.7 and 6.8 will present this relationship for each of the four ethnic groups separately. Again, male farm workers in the two age cohorts will be considered.

Most of the results presented in Tables 6.7 and 6.8 are not significant, which implies that ethnic group membership is important for the migratory status of the worker. Except in the case of the older blacks, whether a worker is skilled or unskilled did not influence migratory status; thus a skilled farm worker is not more likely to be nonmigratory than an unskilled farm worker. The significant relationship shown by the older blacks has the same direction as the relationship in Table 6.6, in which doing some skilled farm work increased the probability of being nonmigratory.

The relationships between education and migratory status and between occupational skills and migratory status reveal that ethnic group membership plays the dominant role in whether a farm worker is migratory or nonmigratory. If ethnic group membership were to be ignored in examining these relationships, we would be led to the conclusion that fewer years of education, or doing unskilled work, increase the probability for all farm workers of being migratory. However, within the four ethnic categories, these relationships take different directions; but the results — except those for older blacks — are not significant. This indicates that within each of the ethnic categories, education and skills have almost no influence on the worker's migratory status. One of the relationships shown by the older blacks is quite different and very surprising: for them, *more* years of education was associated with being *migratory*, which is quite the opposite of the general direction of this relationship — i.e., that *more* years of education are associated with being *non*migratory.

Thus it is ethnic group membership, and *not* education or skills, that is the most influential characteristic in determining whether a farm worker is migratory or not.

2.3. *Social Background and Migratory Status*

The type of job the worker's father had while the worker was in his teens will be used (as in Chapter 5) as an approximation for the social background of the worker. As the number of available jobs in farm work has declined consider-

Table 6.7. Occupational Skills and Migratory Status of Male Farm Workers Aged 25-34 Years in Four Ethnic Groups

Ethnic group membership and migratory status

Occupations	White			Black			Puerto Rican			Mexican		
	Migratory %	Non-migratory %	Total % (N)	Migratory %	Non-migratory %	Total % (N)	Migratory %	Non-migratory %	Total % (N)	Migratory %	Non-migratory %	Total % (N)
Unskilled	6	94	100 (493)	64	36	100 (340)	71	29	100 (262)	83	17	100 (52)
Some skill	7	93	100 (376)	56	44	100 (135)	76	24	100 (89)	80	20	100 (20)
Total	6	94	100 (869)	62	38	100 (475)	73	27	100 (351)	82	18	100 (72)
	$X^2 = 0.6$ 1 df. Phi = 0.03			$X^2 = 2.5$ 1 df. Phi = 0.07			$X^2 = 0.8$ 1 df. Phi = 0.05			$X^2 = 0.1$ 1 df. Phi = 0.04		

Table 6.8. *Occupational Skills and Migratory Status of Male Farm Workers Aged 45-54 Years in Four Ethnic Groups*

Occupations	Ethnic group membership and migratory status											
	White			Black			Puerto Rican			Mexican		
	Mi-gratory %	Non-migratory %	Total % (N)	Mi-gratory %	Non-migratory %	Total % (N)	Mi-gratory %	Non-migratory %	Total % (N)	Mi-gratory %	Non-migratory %	Total % (N)
Unskilled	7	93	100 (436)	49	51	100 (293)	79	21	100 (163)	81	19	100 (36)
Some skill	11	89	100 (245)	35	65	100 (68)	65	35	100 (20)	75	25	100 (8)
Total	9	91	100 (681)	47	53	100 (361)	78	22	100 (183)	80	20	100 (44)

White: $X^2 = 3.1$, 1 df., Phi = 0.07

Black: $X^2 = 4.2$, 1 df. Sign. at .05, Phi = 0.11

Puerto Rican: $X^2 = 2.0$, 1 df., Phi = 0.10

Mexican: $X^2 = 0.1$, 1 df., Phi = 0.05

Table 6.10. Social Background and Migratory Status of Male Farm Workers Aged 25-34 Years in Four Ethnic Groups

Job of worker's father during worker's teens	White			Black			Puerto Rican			Mexican		
	Migratory %	Non-migratory %	Total % (N)	Migratory %	Non-migratory %	Total % (N)	Migratory %	Non-migratory %	Total % (N)	Migratory %	Non-migratory %	Total % (N)
Hired farm worker	13	87	100 (149)	62	38	100 (154)	77	23	100 (217)	84	16	100 (43)
Farm operator	4	96	100 (270)	63	37	100 (90)	59	41	100 (37)	86	14	100 (7)
Other	6	94	100 (423)	64	36	100 (191)	62	38	100 (84)	75	25	100 (16)
Total	6	94	100 (842)	63	37	100 (435)	72	28	100 (338)	82	18	100 (66)

Ethnic group membership and migratory status

White: $X^2 = 13.4$, 2 df. Sign. at .05, Phi = 0.13

Black: $X^2 = 0.3$, 2 df., Phi = 0.02

Puerto Rican: $X^2 = 10.2$, 1 df. Sign. at .05, Phi = 0.17

Mexican: $X^2 = 0.7$, 2 df., Phi = 0.10

Undefined = 91

Table 6.11. Social Background and Migratory Status of Male Farm Workers Aged 45-54 Years in Four Ethnic Groups

Job of worker's father during worker's teens	Ethnic group membership and migratory status											
	White			Black			Puerto Rican			Mexican		
	Mi-gratory %	Non-migratory %	Total % (N)	Mi-gratory %	Non-migratory %	Total % (N)	Mi-gratory %	Non-migratory %	Total % (N)	Mi-gratory %	Non-migratory %	Total % (N)
Hired farm worker	12	88	100 (92)	43	57	100 (124)	77	23	100 (122)	79	21	100 (14)
Farm operator	5	95	100 (293)	45	55	100 (85)	72	28	100 (25)	76	24	100 (17)
Other	10	90	100 (272)	53	47	100 (117)	79	21	100 (28)	75	25	100 (8)
Total	8	92	100 (657)	47	53	100 (326)	77	23	100 (175)	77	23	100 (39)

Undefined = 76

White: $X^2 = 6.1$, 2 df. Sign. at .05, Phi = 0.10

Black: $X^2 = 2.8$, 2 df., Phi = 0.09

Puerto Rican: $X^2 = 0.4$, 1 df., Phi = 0.05

Mexican: $X^2 = 0.0$, 2 df., Phi = 0.00

ably over the years, the relationship between the job of the worker's father and the worker's migratory status will be studied in the two age cohorts of male migratory workers, as was done in determining the relationships between education and migratory status, and between occupational skills and migratory status: see Table 6.9.

Table 6.9. *Social Background and Migratory Status of Male Farm Workers Aged 25-34 Years and 45-54 Years*

Job of the worker's father during the worker's teens	Migratory status Age cohort 25-34 years			Migratory status Age cohort 45-54 years		
	Migratory	Nonmigratory	Total	Migratory	Nonmigratory	Total
	%	%	% (N)	%	%	% (N)
Hired farm worker	57	43	100 (564)	48	52	100 (352)
Farm operator	24	76	100 (406)	20	80	100 (420)
Other	30	70	100 (717)	28	72	100 (425)
Total	38	62	100 (1,687)	32	68	100 (1,197)

Undefined = 91 Undefined = 76
$X^2 = 138.2$ $X^2 = 72.3$
2 df.   Sign. at .05 2 df.   Sign. at .05
Phi = 0.29 Phi = 0.25

In both age cohorts, workers whose fathers were hired farm workers were more likely to be migratory than workers whose fathers had some other occupation, e.g., operating a farm or doing nonfarm work. As this relationship may differ significantly in each of the ethnic groups in the sample, Tables 6.10 and 6.11 are presented to show the results of Tables 6.9 for each ethnic group separately.

Most of the results of Tables 6.10 and 6.11 are not significant: the job of the father hardly seemed to matter for members of ethnic minority groups in both age cohorts. Only the younger Puerto Ricans showed significant results: those whose fathers were hired farm workers were more likely to be migratory than those whose fathers operated farms or had other jobs, and this relationship has the same direction as was observed in Table 6.9. The results also indicate that the white workers aged 25-34 years whose fathers were hired farm workers were slightly more likely to be migratory than other white workers.

There were both migratory and nonmigratory workers among the fathers who were hired farm workers. To find out whether the father's migratory status has any bearing on the worker's migratory status, Table 6.12 presents the worker's migratory status in relationship to that of the father, for those workers whose fathers were hired farm workers.

Table 6.12. *The Father's Migratory Status and that of the Worker*[a]

Migratory status of father	Migratory status of worker		Total	
	Migratory	Nonmigratory		
	%	%	%	(N)
Father migratory	65	35	100	(482)
Father nonmigratory	49	51	100	(1,667)
Total	52	48	100	(2,149)

Undefined = 332
$X^2 = 41.2$ 1 df.   Sign. at .05
Phi = 0.14
[a] Only workers whose fathers were hired farm workers when the workers were in their teens are included.

Table 6.12 shows that those workers whose fathers were migratory were more likely to be migratory than those workers whose fathers were nonmigratory. To check for the influence of ethnic group membership, this relationship is presented for each of the ethnic groups separately. Only the blacks showed significant results, as is shown in Table 6.13.[5]

Table 6.13. *The Father's Migratory Status and that of the Worker, for Black Farm Workers*[a]

Migratory status of father	Migratory status of worker		Total	
	Migratory	Nonmigratory		
	%	%	%	(N)
Father migratory	75	25	100	(32)
Father nonmigratory	43	57	100	(122)
Total	49	51	100	(154)

$X^2 = 9.4$ 1 df.   Sign. at .05
Phi = 0.25
[a] To obtain this information, the 25 percent subsample had to be used for financial reasons (as in Chapter 5).

Table 6.13 shows that black farm workers whose fathers were migratory were more likely to be migratory than those black farm workers whose fathers were nonmigratory.

Examining the relationship between the job of the worker's father during the worker's teens and the worker's migratory status within two age cohorts has made it clear that farm workers whose fathers were hired farm workers are more often migratory than farm workers whose fathers had other jobs. Within each of the ethnic minority groups, however, the father's occupation has almost no effect on the worker's migratory status, except in the case of the younger Puerto Ricans. Young white farm workers whose fathers were hired farm workers are also slightly more often migratory than the other young white farm workers. Furthermore, considering only those workers whose fathers were migratory during the worker's teens, we find that it is only among the black farm workers that the migrancy of the father is related to the migrancy of the worker. This relationship is not significant among the whites, Puerto Ricans, and Mexicans, very likely because the whites were so overwhelmingly nonmigratory and the Puerto Ricans and Mexicans are so overwhelmingly migratory.

Here again, we see that ethnic group membership is an influential factor in determining the migratory status of the farm workers on the East Coast. On the other hand, the worker's social background seldom affects migratory status, as taking each of the ethnic groups separately shows.

2.4. Age and Migratory Status

As younger workers seem to be particularly attracted to migratory farm work, the relationship between age and the worker's migratory status is presented in Table 6.14.

Table 6.14. Age and Migratory Status[a]

Age	Migratory status		Total	
	Migratory	Nonmigratory		
	%	%	%	(N)
Less than 30 years	38	62	100	(3,529)
30 – 49 years	32	68	100	(3,616)
50 years or older	22	78	100	(2,199)
Total	32	68	100	(9,344)

Undefined = 20
$X^2 = 171.9$ 2 df.   Sign. at .05
Phi = 0.14

[a] This table includes the 122 workers who were in the ethnic category labeled "other," but exludes workers who spent at least one week in housekeeping, school, retirement, or self-employment (see page 136) during the fifty-two-week survey period.

Table 6.14 shows that workers aged thirty years or less comprised the highest percentage of migratory workers, while workers aged fifty years or more comprised the lowest percentage.

In Table 6.15 the relationship between age and migratory status is presented for each ethnic group separately. Only the black farm workers in the sample showed significant results: almost two thirds of the blacks aged thirty years or less were migratory, while slightly more than one third of the blacks aged fifty years or more were migratory. This indicates that most of the differences in percentages in Table 6.14 are accounted for by black workers; it also shows that the blacks tended to stop doing migratory farm work as they grew older (which confirms findings mentioned on pages 133-134).

2.5. Family Characteristics and Migratory Status

Migratory farm work appears to be attractive to workers with large families because (as Chapter 5 showed) it offers the workers the opportunity to bring their families with them and thus enables all the family members to work in the fields and increase the family's income. The analysis of mobility (Chapter 4) showed, however, that despite this opportunity to increase earnings, the majority of the migratory farm workers traveled without their families.

To find out more about migratory status and family size, Table 6.16 makes two comparisons: on the left hand side of the table, the size of each farm worker's family (counting all family members, not just those traveling with the worker) is related to the migratory status of all workers; on the right hand side, the same relationship is shown, but only those migratory workers who traveled with all their family members are included.

Both sides of Table 6.16 show that having a large family (seven or more people) tended to be associated with being migratory. When this relationship is examined in each ethnic group separately, the results are not significant.[6] This is an important correction and qualification of the general assumption that migratory farm work is particularly attractive to larger families. Again, ethnic group membership, and *not* family size, in large part determines whether or not the farm worker is migratory. Large families are found among migratory farm workers because the ethnic minorities which have larger families than whites do this type of work.

Table 6.15. Age and Migratory Status within Four Ethnic Groups[a]

Age	Ethnic group membership and migratory status											
	White			Black			Puerto Rican			Mexican		
	Mi-gratory %	Non-migratory %	Total % (N)	Mi-gratory %	Non-migratory %	Total % (N)	Mi-gratory %	Non-migratory %	Total % (N)	Mi-gratory %	Non-migratory %	Total % (N)
Less than 30 years	4	96	100 (454)	64	36	100 (155)	80	20	100 (172)	93	7	100 (53)
30-49 years	5	95	100 (468)	52	48	100 (271)	70	30	100 (127)	88	12	100 (34)
50 years or more	6	94	100 (321)	36	64	100 (144)	84	16	100 (55)	100	–	100 (13)
Total	5	95	100 (1,243)	52	48	100 (570)	77	23	100 (354)	92	8	100 (100)
Undefined = 33	$X^2 = 0.7$ 2 df. Phi = 0.02			$X^2 = 24.3$ 2 df. Sign. at .05 Phi = 0.21			$X^2 = 5.8$ 2 df. Phi = 0.13			$X^2 = 1.8$ 2 df. Phi = 0.13		

[a] To obtain this information, the 25 percent subsample had to be used for financial reasons (as in Chapter 5).

Table 6.16. *Family Size^a and Migratory Status*

Size of family	Migratory status for all workers			Migratory status for all workers excl. those who traveled with some or no family members		
	Migratory	Nonmi- gratory	Total	Migratory: all family members traveled	Nonmi- gratory	Total
	%	%	% (N)	%	%	% (N)
3 or less	31	69	100 (4,263)	6	94	100 (3,146)
4 - 6	29	71	100 (3,177)	7	93	100 (2,436)
7 or more	42	58	100 (1,375)	14	86	100 (922)
Total	32	68	100 (8,815)	7	93	100 (6,504)

Undefined = 239   Undefined = 152
$X^2 = 85.9$ $X^2 = 62.8$
2 df.   Sign. at .05   2 df.   Sign. at .05
Phi = 0.10   Phi = 0.10

^a Family size was computed by counting the interviewee, his or her spouse, and all resident and nonresident dependent children.

A high frequency of broken marriages and fatherless families has often been observed among migratory farm workers. To find out whether marital status has any bearing on migratory status, the relationship between the worker's marital status and being migratory or nonmigratory is presented in Table 6.17. As it is quite likely that male workers with broken marriages may have different reasons for choosing to do migratory farm work than female workers with broken marriages, this relationship will be presented separately for male and for female workers.[7]

Table 6.17 shows that three quarters of the married farm workers in the sample were nonmigratory farm workers. Looking at the marital status category with the highest percentage of migratory workers, we find that for all farm workers and for male farm workers, the "was married" category comprised, relative to the other categories, the highest percentages (42 percent and 48 per-

Table 6.17. *Marital Status and Migratory Status of Male and Female Farm Workers*

Marital status	All[a] farm workers			Male farm workers			Female farm workers		
	Migratory	Non-migratory	Total	Migratory	Non-migratory	Total	Migratory	Non-migratory	Total
	%	%	% (N)	%	%	% (N)	%	%	% (N)
Married	25	75	100 (5,662)	26	74	100 (4,900)	17	83	100 (762)
Was married	42	58	100 (1,285)	48	52	100 (990)	23	77	100 (295)
Never married	40	60	100 (2,744)	41	59	100 (2,448)	33	67	100 (296)
Total	32	68	100 (9,691)	33	67	100 (8,338)	22	78	100 (1,353)

$X^2 = 270.1$
2 df. Sign. at .05
Phi = 0.17

$X^2 = 267.3$
2 df. Sign. at .05
Phi = 0.18

$X^2 = 31.8$
2 df. Sign. at .05
Phi = 0.15

[a] The data used in this table are slightly different from the data used in the other tables, as "all farm workers" excludes those workers who spent at least one week in housekeeping or school during the fifty-two-week period, but includes those workers who spent at least one week in retirement or self-employment (548 workers in the total sample of 12,666). The category labeled "other" is excluded from this table.

Table 6.18. *Marital Status and Migratory Status of Male and Female White Farm Workers*

Marital status	All white farm workers			Male white farm workers			Female white farm workers		
	Migratory	Non-migratory	Total	Migratory	Non-migratory	Total	Migratory	Non-migratory	Total
	%	%	% (N)	%	%	% (N)	%	%	% (N)
Married	4	96	100 (3,472)	4	96	100 (2,976)	3	97	100 (496)
Was married	18	82	100 (476)	22	78	100 (352)	6	94	100 (124)
Never married	6	94	100 (1,363)	7	93	100 (1,190)	5	95	100 (173)
Total	6	94	100 (5,311)	6	94	100 (4,518)	4	96	100 (793)

$X^2 = 168.8$
2 df.   Sign. at .05
Phi = 0.18

$X^2 = 198.2$
2 df.   Sign. at .05
Phi = 0.21

$X^2 = 3.44$
2 df.
Phi = 0.07

Table 6.19. *Marital Status and Migratory Status of Male and Female Black Farm Workers*

Marital status	All black farm workers			Male black farm workers			Female black farm workers		
	Migratory	*Non-migratory*	*Total*	*Migratory*	*Non-migratory*	*Total*	*Migratory*	*Non-migratory*	*Total*
	%	%	% (N)	%	%	% (N)	%	%	% (N)
Married	45	55	100 (1,229)	47	53	100 (1,017)	40	60	100 (212)
Was married	51	49	100 (628)	56	44	100 (474)	34	66	100 (154)
Never married	67	33	100 (646)	68	32	100 (578)	63	37	100 (68)
Total	52	48	100 (2,503)	55	45	100 (2,069)	41	59	100 (434)

$X^2 = 83.4$
2 df.   Sign. at .05
Phi = 0.18

$X^2 = 68.5$
2 df.   Sign. at .05
Phi = 0.18

$X^2 = 17.2$
2 df.   Sign. at .05
Phi = 0.18

cent respectively) of migratory workers. For the female workers the "never married" category comprised the highest percentage (33 percent) of migratory workers. Thus it is the divorced, separated, or widowed male farm workers and the female farm workers who had never married who are most likely to become migratory farm workers.

As ethnic group membership has proved to be such an influential factor as far as migratory status is concerned, the relationship between marital and migratory status was studied in each ethnic group separately, but only the whites and blacks showed significant results. These are presented in Tables 6.18 and 6.19. In Table 6.18 the workers who were no longer married comprised a surprisingly high percentage (22 percent) of male white migratory farm workers, indicating that migratory farm work attracts male white workers who are divorced, separated, or widowed.

In Table 6.19 the high percentage of black migratory workers in the "never married" category is certainly related to the fact that these workers were relatively young. Table 6.19 also shows that only a relatively low percentage of divorced, widowed, or separated female black farm workers were migratory. This finding counters the general impression that broken marriages and especially fatherless families are particularly common among black migratory workers, and that such families are especially attracted to migratory farm work. The table also shows that nonmigratory farm work is more attractive to black widowed, divorced, or separated women than migratory work. The impression that the black migratory family is often fatherless may stem from the fact that, when all black female farm workers are compared to female farm workers in each of the other ethnic groups, the black women comprised the highest percentage in the "was married" category.[8] As most of the research on migratory farm workers has focused on the blacks and has considered them to be typical of all migratory farm workers, and as the migratory farm workers have not been studied in comparison to the nonmigratory farm workers, researchers have been (mis)led to believe that migratory farm work attracts female workers with broken marriages. The fact is that, besides the blacks who never married, the only farm workers who were clearly attracted to migratory farm work were the widowed, divorced, or separated male white workers.

3. ETHNICITY: THE DETERMINANT FACTOR

Migratory farm workers have generally been observed to be uneducated, unskilled, and usually young, and to have broken marriages or quite large families. At first sight, considering the worker characteristics which are related to migrancy seems to confirm this. Comparing migratory to nonmigratory farm workers shows that the migratory workers are usually uneducated and unskilled, that they are young, and that large families are relatively overrepresented in this category. Also, their fathers are more likely to be hired farm workers; furthermore, a relatively high percentage of divorced, separated, or widowed workers is found among migratory men.

This general picture has, however, proved to be *only part* of the story. When the relationships between the socioeconomic characteristics and migratory status are analyzed within each of the four ethnic groups separately, it becomes clear that ethnic group membership is unquestionably the most important factor in farm labor: within the ethnic groups, only a few relationships between these socioeconomic characteristics and migratory status are significant. We must conclude that even in one of the lowest paid and least prestigious occupations, occupational opportunities for the four ethnic groups differ greatly. The picture presented by this configuration of significant and not significant relationships can only lead to the generalization that, in terms of the role ethnicity plays in determining socioeconomic positions, the farm workers can be divided into three categories: (1) Puerto Ricans and Mexicans, (2) whites, and (3) blacks.

(1) Most of the Puerto Rican and Mexican farm workers (75 and 86 percent respectively) who were interviewed in the fourteen states on the East Coast were migratory, and thus may be located at one end of a migratory — nonmigratory continuum. In comparison to the nonmigratory farm workers, it is neither their lack of education or skills, nor their social background (except in the case of the young Puerto Ricans), nor their age, nor the size of their families, nor their marital status which is associated with being migratory. For this group, being migratory clearly has more to do with being Puerto Rican or Mexican than anything else: ethnicity largely determines the quality of their lives and their chances for the future.

(2) The white farm workers are located at the other end of the migratory — nonmigratory continuum (95 percent were nonmigratory). As is the case with the Puerto Ricans and Mexicans, most of the socioeconomic characteristics of the white farm workers are not associated with migratory status. Thus in general among farm workers, being white saves the worker from the dismal situation of trying to earn a living by migrating. It is only the young white workers' social

background (determined by whether or not the father was a hired worker) and, in the case of all white workers being divorced, separated, or widowed, that is associated with being migratory.

(3) On the one hand, we find that the Puerto Ricans and Mexicans are predominantly migratory farm workers; the whites, on the other hand, are predominantly nonmigratory. The black farm workers present a very different picture. The number of blacks in the sample of East Coast farm workers who did migratory work almost equals the number who did nonmigratory farm work. Among these workers, and especially among those aged 45-54 years, *more* years of education were shown to be associated with being migratory, while for farm workers in general, *fewer* years of education are associated with being migratory. Among blacks aged 45-54 years, doing unskilled work was also associated with being migratory. This leads to the conclusion that if the worker is an older black, having more years of education will probably *not* give him or her a better chance of getting the more skilled jobs in migratory farm work.

It is also only among black farm workers that being younger (that is, less than thirty years old) is associated with being migratory. This to some extent explains why among blacks, never having been married is associated with being migratory; it also implies that black farm workers do not continue to do migratory farm work for many years.

A question to which this investigation provides no answer is whether the young black workers are forced into migratory farm work for lack of other work opportunities, or choose it and use it as a stepping-stone to finding employment in the North. Further research on the motivations for and complex process of joining and leaving the migratory stream would provide useful findings on this question.

Compared to the women in the other ethnic categories, female blacks were shown to comprise the highest percentage of divorced, separated or widowed women. Yet it can definitely not be said that migratory farm work attracts divorced, separated, or widowed black women more than nonmigratory farm work.

This analysis clearly shows that simply stating that migratory farm workers are uneducated and unskilled, or usually young and from broken families, is quite erroneous and certainly misleading. Such statements ignore the impact of ethnicity on farm labor and its determinant role in the worker's socioeconomic opportunities; they furthermore overlook the diversity of the associations between certain socioeconomic characteristics and migratory status. The ethnic groups show very significant differences in these associations, which indicates that in terms of shaping policies and legislation to benefit these workers, each group should be distinguished and to some extent dealt with separately, because their problems "on the season" are different. The analysis also underscores the necessity, in investigating the socioeconomic situation of migratory farm workers, of comparing them to the workers who are occupationally closest to them, the nonmigratory farm workers, to find out which problems are typical of migratory workers and which are typical of farm workers in general. Policies designed to help these workers are desperately needed and can only be effective if it is understood that these workers should be closely linked to the nonmigratory farm workers and dealt with within the *wider context of the entire system* of agricultural production.

In order to improve particularly the migratory farm workers' occupational possibilities, education and training for these workers are urgently needed, but they must be linked to the creation of appropriate occupational opportunities. Such education and training must also be integrated into more general policies aimed at solving the problems of the rural poor by creating nonfarm employment in rural areas.

NOTES

1. Unfortunately, this analysis focused on the black-white dichotomy and did not treat Puerto Ricans and Mexicans separately.
2. These workers were defined as having spent one week or more in school, housekeeping, retirement, or self-employment during the fifty-two-week survey period.
3. Unfortunately, the number of women in the sample was too small to make a separate analysis of the female workers worthwhile.
4. The variation in N and the values for N, which are sometimes rather large, make judging the significance of the results quite difficult because Chi-square depends on the size of N. For this reason Phi has been added to neutralize the variation in N. However, we will first look at the differences in the percentages and the direction of the relationship.
5. Because the results for the other ethnic groups were not significant, the tables showing them have been excluded.
6. Table 6.16 shows higher percentages among the migratory workers with the largest families because the blacks, Puerto Ricans, and Mexicans had larger families than the whites. In the 25 percent subsample, for the category labeled "all family members traveled" and for the total of nonmigratory farm workers, the following percentages were found for families comprising seven or more members: whites, 15 percent; blacks, 19 percent; Puerto Ricans, 23 percent; and Mexicans, 33 percent.
7. Cross tabulation involves the risk of certain variables acting as intervening variables. For this reason, a correlation matrix was set up so that the variables which are most likely to disturb the relationships described in this chapter could be controlled for. The variables that are not controlled for have correlation coefficients which are considerably below .22. It was only in the case of family size that the correlation with the other variables could not be checked. In the case of marital status, "being married" was correlated with the other variables. The highest correlation coefficient (.21) was observed for the relationship between being married and age.
8. The results showed that 35 percent of the female black farm workers were in the "was married" category (154 out of 434 workers); for female white workers this percentage was 16 (124 out of 793), for female Puerto Ricans it was 28 (10 out of 36 workers), and for female Mexicans it was 8 (7 out of 88 workers). The results also showed that 25 percent of all black farm workers were in the "was married" category (628 out of 2,503 workers); for all white workers this percentage was 9 (476 out of 5,311 workers), for all Puerto Ricans it was 11 percent (164 out of 1,463 workers), and for all Mexicans it was 4 percent (18 out of 413 workers).

7

CONCLUSIONS AND POLICY IMPLICATIONS

The way of life and work of migratory farm workers on the East Coast of the United States has been investigated from several angles by exploring the rather fragmentary body of knowledge on these workers, by analyzing the data gathered in the fourteen-state survey of their geographic mobility, earnings and socioeconomic characteristics, and by comparing them to the occupational group to which they are closest: the nonmigratory farm workers. The difference between the popular image of these workers — as documented by filmmakers, reporters, and journalists, as well as by social scientists making qualitative observations — on the one hand, and the facts revealed by the statistical analysis of the survey data on the other, proved to be particularly surprising and provided a picture of the migratory farm worker that is quite different from what was expected. The conclusions reached are therefore of great significance for policy makers concerned with improving the socioeconomic situation of these workers.

1. THE MOST SIGNIFICANT FINDINGS

The historical overview of migratory farm workers (Chapter 2) recounted how

---

Notes to this chapter may be found on page 183.

revolutionary developments and structural changes in agriculture during the nineteenth and first part of the twentieth centuries affected the demand for migratory agricultural workers. Foreign workers were brought to the West Coast to provide cheap labor to satisfy this demand. First it was the Chinese, then the Japanese, and thereafter the Mexicans and the Philippinos that did migratory farm work. At present it is again the Mexicans who are crossing the border into the United States to do farmwork, often entering illegally and creating an increasingly chaotic situation at the Mexican border.

The situation on the East Coast was quite different, however. The influx of foreign workers was not as large, and it could be more easily controlled. Black workers from the southern states probably started to fulfill the need for migratory farm work during the Reconstruction years and continued to do so thereafter. When a shortage of workers developed in the emergency situation created by World War II, workers were imported from the Bahamas, Jamaica, and Honduras. After World War II, Puerto Rican workers and workers from the West Indies were brought in under the provisions of Section H-2 (Public Law 414) to do farm work on the East Coast; in recent years, Mexicans from Texas have also joined the East Coast migratory stream. In this way, workers from several quite different ethnic minority groups have come to be part of the East Coast migratory stream.

The socioeconomic and political position of farm workers in the United States is extremely weak (Chapters 2 and 3). Time and again, these workers have been excluded from social legislation, even when it has covered most other categories of workers. The farm workers, who are poor, have little education, and have no trade unions to fight for their rights and for better working conditions, are no match for the amply financed and powerful agricultural employers' organizations, with their effective lobbies in Washington, D.C. During the 1950s and 1960s, when deep concern began to grow in the United States about the poor and the underprivileged, some legislation was passed which was meant to help farm workers, but most of it can best be described as "too little for too few."

The results of the analysis of the interstate mobility of migratory farm workers on the East Coast (Chapter 4) reveal that the majority of these workers move to and from only two states, rather than continually traveling from state to state during the season. Thus these workers are *not* as mobile as they are thought to be. The image they have of constantly being on the move has apparently been created by the presence of small numbers of workers in almost all of the states during a given period of each year, but this image does not reflect the actual situation. In fact, the data indicate that in 1969-70, when the unemployment insurance survey was taken, black migratory farm workers on the East Coast did *not* travel to more states than they did fifteen years earlier (page 81).

The most surprising conclusion drawn from this investigation is that ethnic group membership is *the* most important factor in migratory farm work. The three largest ethnic minorities (blacks, Puerto Ricans, and Mexicans) each have their own home base states, and their degrees of interstate mobility differ; the Mexicans are by far the most mobile ethnic minority.

Exploring whether certain socioeconomic characteristics of the migratory workers influence their degree of interstate mobility has proved to be most interesting because of what it reveals about whether the worker travels with or without the family. While most of the Mexicans in the sample (83 percent) traveled with their families, most of the Puerto Ricans (85 percent) left their families behind. The second largest category of workers that traveled with all or some of their family members was the blacks (40 percent). In absolute numbers, black families almost equal Mexican families, and thus the problems of migratory families in the East Coast stream are to a great extent the problems of Mexican and black families. Once the worker has decided to bring his or her family along "on the season," the presence of school-age children does not affect migratory patterns. Furthermore, there is no evidence that having school-age children is a reason for leaving the family at the home base.

The analysis of the earnings of migratory and nonmigratory workers (Chapter 5) uncovered very *substantial differences in earnings*. The extent of these differences is very striking because these workers are in one of the most poorly paid occupational categories in the United States. The earnings differences among migratory workers do not correspond to the experience or skills the worker has, but they can to a considerable extent be associated with the number of weeks the worker is employed and the ethnic group to which the worker belongs. The Mexicans were in the worst position, having the lowest average earnings; thereafter came the Puerto Ricans and the blacks; the whites earned the most. The earnings analysis clearly evidences the great importance for migratory farm workers of ethnic group membership. Mexican migratory workers, for no apparent reason other than that they are Mexicans, earned an annual average of $942 less than white migratory workers. Puerto Ricans were slightly better off, earning $763 less than whites; blacks, earning $357 less, had earnings which came closest to the whites' earnings. Earnings are also clearly influenced by the worker's sex, age, years of schooling, and whether the worker travels with or without the family. It should be noted that many of these factors are quite beyond the workers' control: a worker can do very little about the lack of remuneration for experience or skills in migratory farm work, and sex, ethnic group membership, and age are facts of life which cannot be changed. Thus it is the migratory farm workers in particular who are caught in a situation about which they can do almost nothing, and their opportunities for increasing annual earnings in farm work are extremely limited. Earnings increases were shown to result almost exclusively from increases in the number of weeks of work done, or increases in the number of family members (that is, workers) the worker brings along. But here again, the amount of work a worker can do is in large part beyond his or her control: the timing of and demand for farm labor, the crew leader, and the weather determine how much the worker will earn; also, not all workers have families to bring with them.

More years of schooling were shown to increase the earnings of migratory farm workers, but the living and working conditions of these workers are such that they do not encourage enrollment in adult education programs. As farm workers comprise one of the lowest paid categories of workers in the United States, the substantial difference — $1,293 — between the estimated average annual earnings of the migratory workers ($3,493) and nonmigratory workers ($4,786) in the fourteen-state sample must not be taken lightly. The quite different ways in which certain socioeconomic factors influence the earnings of migratory and nonmigratory farm workers necessitate further research on socioeconomic characteristics that are associated with the migratory status of the worker.

The nonmigratory farm workers in the sample not only have higher earnings than migratory workers; their earnings patterns are also more similar to those of the nonfarm (industrial) workers: thus experience or occupational skills pay off for the nonmigratory farm worker, and age and education also substantially increase earnings. There appears, however, to be no discrimination against Mexicans and Puerto Ricans in nonmigratory farm work, while discrimination against black workers persists. That the earnings patterns of the nonmigratory workers are more similar to those of nonfarm workers is also demonstrated by the fact that among nonmigratory workers, marital status has a positive effect on earnings, while it does not among the migratory workers. Thus we see that migratory workers not only have lower earnings than nonmigratory workers, but also have fewer options for improving their situation. Furthermore, in terms of earnings and factors influencing them, they are much less similar than was expected to the category that is occupationally closest to them.

It should be noted that among both migratory and nonmigratory farm workers, men were shown to earn considerably more than women. The high "cost" of being a woman in farm work can probably be explained by two facts: (a) caring for small children while working in the fields is usually considered to be the women's responsibility, and the women's work is often interrupted as a result; this leads to fewer hours of work being done and consequently to lower earnings; (b) certain lower-paying jobs (picking beans, for instance) are considered to be women's work.

The characteristics distinguishing migratory from nonmigratory farm workers were investigated in Chapter 6. At first glance, the data seem to corroborate the stereotype image of the migratory workers, showing them to be uneducated, unskilled, and young, and often members of broken and/or large families. But when several socioeconomic characteristics are considered within each ethnic group separately, a much more complex picture emerges: each of the four ethnic groups in farm work on the East Coast has quite different and distinct occupational opportunities. The white workers are at one end of a migratory— nonmigratory continuum, comprising nonmigratory workers almost exclusively. At the other end of the continuum are the Puerto Ricans and Mexicans, who mainly comprise migratory farm workers. The black migratory workers are completely different: they are quite evenly spread between the migratory and nonmigratory categories.

Relating several socioeconomic characteristics (education and skills, social background, age, family composition, and marital status) to whether a worker is migratory or nonmigratory showed no significant relationships for the whites, Puerto Ricans, and Mexicans. Among the blacks, however, several significant differences between migratory and nonmigratory farm workers were found, indicating that factors other than ethnic group membership influence the black workers' migratory status. It would seem that blacks have more opportunities than other workers to alternate between migratory and nonmigratory farm work. Also, older black migratory farm workers with at least nine years of schooling are significantly more apt to be migratory than older black workers with less schooling. Furthermore, black migratory farm workers are rather young, which implies that black workers do not stay in the migratory stream for very long, but use it as a stepping-stone to other types of employment, usually in the North, where job opportunities are thought to be more abundant.

Studying black farm workers separately uncovered several other interesting facts about them. For instance, having a father who was a migratory farm worker increases the probability that the black farm worker is migratory. Another interesting finding is that broken marriages are not characteristic of black migratory farm workers; furthermore, in contrast to what is generally assumed, female black workers with broken marriages are not particularly attracted to migratory farm work. Both the migratory and the nonmigratory female black workers have, in comparison to the female workers in the other ethnic categories, the highest percentage in the "was married" category.

We have clearly demonstrated that ethnic group membership is the determinant factor in distinguishing migratory from nonmigratory farm workers. The literature and our analysis of the survey data indicate that the migratory farm worker problem cannot be solved simply by adapting and/or improving education and training, or by providing nonfarm employment. There is much more to it because, as we have seen, the varying degrees of occupational discrimination against different ethnic groups have a significant impact on farm workers.

2. INTERPRETING THE FINDINGS IN TERMS OF POLICY IMPLICATIONS

The determinant role which ethnic group membership plays in farm work in the United States should be considered in light of ongoing research on economic discrimination against ethnic minority workers in the labor force in general.

2.1. Discrimination in Agriculture

Migratory farm workers on the East Coast of the United States live and work under the most distressing conditions, with little hope of improving their situation. The "participant-observer" type of studies on East Coast migratory workers have described the dismal lives of certain groups of blacks in the migratory stream, but the data collected during the 1970 unemployment insurance survey revealed that in some ways, the blacks are better off than the other ethnic minority groups in migratory farm work. The survey also exposed quite considerable differences between the four ethnic groups that were distinguished. While the large majority of the nonwhite farm workers was migratory, the migratory workers did not comprise a homogeneous group. Substantial differences in both the earnings and the mobility patterns of the ethnic minority groups in migratory farm work were found.

Because of the lack of remuneration for experience and occupational skills, and the lack of attachment to an employer, migratory farm work seems to be unstructured and impersonal: all the agricultural employer needs is a pair of hands — *any* pair of hands — to do the jobs which cannot as yet be done by machines. As bad as these impersonal employment relationships are, the facts revealed by investigating the role of ethnic group membership in farm work demonstrate that this is not the worst aspect of migratory farm work, for on top of this, discrimination against the various ethnic groups was shown to be considerable and to vary. This implies that the employers take advantage of the weaker socioeconomic positions of the various nonwhite ethnic minorities. That is why Mexican migratory workers earn the least, while Puerto Ricans are only a little better off, and blacks have earnings that come closest to white workers' earnings, but still earn significantly less on the average.

These findings are amazingly similar to Szymanski's observations on economic discrimination in the working class as a whole, which are based on a synthesis of two main views on the relationship between capitalism and racism (Szymanski 1975:1-21).[1] Szymanski's reasoning is that on the one hand, the blacks are gradually being integrated into the working class in the United States because the logic of capitalism undermines economic discrimination against them; on the other hand, racism itself is not being eliminated: "While it is true that capitalism necessarily generates racism, it is not true that Blacks are the perpetual victims of that racism." (1975:3) Szymanski found that in four major industrial cities, the blacks, though they were not yet integrated in the more prestigious occupations, were generally moving out of their traditional menial jobs into semi-skilled and skilled occupations. He placed this development in its historical perspective: the blacks were becoming integrated into the working class in the same way that the Irish, the Poles, and the Italians did before them. As the blacks left their unpleasant jobs, vacancies were filled by the most recent immigrants, mainly Spanish-speaking workers such as Puerto Ricans and Mexicans, or West Indian workers. Szymanski found that the gap between the incomes of the blacks and the whites was slowly decreasing and that this process was moving much more rapidly among black and white women. Compared to the blacks, the incomes of Puerto Ricans and Mexicans had worsened between 1960 and 1970.

The validity of Szymanski's reasoning on the relationship between capitalism and racism is questionable, and Szymanski himself provided the reasons for doubt. In stressing the historical perspective, he remarked that before the Irish, Polish, and Italians, the "...very first menial laborers for the emerging capitalist enterprise in the U.S. were women and children of native farm families who went to work in the textile mills of New England in the early part of the 19th century." (1975:4) These workers were later replaced by Irish immigrants, which suggests that the Irish — and the Polish and Italians who later took over their unpleasant jobs — were exploited not so much because they were members of ethnic minorities, but because of their economic position, which, like that of the women and children of the poor whites, was very weak. Thus a weak economic position, aggravated by different cultural backgrounds and the fact that in most cases, the immigrants did not speak English, made these workers easy victims of exploitation in the early capitalist system. As the Irish, Polish, and Italians became integrated into the industrial labor class, the blacks took over their jobs. The relationship between capitalism and racism is clearly embedded in a broader relationship between capitalism and the exploitation of those who are economically weakest.

The facts which this investigation has brought to light on migratory farm workers concur with Szymanski's findings. As was mentioned above, the blacks are closest to the whites in their earnings, while the Mexicans and Puerto Ricans suffer the most from discrimination. The blacks appear to use migratory farm work as a stepping-stone to better jobs. The fairly recent appearance of Mexicans and Puerto Ricans in the East Coast migratory stream suggests that the blacks are leaving migratory farm work and may be on their way to becoming integrated into the skilled and semi-skilled working class, and that their jobs are being taken over by Mexicans and Puerto Ricans — the new "immigrants" — who are in the weakest position economically.

There appears to be *no* discrimination in nonmigratory farm work against the few Mexicans (1 percent) and Puerto Ricans (4 percent), while there is considerable discrimination against the blacks. This may indicate that, in nonmigratory farm work, which offers more opportunities for establishing an attachment to a certain employer, a weak economic position combined with differences in culture and language are easier to overcome than a weak economic position combined with a dark skin.[2] To find out whether this is the case, further research should be done on the position of the small number of Mexicans and Puerto Ricans who do nonmigratory farm work.

Szymanski also reasoned in his article that it makes sense in the more backward capitalist economies to perpetuate racism in order to ensure that an adequate number of submissive and willing workers can be recruited. It is known that agricultural production systems in general — including that of the United States — are not the most advanced modern capitalistic production organizations. The findings on migratory farm workers appear to indicate that the discrimination in this category of workers may be an example of the backward capitalist mechanism which Szymanski described.

2.2. Structural Problems

The quotation on page 11 states that the demand for migratory farm workers is created by the particular way in which agricultural production is organized (U.S. Congress, Senate, Committee on Labor and Public Welfare, 1960:6). This is of course only half the story, because it approaches the migratory farm labor problem from the viewpoint of demand only. Agricultural production in the United States requires cheap migratory labor because it is organized in the same way as economic production in general: in the capitalist way. The driving force in a capitalist enterprise is the maximization of profits: the agricultural employer specializes in certain crops and mechanizes his production process to increase profits; he depresses the labor costs for the same reason. In a free market economy, however, cheap labor can only be used if more than enough workers are available and are willing to work for the wages offered.

This brings us to the supply side of the migratory farm labor problem. In a country where farm workers had no unemployment insurance until January 1978, and where unemployment in agriculture is high,[3] it is quite logical that a large pool of cheap labor is available. The choices for these workers are simple: migratory farm work or no work at all.

Thus we have the two sides of the migratory farm worker problem: the demand side, with the employer who runs his enterprise according to the rules of the capitalist "game"; and the supply side, with the unemployed farm worker who needs money to support him- or herself and perhaps a family as well. For decades this situation has precipitated ruthless exploitation of the migratory farm workers. The great differences between migratory farm workers and the workers in the occupational category closest to them, nonmigratory farm workers, underscore the disadvantages the migratory workers must suffer. Improvements in the position of the black workers (as observed by Szymanski) and their increasing integration, compared to other minority workers, into the industrial working class probably explain why black migratory farm workers are less affected by discrimination in earnings in migratory farm work than Puerto Ricans and Mexicans.

If the results of this investigation are interpreted in light of Szymanski's observations, they suggest that in the long run, the black migratory farm workers on the East Coast will be replaced by Puerto Ricans and Mexicans. White nonmigratory workers will to a lesser extent be replaced by blacks, and subsequently by Puerto Ricans and Mexicans, but this will probably be less pronounced because nonmigratory farm work will continue to provide jobs for a residual group of white workers who have no other alternative (see page 122).

As long as cheap farm labor is available, exploitation will continue to exist in agriculture in the United States. The pool of unemployed black farm workers may be becoming smaller, but (illegal) Mexican immigrants and Puerto Ricans, who leave their countries because of widespread unemployment at home, will ensure that there will be a large supply of cheap and willing workers for quite some years to come. The power of the well-organized, amply financed agricultural employers' organizations and the dependence of uneducated, unskilled, and nonorganized workers on farm jobs guarantee that these workers will continue to be exploited in the future. The victims of this kind of discrimination may change, but exploitation will remain. A solution to the migratory farm labor problem cannot be found unless the existing economic power structure is altered and the unemployment rate among farm workers is reduced, so that the pool of unemployed workers who are willing to take any job at any pay disappears. Employers will not allow their labor costs to rise and profit margins to fall unless they are forced to do so by the government; workers will not stop doing migratory work if their only options continue to be either such work or no work at all — and thus no earnings. In order to force employers to pay higher wages for farm labor, workers must strengthen their bargaining position by organizing strong unions, for in the United States, the only appropriate instrument for wielding the kind of power that can countervail the power of employers' organizations is unionization. If a surplus of workers who are desperately in need of work is to be discouraged from entering the migratory farm labor stream, effective government policies will be needed to create jobs in the migratory workers' home base areas, to limit child labor, and to halt the legal or illegal entry of foreign agricultural workers. The results of this analysis, especially when assessed in light of Szymanski's observations on the nonfarm labor sector, underscore the primary and urgent need for two structural changes in agriculture: *unionization* and the *restriction of the number of unskilled, uneducated, and jobless workers entering the migratory farm labor streams*. Unless these changes are made, there can be no hope of improving the plight of these workers.[4] Once these two structural changes have been realized, a solution to the migratory farm labor problem could be found by helping those workers who want to move out of the stream to settle down and adjust to the nonmigratory way of life, and by creating better living and working conditions for those who stay in the stream. Besides these two structural changes, the following measures should be taken to improve the operation of the migratory farm work system on the East Coast.

1. *Bilateral cooperation between the states.*   Analysis of the migratory workers'

mobility showed that the majority of these workers work in two states. Because only two states — rather than several — would be concerned with most of the workers, it should be possible for the (government or private) agencies dealing with migratory farm workers in those states to coordinate their activities and work together closely, so that they can effectively help the workers. For example, if a worker has been employed in Florida and New Jersey and has joined an adult education or vocational training course in Florida, it should be possible, through interstate cooperation, for him or her to continue the course in New Jersey. Similarly, health and welfare programs for the migratory farm workers and schooling of their children could more easily be coordinated between two states than among several states.

As most of the workers leave their families at the home base, it is essential that the home base states take responsibility for their families' health, education, and welfare. Furthermore, agencies in the East Coast states where migratory farm workers are employed during the season must become more conscious of the fact that the migratory families who are on the road are very likely to be Mexican or black, and should be equipped to deal with their particular problems.

Lastly, through bilateral cooperation between the states supplying farm labor and those demanding it, the Annual Worker Plan should be set up in such a way that the workers' itineraries are arranged to guarantee the farm workers a certain minimum number of days of work — and thus a guaranteed income — during the trip to the North and back.

2. *More recognition of the significance of ethnic group membership in migratory farm labor.* Since ethnic group membership is the key factor in migratory farm work, it should be given more attention by the people working in the various agencies dealing with migratory families, and it should be taken into account in setting up programs for these families. A report prepared by the Utah Migrant Council (Jones 1973:21-27), which helps migratory farm workers to leave the migratory stream and settle down, illustrates the importance of this point. In describing the success of the program, which deals mainly with Mexican Americans, the report indicated that:

Perhaps the most important reason for this success is the fact that the entire staff of the UMC is made up of former migrants who are bilingual and are committed to improving the circumstances of their brothers who remain in the fields. The spirit which develops between the migrants and the Council goes far beyond that of an agency towards a client. It is rather a relationship among people of common values, language and blood. This creates an understanding that does not exist when the migrant encounters other agencies. (Jones 1973:27)

3. *Creating a job structure in farm work.* The data on earnings show not only that the earnings of migratory farm workers are considerably lower than those of nonmigratory farm workers, but also that the job structure in migratory farm work is quite different from that in nonmigratory farm work. Migratory farm workers who have experience or occupational skills are not paid more, and they receive less than nonmigratory workers for more years of education. The non-migratory farm workers, on the other hand, are paid substantially higher wages for experience, education, and occupational skills. These differences suggest that there is more job structure in nonmigratory farm work than in migratory farm work; they also imply that there are incentives in nonmigratory work which encourage the worker to get more education, experience, and skills, but that these incentives are lacking in migratory work.

Generally speaking, farm work is considered to lack job structure. As Becket wrote: "...'unstructured' is the most descriptive term which can be applied to the farm labor scene." (1960:7) This means that the farm workers are denied the opportunity to climb the career ladder — by not being paid for experience and skills, for example, as is the case with the migratory farm workers especially. To remedy this problem, Becket strongly recommended the creation of a classification system and more structure in farm employment (1960:7-11). He proposed a structural model with six levels, each of which is based on the workers' education and experience and is linked to a particular wage level. Differences between the levels would create incentives for the workers to improve their positions in farm work. At present, the farm worker who really wants to improve his or her position must leave farm work and choose some other occupation, because there is no "career ladder" to climb in the farm labor sector. Becket argued that if a well-trained, skilled, and experienced agricultural work force is to be maintained, such a classification of farm jobs is a necessity, and experience and education will have to be remunerated. His structural model for farm labor would include seasonal as well as regular jobs and would create incentives for the lowest wage level in the model (the casual laborers) by encouraging workers to show that they can be depended upon.

The question arises of whether migratory farm workers would really benefit from more job structure in farm labor. In order to improve their positions in such a structure, they would have to be able to get beyond the lowest wage level, but opportunities for doing this are not readily available in migratory farm work. Theoretically, the incentive for workers to demonstrate that they can be depended upon might be a good solution, but the fact is that the employer will probably not give the migratory worker a chance to prove his or her dependability: employers are more likely to leave the jobs requiring dependability to the year-round worker they know well, rather than giving them to a migratory worker who is a virtual stranger. (The employer is apt to do this even if the migratory worker has certificates proving that he or she is trained to do skilled work.) Of course, if an employer wants a migratory worker to return the following year, he can express this by paying higher wages, but the only reward the migratory worker gets is more money: he or she will not be able to move up the career ladder. Furthermore, as the analysis of earnings indicated, attachment to an employer generally does not result in higher pay: even the nonmigratory farm workers receive only small increases in earnings when they work for the same employer for longer periods. Although the creation of a job structure in farm work would appear to offer some improvements that would be beneficial to both the workers and the employers, whether the migratory workers would actually gain anything from it is not entirely clear: they would certainly require special attention within the farm labor job structure to ensure that they are rewarded for more experience and skills.

4. *Further research on the role of women in farm labor.* Some mention was made in the earnings analysis of the position of women in farm labor, but such issues as whether women receive less pay for certain jobs than men, and whether they work fewer hours or days during a given week, or are employed in the lower-paying, so-called "women's jobs," need to be explored much more thoroughly. Special attention should be given to the division of labor — including caring for children and doing housework — between men and women, not only in the fields but also in the farm labor camps.

For years, migratory farm workers have been the subject of much talk, of reports by journalists, and of some significant research by both government and private agencies. Recommendations and proposals have been made to improve their living and working conditions — for example, by raising wage rates, teaching the workers more diversified farm skills, increasing the number of farm jobs by planting more diversified crops, organizing the work more efficiently, or enacting social legislation which would cover these and other farm workers, etc. But low earnings and the need to travel to remain employed continue to be the main problems confronting migratory farm workers, not only in comparison with nonfarm (industrial) workers but even in comparison with nonmigratory farm workers.

In the discussion of social legislation covering migratory workers, it became clear that although laws have been passed to help these workers — e.g., by improving the crew leader system, the workers' housing and health facilities, and their children's education and care — the effects have unfortunately been marginal and haphazard (see Friedland and Nelkin 1971). Considering several more comprehensive policy proposals should clarify why these and some other, more incidental proposals have resulted in so little improvement.

2.3. The Inefficacy of the Policies and Proposals

Most studies on migratory farm workers have two basic weaknesses: (1) they accept the premise that agricultural employers must have a supply of temporary, out-of-state workers in order to harvest their crops; and (2) they accept the existing network of power relations in agriculture. Because of this, most of the recommendations made in these studies aim at only marginal improvements: they entail no radical and/or structural changes in the existing system.

Studies such as the ones by Metzler (1955) and by Larson and Sharp (1960) have in fact provided only marginal solutions: they have pointed out the existing problems and suggested measures for increasing the *efficiency* of the migratory farm labor system — e.g., by spreading the demand for labor more evenly over the year, making wage levels and other working conditions attractive enough to appeal to the required number of workers, and improving the management of the workers — but they have not questioned the migratory farm labor system as such. Such studies aim at nothing more than a more efficient operation of the present — unsatisfactory — migratory farm labor system, and they will therefore not be considered further, for they can offer very little to the migratory farm worker. We will focus instead on the reports and proposals which take a comprehensive approach to improving the dismal situation of the migratory farm workers.

The United States government has not been insensitive to the problems of the migratory farm workers: it has carefully and repeatedly investigated these problems and has earnestly recommended changes. During the 1960s, legislation was enacted to bring some relief to the migratory farm workers. Well meant as this legislation may have been, it is not effective. Its major drawback is that its enforcement is dependent on the willingness of the employer or the crew leader, or both, to cooperate. Consequently, law enforcement is a serious problem in farm work. Obviously, for a law enforcement officer, it is much more important to maintain good relations with the employers, who are year-round members of the community, than to fight for the rights of the poor and powerless migratory workers. Government measures leave the existing power relations in agriculture unchanged.[5] In a discussion of farm manpower policies and the diversification and development of the rural economy (Fuller 1966), the farm worker agencies with outreach facilities (the agricultural extension services and employment services structure of the Department of Labor) were said to have "...acquired political alliances with commercial farming and with the leadership of farm organizations which tend to constrain them with respect to other sectors of rural communities." (1966:109-110) Thus the primary commitment of the local officers in these government agencies seems to be to the employer and not to the worker.

The marginality of the government's policies is also evidenced by the Federal Unemployment Insurance Amendments of 1976, which became effective on 1 January 1978. On the basis of the 1970 unemployment insurance survey data, it was estimated that these amendments only covered about two fifths of all hired agricultural workers when they went into effect. Farm workers who benefited from the unemployment insurance program were estimated to receive an average of $386 yearly. The annual earnings of the beneficiaries averaged $2,843, which is considerably less than the average annual earnings ($4,383) of the farm workers who are covered by unemployment insurance and who are in the labor force all year-round (Elterich 1978a:23-33). Thus the impact of the benefits on the incomes of farm workers is not impressive: despite these benefits, the migratory farm workers remain the poorest of the poor. The amendments, like so much of the social legislation for these workers, provide too little for too few: the system itself is *not* changing.

Fortunately, not all research on migratory farm work has resulted in recommendations that can only be described as marginal. Although Nelkin (1970:73-79) accepted the premise that agricultural employers need temporary out-of-state workers, and implicitly accepted the existing network of power relations in agriculture in the solutions she presented, she recognized that the problems cannot be solved without altering these relations. In describing the weaknesses of the system and making recommendations for improving the migratory farm workers' situation, she observed the following:
— employers know very little about labor management practices (and consequently cause considerable labor wastage);
— the crew leaders' power is far too great;
— inexperienced workers receive no training and thus cannot become skilled;
— the job structure in migratory farm work lacks stratification, hence there are no opportunities for occupational mobility;

— information on wages, crops, and the location and hours of work is inadequate;
— better housing is needed;
— the agencies that deal with migratory farm workers need to coordinate their efforts;
— all farm workers should be covered by the same social legislation as nonfarm workers;
— stable employment relationships with a minimum of seasonality and unpredictability are needed in agriculture.

Nelkin also pointed out that she is well aware that it is the existing network of power relations in agriculture that prevents a solution to the migratory farm labor problem: "It is unrealistic to assume that appropriate labor practices in agriculture will ever be introduced without either severe government regulations or a more equitable distribution of bargaining power." (1973:77) She did *not*, however, mention the relationship between the rate of unemployment and the migratory farm labor problem — i.e., the fact that in a capitalistic agricultural structure, a high unemployment rate will inevitably lead to the exploitation of the workers.

In New York state, a realistic plan for replacing migratory farm workers with local workers was proposed by Montero (1966), who questioned whether the migratory farm labor system is really essential to the agricultural economy, given its inherent social disadvantages. She concluded that it is not and proposed the following policy measures for New York state to create an agricultural system without migratory farm workers (1966:11-24).

(1) A land-use policy must be established to ensure that the demand for labor is spread more evenly over the harvest season, thus reducing the sharp peaks in demand at certain times and places. Greater diversification of crops should also be introduced. Although this may be less efficient for the individual farmer, it need not be inefficient in general because if a certain area is taken as a whole, it would allow a better use of resources, including labor.

(2) The wages for farm labor must be increased to encourage a more efficient use of labor and stimulate mechanization, thus reducing the need for migratory labor.

(3) A policy for hiring local workers must be established. Montero pointed out that the Annual Worker Plan actually encourages workers to migrate by scheduling worker itineraries in advance. This discourages local labor from seeking employment in harvest work: "Thus, while in theory migrants are the marginal labor supply brought in only to supplement when there is a shortage, in practice,

where early commitments are made to hire migrants, local workers become the marginal supply." (1966:18)

(4) Employment relationships must become stabilized and more structured. The relationships between the employer and the seasonal worker are far too casual and impersonal: they change from year to year or even from day to day, and no attachment can be built up. Montero argued that the impersonal character of seasonal farm work could be diminished by giving the employment relationship a certain structure and content. This should include a guaranteed minimum wage and an established number of hours of work per month, as well as such additional benefits as overtime pay, wage increments based on the duration of service, and training for more skilled jobs. More extensive pooling of labor by the farm employers would also have a stabilizing effect.

These proposals would be quite feasible for agriculture in New York state *if* it were recognized, once and for all, that the "inherent social disadvantage" of the migratory farm labor system is not acceptable. Such proposals would not, however, solve any of the problems of the migratory workers who arrive from the South without any alternative to farm work except unemployment.[6] These proposals show an awareness of how the migratory farm worker problem is linked to unemployment, but leave many problems unsolved. Because they aim to reduce the need for farm workers to migrate, they would require that a policy of job creation be initiated simultaneously at the home bases (especially in Florida, Texas, and Puerto Rico). They would offer no solution for the problem of foreign workers who (legally or illegally) cross the borders and would also not tackle the problem of the existing power relations in agriculture. Even if the migratory farm labor system were eliminated, the local farm workers would need to organize themselves into unions in order to bargain with their employers for better working conditions.

The question now arises of why these social policies, recommendations, and proposals have yielded so little benefit to farm workers. It is certainly not a lack of interest or of proposals that has stood in the way of solving the problems of these workers: although many of the recommendations may not approach the problem comprehensively, most would certainly give some relief. Why have the state and federal governments in the United States repeatedly failed to do away with the privileges which agricultural employers can enjoy because they exploit a pool of uneducated and unskilled laborers who need work? Why have they excluded farm workers from labor legislation, and even from legislation granting farm workers the right to unionize?

One important factor in explaining this situation is the fact that for too long, farm labor policies have been considered to be separate from national manpower policies (Fuller 1967:97-101). This is because labor relations in agriculture used to be stereotyped: the farmer and the farmhand worked together as a unit, sharing each other's interest and needs; they did not seem to need any government regulation. In this seemingly idyllic situation, the employers were able to build up powerful organizations which have successfully maintained a supply of cheap labor for years. The ways in which the employers' organizations operate is probably best illustrated by the pressure they exerted on the government to maintain the bracero program (see Chapter 2). The discontinuation of this program against the employers' wishes indicates that their influence is starting to diminish, as does the fact that, since the 1960s, farm labor policies have not been considered separate from national manpower policies. Another hint that the agricultural employers' power is declining is the new approach to migratory farm labor problems taken in 1971, when the Rural Manpower Service set up the National Migrant Worker Program (Jones 1973:21-22). Until then, the focus of the Rural Manpower Service, as far as migratory farm work was concerned, had generally been on the employer and his needs — i.e., on securing enough migratory workers at the right time. At the beginning of the 1970s, thinking in the Service changed because there were more farm workers than farm jobs, and it is now felt that it should focus more on the workers' needs. An important part of the work of the National Migrant Worker Program is to help workers settle down outside the migratory stream. As the report on the Utah Migrant Council (page 172) showed, the Program has had some success. Its success, however, will in the end depend largely on the availability of jobs in rural areas, and such jobs are very often not available. Several job creation programs have been started in recent years: the Emergency Employment Act, the first nationwide Public Service Employment program since the Depression years, was enacted in 1971 and was designed to provide transitional jobs and the necessary public services in times of high unemployment. Continuing high unemployment led in 1973 to the enactment of the Comprehensive Employment and Training Act, which emphasized local participation in federally sponsored programs. It has been observed, however, that the rural areas tend not to get adequate finances for dealing with their needs and thus have only limited facilities for training and job creation (Martin 1978:30-32). Furthermore, unless the necessary conditions for controlling the influx of new, unemployed farm workers into the stream are created, and unless strong unions for farm workers are organized, there probably will continue to be a large number of migratory workers who need to be helped in settling outside the migratory stream, as well as a pool of cheap labor which is available to the agricultural employers. As long as this is the case, employers will have no incentives to develop the kind of labor relations which exist outside agriculture.

3. THE FUTURE OF MIGRATORY FARM WORK

Will the agricultural system continue to require a migratory farm work force in the coming years, or will the ongoing technological developments and changes in scale in agriculture soon render the migratory farm workers obsolete? If this happens, would a possible solution to the present migratory farm worker problem be to simply wait until the system dies out? Does this mean that policies aimed at benefiting these workers are in fact no longer needed? The easiest answer to these questions has been provided by some of the northern states, where it has occasionally been argued that without outside interference, increasing mechanization will simply make the migratory farm worker disappear (Friedland and Nelkin 1971:258).

It has also been predicted that mechanization, instead of putting an end to migratory labor, will intensify the workers' problems because different crops will become mechanized to varying degrees, causing a very uneven distribution of work during the season and an even more acute, but briefer, need for seasonal workers. This would mean that the migratory workers would either have to become even more mobile to find work, or would have to wait out longer intervals without employment. The employers' recruitment problems would also increase because recruiting large numbers of workers for short periods is a difficult task (U.S. Department of Labor 1959:68; Shotwell 1961:194).

The future of the migratory farm workers has been described as follows:

Mechanization has already eliminated a great many farm jobs and indications are that it will eliminate a great many more.

The implication is clear. Each year, the States through which migrants travel will find themselves with larger and larger numbers of migrants who cannot find farm work to support themselves. Unless migrants can be channeled into the nonfarm economy as farm jobs disappear, many of them will be left without any means of earning a living. (Jones 1973:21)

An article on the structure of the labor force and mechanization in the Florida citrus industry ("Florida Citrus..." 1970)[7] forecasted a considerable shift in the demand for seasonal labor due to mechanization. Between 1975 and

1980, the demand for less skilled workers was to decrease by about 15 percent and the demand for skilled and semi-skilled workers was to almost double during the peak of the harvest season. This would mean that there would be a need in the future for more skilled migratory workers in the East Coast stream.

What this kind of statement about the migratory farm workers ignores is the fact that their future does *not* depend only on the demand side of agriculture — on the technical developments in agricultural production; it also depends on the employment situation both in the migratory workers' home base areas and throughout the United States. It has been suggested that the number of workers who are migratory varies inversely with the business cycle: that is, the number of migratory farm workers decreases in periods of prosperity and increases in periods of depression (Ducoff 1951:223). Furthermore, "...during periods of economic boom, demand for unskilled labor is high and some farm migrants can find nonfarm employment. But during periods of economic slow-down, problems begin to surface." (Cronemeyer 1972:9) The farm labor problem has also been closely related to the national unemployment rate, and this has led to questioning the effectiveness of minimum wage rates in agriculture and of training programs for farm laborers in all situations except those where the national unemployment rate is reasonably low (Schultz 1967:58-59).

The unemployment rate in the United States rose steadily in the years between 1970, when the unemployment insurance survey was taken, and 1975, when it was as high as 8.5 percent (*Economic Report of the President* 1976: Table B-22). Since then it has slowly decreased to 7.7 percent in 1976, 7 percent in 1977, and 6 percent in 1978 ("Current Labor Statistics" 1979:74). The unemployment rate for agricultural wage and salary workers was 11.7 percent in 1976, 11.1 percent in 1977, and 8.8 percent in 1978 ("Current Labor Statistics" 1979:74), which is high enough to cause workers to migrate in a desperate search for work. This makes it unlikely that the migratory farm labor problem will disappear by itself in the near future. The increasing demand for more skilled workers in seasonal farm work (see "Florida Citrus..." 1970:20-26) will affect only a small number of migratory workers and will mean that these workers must be encouraged to acquire new skills. Problems will continue to exist for the rest of the workers, who do not have enough work and therefore have to leave the migratory stream. Thus the migratory farm worker's future will be very gloomy indeed unless the two conditions described above are fulfilled.

First, effective government measures must be implemented to halt the entry of new, economically weak workers into the migratory farm labor stream.[8] At the same time, nonfarm job opportunities must be created to absorb the existing surplus in farm labor; nonfarm jobs for migratory workers should be in the home base areas. If this is not done, the agricultural employers will continue to be able to economically exploit the farm workers who are desperately in need of work.

Second, a more equitable distribution of power in bargaining is urgently needed throughout the network of power relations in agriculture. The appropriate instrument for breaking the grip that agricultural employers have on farm workers in the United States is creating strong unions. By passing laws that will put an end to discrimination against farm workers resulting from their exclusion from social and labor legislation, the government can, at both the federal and state levels, encourage farm workers to unionize.

If the necessary steps are taken to fulfill these two conditions, policies and programs aimed at alleviating the problems of the migratory farm workers will be more likely to be successful because the vacancies left by workers who settle down outside the migratory stream will no longer be filled by other workers.

During the past forty years, many social policies intended to benefit the migratory workers have been implemented in the United States. Yet despite all those efforts and after so many years, the migratory farm workers' living and working conditions, as described in Shotwell's *The Harvesters* (1961) and Friedland and Nelkin's *Migrant* (1971), are still strikingly similar to those described by Steinbeck in 1939 in *The Grapes of Wrath*! One can only conclude that the social legislation and policies designed to benefit the migratory farm worker have either overlooked, or seriously underestimated, very significant aspects of the system of agricultural production in the United States.

NOTES

1. Szymanski studied occupations, types of industries, and incomes. This investigation is limited to agriculture and deals with farm workers only.

2. This does not necessarily contradict Szymanski's observation that blacks outside the South were more rapidly improving their economic position than new immigrants from Latin America (other than male Mexicans). This investigation does not distinguish between southern and non-southern blacks, and the question of whether or not the workers are immigrants is also not considered.

3. In 1969 the official unemployment rate for agricultural wage and salary workers was 6 percent, compared to a national average rate of 3.5 percent (*Manpower Report of the President* 1971:122).

4. It is interesting to note that Bryce (1970:413-428), in a rather general discussion of alternative policies for increasing the earnings of migratory farm workers, dealt with the structural side of the earnings problem. Arguing that in general, three alternative policies – an increase in the demand for the workers' services, a minimum wage, and a reduction in the supply of workers – could increase the earnings of a given category of workers, he proposed the following as a set of policies that could increase migratory farm worker earnings:

(1) on the supply side: limitation by law of the number of children working on farms; cessation of the hiring of illegal aliens; and training, orientation, and hiring of migratory workers in the nonfarm sector;

(2) on the demand side: more efficient organization of work;

(3) in terms of organization: a trade union;

(4) for those who remain below the poverty line: a supplementary income.

Bryce said nothing, however, about differences in the opportunities which the various ethnic categories have in migratory farm work, differences in the earnings of these categories, and the reasons for these differences.

5. Except in California, where the California Agricultural Labor Relations Act passed in 1975 requires employers to deal only with the unions representing the workers. Idaho, Kansas, and Arizona have also passed laws regulating farm labor relations.

6. Montero recognized this, but did not deal with it because her paper addressed itself only to finding alternatives to migratory labor in New York state.

7. This article summarizes J. Kamal Dow's *Historical Perspective of the Florida Citrus Industry and the Impact of Mechanical Harvesting on the Demand for Labor* (Department of Agricultural Economics, University of Florida, April 1970).

8. President Carter deserves credit for again taking up the hot issue of the illegal aliens and for working out a plan to reduce the increasing influx of illegal aliens, and register and take care of the millions of illegal aliens already in the United States. However, unless control on the long Mexican border and in the fields where the aliens work is carried out very efficiently, these plans may not be the final answer to this problem. What probably will happen is that once the illegal workers have become legal members of the work force, they will leave the jobs they are doing (in which they are afraid to demand higher wages and better working conditions because they are illegal) and create vacancies at the bottom of the occupational ladder. These vacancies will be filled by new illegal aliens. As long as there is unemployment in Mexico and work in the United States, Mexican workers will find ways to cross the border and employers will find ways to employ them (see *Economist* 1977:13 August).

APPENDIX A

QUESTIONNAIRE

		Code
FARM LABOR SURVEY Northeast Agricultural Experiment Stations Cooperating (NE-58) WORKER QUESTIONNAIRE Confidential. For Statistical Use Only	*Interviewer.* _____ *Place: Work site (1)* *Local address (2)* *Other* _____ *(3)* *Time: Start* ___ : *End* ___ : *Date:* ___ / ___ / ___ *Employer ID Number* *Checked: Supervisor* *Office Edit*	⊏⊐⊩⊏⊐ ⊏⊐ ⊏⊐⊏⊐⊏⊐⊏⊐ ⊏⊐⊏⊐⊏⊐ ⊏⊐⊏⊐⊏⊐⊏⊐⊏⊐⊏⊐ ⊏⊐⊏⊐⊏⊐⊏⊐⊏⊐⊏⊐⊏⊐⊏⊐⊏⊐ ⊏⊐⊏⊐ ⊏⊐⊏⊐

1. Name _____

   Sex |☐| *male (1)* |☐| *female (2)*   ⊏⊐

2. What is your present address?
   (Where are you living now while you are working at this job?)

   Address _____ City _____
   County _____ State _____

   City ⊏⊐⊩⊏⊐⊩⊏⊐
   County ⊏⊐⊩⊏⊐⊩⊏⊐
   State ⊏⊐⊩⊏⊐

3. In what state or country were you born? _____   *birthplace* ⊏⊐⊏⊐⊩⊏⊐

   IF FOREIGN COUNTRY: Are you a U.S. citizen? |☐| *yes (1)*
   |☐| *no (2)*   ☐

   ETHNIC GROUP: |☐| *Wh (1)* |☐| *Bl (2)* |☐| *PR (3)* |☐| *Mex (4)*
   |☐| *oth (5)*   ☐

4. How old were you on your last birthday? _____   ⊏⊐⊩⊏⊐⊩⊏⊐ *years*

5. What was the highest grade you completed in school? _____   ⊏⊐⊩⊏⊐⊩⊏⊐ *grade*

6. Are you: |☐| *Married (1)* |☐| *Widowed (2)* |☐| *Divorced (3)*
   |☐| *Separated (4)* |☐| *Never married (5)*   ☐

7. Do you own a: |☐| *House (1)* |☐| *Mobile Home (Trailer) (2)*
   |☐| *None (3)*   ☐

8. Are you related to this employer? |☐| *yes (1)* |☐| *no (2)*   ⊏⊐

9. How many years have you been doing some farm work for wages?   ⊏⊐⊩⊏⊐⊩⊏⊐ *years*

10. How many years have you done some farm work for this employer?   ⊏⊐⊩⊏⊐⊩⊏⊐ *years*

11. During the past 12 months did you leave home overnight to do temporary work . . .
    in another state? |☐| *yes (1)* |☐| *no (2)*   ☐
    in another county in this state? |☐| *yes (1)* |☐| *no (2)*   ☐

185

12. Now I would like to ask you some questions about each week of employment in the past 12

Line Number	Did you work during the week ending . . . ? 1970	Yes	No	Status Code	What state were you in?		State Code	IF WORKED: What kind of work did you do that week?										
								Farm	Non-farm	Self-employed	Unpaid	What kind of farm (business) is this?	Ind. Code	What kind of work did you do?	Occup. Code	How much did you earn that week before deductions?		
01	Oct. 31																	.00
02	Oct. 24																	.00
03	Oct. 17																	00
04	Oct. 10																	.00
05	Oct. 3																	.00
06	Sept. 26																	.00
07	Sept. 19																	.00
08	Sept. 12																	.00
09	Sept. 5																	.00
10	Aug. 29																	.00
11	Aug 22																	.00
12	Aug 15																	.00
13	Aug. 8																	.00
14	Aug. 1																	
15	July 25																	.00
16	July 18																	.00
17	July 11																	.00
18	July 4																	.00
19	June 27																	.00
20	June 20																	.00
21	June 13																	.00
22	June 6																	.00

RECORD SECOND JOBS BELOW:

											.00
											.00
											00
											.00
											.00
											.00

months.

Line Number	IF WORKED: Did you receive any extra pay (bonus, incentive) in addition to these wages?			Did you receive any ___ at no cost to you?				IF NON-FARM WORK: What is the name and address of your employer?	Any other job that Week?			IF NO WORK: What did you do that week?						
	No	or Amount		House	Meals	Trans	Other		Yes	No	Code	Use codes below	Did you receive any unemployment benefits?					
													No	or Amount		State		Code
01			.00												.00			
02			.00												.00			
03			.00												.00			
04			.00												.00			
05			.00												.00			
06			.00												.00			
07			.00												.00			
08			.00												.00			
09			.00												.00			
10			.00												.00			
11			.00												.00			
12			.00												.00			
13			.00												.00			
14			.00												.00			
15			.00												.00			
16			.00												.00			
17			.00												.00			
18			.00												.00			
19			.00												.00			
20			.00												.00			
21			.00												.00			
22			.00												00			

			.00				
			.00				
			.00				
			.00				
			.00				
			.00				

NO WORK CODES:

1=looked for work	6=paid vacation
2=bad weather	7=unpaid vacation
3=wanted work, but not looking	8=in school
	9=sick, injured
4=traveling to new job	10=keeping house
5=retired	11=other

Line Number	Did you work during the week ending . . . ? 1970	Yes	No	Status Code	What state were you in?	State Code	Farm	Non-Farm	Self-Employed	Unpaid Work	What kind of farm (business) is this?	Ind. Code	What kind of work did you do?	Occup. Code	How much did you earn that week before deductions?
							IF WORKED: What kind of work did you do that week?								
23	May 30														.00
24	May 23														.00
25	May 16														.00
26	May 9														.00
27	May 2														.00
28	April 25														.00
29	April 18														.00
30	April 11														.00
31	April 4														.00
32	March 28														.00
33	March 21														.00
34	March 14														.00
35	March 7														.00
36	Feb. 28														.00
37	Feb. 21														.00
38	Feb. 14														.00
39	Feb. 7														.00
40	Jan. 31														.00
41	Jan. 24														.00
42	Jan. 17														.00
43	Jan. 10														.00
44	Jan. 3														.00

RECORD SECOND JOBS BELOW:

												.00
												.00
												.00
												.00
												.00
												.00

Line Number	IF WORKED: Did you receive any extra pay (bonus, incentive) in addition to these wages?			Did you receive any ___ at no cost to you?				IF NON-FARM WORK: What is the name and address of your employer?	Any other job that week?			IF NO WORK: What did you do that week? Did you receive any unemployment benefits?					
	No	or Amount		House	Meals	Trans	Other		Yes	No	Code	Use codes below	No	or Amount		State		Code
23			.00												.00			
24			.00												.00			
25			.00												.00			
26			.00												.00			
27			.00												00			
28			.00												.00			
29			.00												.00			
30			.00												.00			
31			.00												.00			
32			.00												.00			
33			.00												.00			
34			.00												.00			
35			.00												.00			
36			.00												.00			
37			.00												.00			
38			.00												.00			
39			.00												.00			
40			.00												.00			
41			.00												.00			
42			.00												.00			
43			.00												.00			
44			.00												.00			

			.00				
			.00				
			.00				
			.00				
			.00				
			.00				

NO WORK CODES:

1=looked for work	6=paid vacation
2=bad weather	7=unpaid vacation
3=wanted work, but not looking	8=in school
4=traveling to new job	9=sick, injured
5=retired	10=keeping house
	11=other

Line Number	Did you work during the week ending . . . ? 1969	Yes	No	Status Code	What state were you in?	State Code	IF WORKED: What kind of work did you do that week?										How much did you earn that week before deductions?
							Farm	Non-Farm	Self-Employed	Unpaid Work	What kind of farm (business) is this?	Ind. Code	What kind of work did you do?		Occup. Code		
45	Dec. 27																.00
46	Dec. 20																.00
47	Dec. 13																.00
48	Dec. 6																.00
49	Nov. 29																.00
50	Nov. 22																.00
51	Nov. 15																.00
52	Nov. 8																.00
53	Nov. 1																.00
54	Oct. 25																.00
55	Oct. 18																.00
56	Oct. 11																.00
57	Oct. 4																.00
58	Sept. 27																.00
59	Sept. 20																.00
60	Sept. 13																.00
61	Sept. 6																.00
62	Aug. 30																.00
63	Aug. 23																.00
64	Aug. 16																.00
65	Aug. 9																.00
66	Aug. 2																.00

RECORD SECOND JOBS BELOW:

																.00
																.00
																.00
																.00
																.00
																.00

Line Number	IF WORKED: Did you receive any extra pay (bonus, incentive) in addition to these wages?		Did you receive any ___ at no cost to you?				IF NON-FARM WORK: What is the name and address of your employer?	Any other job that week?			IF NO WORK: What did you do that week? Did you receive any unemployment benefits?			
	No	or Amount	House	Meals	Trans	Other		Yes	No	Code	Use codes below / No	or Amount	State	Code
45		.00										.00		
46		.00										.00		
47		.00										.00		
48		.00										.00		
49		.00										.00		
50		.00										.00		
51		.00										.00		
52		.00										.00		
53		.00										.00		
54		.00										.00		
55		.00										.00		
56		.00										.00		
57		.00										.00		
58		.00										.00		
59		.00										.00		
60		.00										.00		
61		.00										.00		
62		.00										.00		
63		.00										.00		
64		.00										.00		
65		.00										.00		
66		.00										.00		

	.00					
	.00					
	.00					
	.00					
	.00					
	.00					

NO WORK CODES:

1=looked for work
2=bad weather
3=wanted work, but not looking
4=traveling to new job
5=retired
6=paid vacation
7=unpaid vacation
8=in school
9=sick, injured
10=keeping house
11=other

Line Number	Did you work during the week ending . . ? 1969	Yes	No	Status Code	What state were you in?	State Code	IF WORKED: What kind of work did you do that week?				What kind of farm (business) is this?	Ind. Code	What kind of work did you do?	Occup. Code	How much did you earn that week before deductions?			
							Farm	Non-Farm	Self-Employed	Unpaid Work								
67	July 26																	.00
68	July 19																	.00
69	July 12																	.00
70	July 5																	.00
71	June 28																	.00
72	June 21																	
73	June 14																	.00
74	June 7																	.00
75	May 31																	.00
76	May 24																	.00
77	May 17																	.00
78	May 10																	.00
79	May 3																	.00
80	April 26																	.00
81	April 19																	.00
82	April 12																	.00
83	April 5																	.00

RECORD SECOND JOBS BELOW:

									.00
									.00
									.00
									.00
									.00
									.00

193

Line Number	IF WORKED: Did you receive any extra pay (bonus, incentive) in addition to these wages?					Did you receive any ___ at no cost to you				IF NON-FARM WORK: What is the name and address of your employer?	Any other job that week?			IF NO WORK: What did you do that week? Use codes below	Did you receive any unemployment benefits?				
	No		or Amount			House	Meals	Trans	Other		Yes	No	Code		No	or Amount		State	Code
67					.00												.00		
68					.00												.00		
69					.00												.00		
70					.00												.00		
71					.00												.00		
72					.00												.00		
73					.00												.00		
74					.00												.00		
75					.00												.00		
76					.00												.00		
77					.00												.00		
78					.00												.00		
79					.00												.00		
80					.00												.00		
81					.00												.00		
82					.00												.00		
83					.00												.00		

				.00				
				.00				
				.00				
				.00				
				.00				
				.00				

NO WORK CODES:

1=looked for work	6=paid vacation
2=bad weather	7=unpaid vacation
3=wanted work, but not looking	8=in school
	9=sick, injured
4=traveling to new job	10=keeping house
5=retired	11=other

13. From the information you have given me, you have indicated that during <u>most</u> of the past 12 months, you were (check current status)

What were you doing during <u>most</u> of:

	Current	1969	1968	1967	1966	1965		
doing farm work for wages (1)	☐	☐	☐	☐	☐	☐	Current	☐
*doing non-farm work (2)	☐	☐	☐	☐	☐	☐		
**operating a farm (3)	☐	☐	☐	☐	☐	☐	1969	☐☐
doing unpaid farm work (4)	☐	☐	☐	☐	☐	☐	1968	☐☐
keeping house (5)	☐	☐	☐	☐	☐	☐		
going to school (6)	☐	☐	☐	☐	☐	☐	1967	☐☐
looking for work (7)	☐	☐	☐	☐	☐	☐		
in military service (8)	☐	☐	☐	☐	☐	☐	1966	☐☐
doing something else (9)	☐	☐	☐	☐	☐	☐		

IF FARM WORK FOR WAGES IS <u>NOT</u> MENTIONED FOR EACH OF THE YEARS, ASK: 1965 ☐☐

Did you do <u>any</u> farm work for wages during the year?

☐   ☐   ☐   ☐   ☐

---

*IF NON-FARM WORK WAS NOT MENTIONED, ASK: Have you <u>ever</u> done non-farm work?   ☐ Yes (1)   ☐ No (2)   ☐

**IF FARM OPERATOR WAS NOT MENTIONED, ASK: Have you <u>ever</u> been a farm operator (as an owner or tenant)?   ☐Yes (1)   ☐No (2)   ☐

FOR WORKERS WHOSE MAJOR JOB WAS FARM WORK DURING THE PAST 12 MONTHS BUT WHO HAVE BEEN A NON-FARM WORKER SOMETIME DURING THE 5-YEAR HISTORY, ASK:

a   Since 1965, your major work changed from non-farm work to farm work. Could you have continued in non-farm work if you wanted to? (Were there other non-farm jobs like yours available for you to take?)   ☐Yes (1)   ☐No (2)   ☐

---

b. Did you look for other non-farm work?

☐ Yes (1)   ☐ No (2)   ☐

---

14 Would you prefer to work as a farm worker or as a non-farm worker?

☐Farm worker (1)   ☐Non-farm worker (2)

☐No preference (3)   ☐

15. FOR PERSONS WHO WORKED ONLY PART OF THE PAST 12 MONTHS:

Why didn't you work year-round during the past 12 months?

Check those volunteered (1)

(a) family to care for
(b) went to school
(c) poor health
(d) work desired not available
(e) no year-round work available
(f) work for which I qualified not available
(g) no need for year-round work
(h) can make more money collecting unemployment insurance
(i) no response
(j) other _____
(k) other _____

16 How many persons including yourself live together in your household?

Who are they? Name	What relationship is ____ to you? Code	How old is ____? 	Did ____ work for wages during the past 12 months? IF YES: Was it mostly farm or non-farm work? Was it year-round or temporary work? How much did ____ earn during the past 12 months?						Total Earnings
			No work	Farm	Non-Farm	Year-Rnd.	Temporary	Code	
1.									.00
2.									.00
3									.00
4.									.00
5									.00
6.									.00
7									00
8									.00
9.									.00
10									.00

Do you have any dependent children who are not living in your household?

11.									.00
12									.00
13									.00
14.									.00

17. What was your father's major job when you were in your teens?
    |☐|Hired farm worker (1) |☐|Farm operator (2) |☐|Other (3) |☐|DK (4) |☐|

18. FOR INTER-STATE MIGRANTS ONLY:
    a. How many years have you worked in (state) at least part of the year? ___ |☐|

    b Would you stay in (state) the year-round if you could earn a steady
       income here? |☐| Yes (1) |☐| No (2) |☐|

    c. When you travel to do farm work, do you usually travel with a group?
       |☐| Yes (1) |☐| No (2) |☐|

    IF YES: How many of the group are your relatives?
       |☐| All (1) |☐| Some (2) |☐| None (3) |☐|

    How many of your family travel with you when you do farm work?
       |☐| All (1) |☐| Some (2) |☐| None (3) |☐|

    d. Why do you travel to do farm work?   check those volunteered

       can make more money   ☐   ☐
       no work available in home community   ☐   ☐
       better weather during summer   ☐   ☐
       enjoy traveling   ☐   ☐
       other_____   ☐   ☐
       other_____   ☐   ☐
       no response   ☐

19. Have you ever received unemployment insurance? |☐| Yes (1) |☐|No (2) |☐|

20. Has any other member of your household ever received unemployment insurance?
    |☐| Yes (1) |☐| No (2) |☐|

21. Does the fact that you might be able to collect unemployment insurance
    benefits make a job more attractive to you?
    |☐| Yes (1) |☐| No (2) |☐| Never thought about it (3) |☐|

22. If you were out of work now and looking for a job would you be able to draw
    unemployment benefits? |☐|Yes (1) |☐|No (2) |☐|DK (3) |☐|

23. How often do you read a newspaper? |☐| Regularly (1)
    |☐| Occasionally (2) |☐| Seldom (3) |☐| Never (4) |☐|

24. How often do you listen to news broadcast on the radio? |☐|Regularly (1)
    |☐| Occasionally (2) |☐| Seldom (3) |☐|Never (4) |☐|

25 How often do you watch the news on TV? |☐| Regularly (1)
    |☐| Occasionally (2) |☐| Seldom (3) |☐| Never (4) |☐|

26. What is your social security number? |☐☐☐| |☐☐☐| |☐☐☐☐|

Mean and standard deviation of the variables used in the migratory farm worker earnings function (Table 5.1)

Variable		Mean	Standard dev.
E	(earnings)	3,493.06	1,826.27
A	(age)	35.61	13.24
A^2	(age squared)	1,443.15	1,041.84
C_1	(9-12 years of education)	0.33	0.47
C_2	(13^+ years of education)	0.02	0.13
W	(weeks of work)	43.65	12.08
R_1	(black)	0.40	0.49
R_2	(Puerto Rican)	0.36	0.48
R_3	(Mexican)	0.13	0.33
R_4	(other, excl. whites)	0.02	0.15
S	(sex: male)	0.94	0.23
J	(occupational skills)	0.24	0.42
F	(job of father: hired farm worker)	0.47	0.50
T	(all family members traveled with worker)	0.20	0.40

No. of observations: 595

Mean and standard deviation of the variables used in the nonmigratory farm worker earnings function (Table 5.2)

Variable		Mean	Standard dev.
E	(earnings)	4,785.90	2,817.16
A	(age)	38.53	14.77
A^2	(age squared)	1,702.34	1,229,24
C_1	(9-12 years of education)	0.50	0.50
C_2	(13^+ years of education)	0.10	0.30
W	(weeks of work)	49.01	8.30
R	(black)	0.16	0.37
S	(sex: male)	0.83	0.37
J	(occupational skills)	0.35	0.48
F	(job of father: hired farm worker)	0.20	0.40
P	(years of employment with employer where interviewed)	7.83	8.67
M	(married)	0.66	0.47

No. of observations: 1,429

Correlation coefficients of the migratory farm worker earnings function (Table 5.1)

	E	A	A^2	C_1	C_2	W	R_1	R_2	R_3	R_4	S	J	F	T
E	1.00	0.05	0.02	0.14	0.16	0.61	0.24	-0.26	-0.07	0.02	0.16	0.11	-0.17	0.12
A	0.05	1.00	0.99	-0.24	-0.01	0.06	0.11	-0.15	-0.08	0.02	0.01	-0.08	-0.04	-0.00
A^2	0.02	0.99	1.00	-0.24	0.00	0.04	0.09	-0.14	-0.07	0.01	0.01	-0.09	-0.03	-0.02
C_1	0.14	-0.24	-0.24	1.00	-0.09	0.07	0.27	-0.20	-0.06	-0.06	-0.09	0.04	-0.13	0.07
C_2	0.16	0.01	0.00	-0.09	1.00	0.07	0.08	-0.10	-0.05	0.07	0.03	0.11	-0.07	0.00
W	0.61	0.06	0.04	0.07	0.07	1.00	0.22	-0.23	0.01	0.05	0.07	0.10	-0.10	0.06
R_1	0.24	0.11	0.09	0.27	0.08	0.22	1.00	-0.62	-0.31	-0.12	-0.08	-0.04	-0.19	0.02
R_2	-0.26	-0.15	-0.14	-0.20	-0.10	-0.23	-0.62	1.00	-0.29	-0.11	0.19	0.00	0.24	-0.35
R_3	-0.07	-0.08	-0.07	-0.06	-0.05	0.01	-0.31	-0.29	1.00	-0.06	-0.14	-0.01	0.09	0.38
R_4	0.02	0.02	0.01	-0.06	0.07	0.05	-0.12	-0.11	-0.06	1.00	-0.01	0.03	-0.10	0.01
S	0.16	0.01	0.01	-0.09	0.03	0.07	-0.08	0.19	-0.14	-0.01	1.00	0.02	-0.04	-0.17
J	0.11	-0.08	-0.09	0.04	0.11	0.10	-0.04	0.00	-0.01	0.03	0.02	1.00	-0.11	0.03
F	-0.17	-0.04	-0.03	-0.13	-0.07	-0.10	-0.19	0.24	0.09	-0.10	-0.04	-0.11	1.00	-0.01
T	0.12	-0.00	-0.02	0.07	0.00	0.06	0.02	-0.35	0.38	0.01	-0.17	0.03	-0.01	1.00

Correlation coefficients of the nonmigratory farm worker earnings function (Table 5.2)

	E	A	A^2	C_1	C_2	W	R	S	J	F	P	M
E	1.00	0.09	0.03	-0.01	0.25	0.35	-0.15	0.20	0.29	-0.10	0.20	0.32
A	0.09	1.00	0.98	-0.33	-0.08	0.01	0.12	-0.02	-0.08	-0.02	0.44	0.25
A^2	0.03	0.98	1.00	-0.31	-0.08	-0.01	0.10	-0.00	-0.10	-0.03	0.42	0.18
C_1	-0.01	-0.33	-0.31	1.00	-0.33	0.03	-0.15	-0.12	0.07	-0.11	-0.11	-0.10
C_2	0.25	-0.08	-0.08	-0.33	1.00	0.04	-0.12	-0.01	0.19	-0.12	0.04	0.07
W	0.35	0.01	-0.01	0.03	0.04	1.00	-0.14	0.11	0.03	-0.04	0.13	0.12
R	-0.15	0.12	0.10	-0.15	-0.12	-0.14	1.00	-0.04	-0.14	0.23	-0.01	-0.06
S	0.20	-0.02	-0.00	-0.12	-0.01	0.11	-0.04	1.00	-0.00	0.05	0.08	0.06
J	0.29	-0.08	-0.10	0.07	0.19	0.03	-0.14	-0.00	1.00	-0.10	-0.04	0.08
F	-0.10	-0.02	-0.03	-0.11	-0.12	-0.04	0.23	0.05	-0.10	1.00	-0.02	-0.01
P	0.20	0.44	0.42	-0.11	0.04	0.13	-0.01	0.08	-0.04	-0.02	1.00	0.18
M	0.32	0.25	0.18	-0.10	0.07	0.12	-0.06	0.06	0.08	-0.01	0.18	1.00

LOGARITHMIC FORMS OF THE EARNINGS FUNCTIONS

In Chapter 5, two earnings functions were presented: one for the migratory and one for the nonmigratory farm workers. The migratory model explained 43 percent of the variation in earnings, and the nonmigratory model explained 39 percent. Tinbergen, in his study of differences in income, remarked that most studies which "...try to show how deeply the social class structure of American society affects income distribution" (1975:11) still leave a large percentage of the variation in earnings unexplained. He mentioned one exception: an unpublished study that explains 78 percent of the variation in the incomes of individuals.

The earnings functions in Chapter 5 showed quite satisfactory results for individual observations. Even so, more than half of the variation remained unexplained. Mincer (1974: Chapter 5) demonstrated that the explanatory power of regression functions showing the impact of schooling, experience, and weeks of employment on individual earnings is increased considerably by including the logarithmic forms of the dependent variable "earnings" and the independent variable "weeks of work." Using this technique, two variables, E (earnings) and W (weeks of work), were replaced by the logarithmic forms in the earnings functions for migratory and nonmigratory farm workers. This resulted in a considerable increase in the explanatory power of the regressions, particularly for the migratory model. The log forms of the two earnings functions are presented on page 201.

The statistical estimates — based on *individual* observations — in the two earnings functions compare well with similar research done by others.

The logarithmic form of the migratory farm workers' function differs from the model presented in Chapter 5 in that the coefficients for the variables A (age), A^2 (age squared), and R_1 (being black) do not show significant results (these were the estimates with the lowest F-values in Table 5.1). Variable G (the interstate mobility of the workers) is significant in the log form. The significance of the mobility coefficient in the log form supports Metzler's finding (1955:48-55, 69) that traveling to two or more states increases earnings (see page 118). The log form definitely shows a greater explanatory power for migratory farm worker earnings than the non-log form.

Table C.1. *Migratory Farm Worker Earnings: Regression Coefficients of Explanatory Variables, Logarithmic Form*

Variable[a]		Coefficient	F-value
C_1	(9-12 years of education)	0.10	7.9
C_2	(13+ years of education)	0.33	6.6
logW	(log weeks of work)	1.10	1,242.9
R_1	(black)	-0.09	2.1[b]
R_2	(Puerto Rican)	-0.17	7.2
R_3	(Mexican)	-0.29	16.4
R_4	(other, excl. whites)	-0.33	7.4
S	(sex: male)	0.38	28.2
J	(occupational skills)	0.05	1.7[b]
F	(job of father: hired farm worker)	0.04	1.4[b]
T	(all family members traveled with worker)	0.10	4.9
G	(worker traveled to two or more states)	0.09	7.5

Constant = 3.61
$R^2_{(adj)}$ = .72
F = 127.3
N = 595

[a] See Chapter 5 for a more extensive description of the variables.

[b] Not significant at the .05 level.

Table C.2. *Nonmigratory Farm Worker Earnings: Regression Coefficients of Explanatory Variables, Logarithmic Form*

Variable[a]		Coefficient	F-value
A	(age)	0.08	246.3
A^2	(age squared)	-0.00	233.9
C_1	(9-12 years of education)	0.18	32.7
C_2	(13+ years of education)	0.36	48.8
logW	(log weeks of work)	0.99	661.9
R_1	(black)	-0.06	3.1
$R_{2,3}$	(Puerto Rican and Mexican)	0.13	5.2
S	(sex: male)	0.32	77.3
J	(occupational skills)	0.20	49.3
P	(years of employment with employer where interviewed)	0.01	8.5
M	(married)	0.22	48.5

Constant = 2.25
$R^2_{(adj)}$ = .53
F = 160.0
N = 1,539

[a] See Chapter 5 for a more extensive description of the variables.

The logarithmic form of the nonmigratory farm workers' function differs from the model in Chapter 5 in that the estimates for variables R_2 and R_3 (Puerto Ricans and Mexicans) show significant results. This is not the case in the non-log form.

Although there was no opportunity to study the possibilities of the log forms extensively, it is interesting to note that the results presented here lend support to researchers who have argued that log forms of earnings functions are superior to non-log forms. The log forms of both earnings functions explain a higher percentage of the variation in earnings and also corroborate the results and conclusions presented in Chapter 5. The log form for migratory farm workers indicates that there is another way of increasing earnings, i.e., traveling to two or more states. Furthermore, the gap between the earnings of black migratory workers and white migratory workers appears to be smaller than in the non-log form. The log form for nonmigratory farm workers indicates that Puerto Rican and Mexican workers actually have higher earnings than white nonmigratory farm workers. More attention should certainly be devoted to this point in future research on farm workers.

BIBLIOGRAPHY

Adams, F.G. 1958. "The Size of Individual Incomes: Socio-Economic Variables and Chance Variation." *Review of Economics and Statistics* 40 (November): 390-398.
Agee, James, and Evans, Walker. 1941. *Let Us Now Praise Famous Men* (Boston: Houghton Mifflin).
Albrecht, Günter. 1972. *Soziologie der geographischen Mobilität. Zugleich ein Beitrag zur Soziologie des sozialen Wandels* (Stuttgart: Ferdinand Enke Verlag).
Allen, Steve. 1966. *The Ground is our Table* (New York: Doubleday).
Anderson, Nels. 1923. *The Hobo: the Sociology of the Homeless Man* (Chicago: University of Chicago Press).
——. 1940. *Men on the Move* (Chicago: University of Chicago Press).
Ball, Gordon A., and Heady, Earl O. 1972. "Trends in Farm and Enterprise Size and Scale." In *Size, Structure, and Future of Farms*. Edited by Gordon A. Ball and Earl O. Heady (Ames: Iowa State University Press).
Bauder, Ward W. 1973. "Minority Workers on New York Farms." *New York's Food and Life Sciences Quarterly* 6.1 (January-March): 16-19 (Ithaca: New York State and Cornell University Agricultural Experiment Stations).
——. 1976a. "Impact of Unemployment Insurance on Hired Agricultural Workers." In Seaver *et al.* 1976: 35-45 (Chapter IV).
——. 1976b. "Puerto Rican Hired Farm Workers." In Seaver *et al.* 1976: 103-116 (Chapter IX).
Bauder, Ward W., and Bratton, C.A. 1972. *The Impact of Extending Unemployment Insurance to Agricultural Workers in New York State*. A.E. Res. 72-2 (Ithaca: Department of Agricultural Economics, New York State College of Agriculture and Life Sciences, Cornell University).
Bauder, W.W., Elterich, J.G., Farrish, R.O.P., and Holt, J.S. 1976. *Impact of Extension of Unemployment Insurance to Agriculture*. Bulletin 804, January (University Park: Pennsylvania State University, College of Agriculture, Agricultural Experiment Station).
Becker, Gary S. 1972. "Comment." *Journal of Political Economy* 80.3, Part II (May/June): 252-255.
Becket, James W. 1969. "A Career Ladder for Farmworkers." *Farm Labor Developments* (December): 7-11 (Washington, D.C.: U.S. Department of Labor, Manpower Administration).
Beijer, G. 1963. *Rural Migrants in Urban Setting: an Analysis of the Literature on the Problems Consequent on the Internal Migration from Rural to Urban Areas in 12 European Countries (1945-1961)* (The Hague: Martinus Nijhoff).
——. 1970. "International and National Migratory Movements." *International Migration* 8.3 (1970): 93-106.
Bell, Colin. 1969. *Middle Class Families: Social and Geographical Mobility* (London: Routledge & Kegan Paul).
Blalock, Hubert M. 1960. *Social Statistics* (New York: McGraw-Hill).
Blau, Peter M., and Duncan, Otis Dudley. 1967. *The American Occupational Structure* (New York: John Wiley & Sons).
Blaug, Mark. 1972. *An Introduction to the Economics of Education* (Harmondsworth: Penguin Books).
Boekestijn, Cornelis. 1961. "Binding aan een streek: een empirisch onderzoek naar de migra-

tie en de animo voor migratie uit de provincie Zeeland onder jongere arbeiders in Wal-
cheren en Zuid-Beveland." Ph.D. dissertation (Amsterdam, Free University).

Bogue, Donald J. 1959. "Internal Migration." In *The Study of Population. An Inventory
and Appraisal*. Edited by Philip M. Hauser and Otis Dudley Duncan (Chicago: University of Chicago Press).

———. 1969. *Principles of Demography* (New York: John Wiley & Sons).

Bourke-White, Margaret, and Caldwell, Erskine. 1937. *You Have Seen Their Faces* (New
York: Viking Press).

Bowles, Samuel. 1972. "Schooling and Inequality from Generation to Generation." *Journal
of Political Economy* 80.3, Part II (May/June): 219-251.

Bratton, C.A., and Fisher, D.U. 1975. "Special Unemployment Insurance Benefits Extended
to Farm Workers." *Rural Manpower Issues*. Mimeo. No. 4, 14 January (Ithaca: Department of Agricultural Economics, Cornell University).

Brooks, Melvin S., and Hilgendorf, Robert L. 1960. *The Social Problems of Migrant Farm
Laborers: Effect of Migrant Farm Labor on the Education of Children* (Carbondale:
Department of Sociology, Southern Illinois University).

Brown, Malcolm J., and Cassmore, Orrin. 1939. *Migratory Cotton Pickers in Arizona* (Works
Progress Administration, Division of Social Research, Washington, D.C.: U.S. Government Printing Office).

Bryce, Herrington J. 1970. "Alternative Policies for Increasing the Earnings of Migratory
Farm Workers." *Public Policy* (Spring): 413-428.

Burawoy, Michael. 1976. "The Functions and Reproduction of Migrant Labor: Comparative
Material from South Africa and the United States." *American Journal of Sociology*
81.5 (March): 1050-1087.

Caldwell, Erskine. 1949. *God's Little Acre* (New York: New American Library of World
Literature; 29th printing, Signet Books).

Campbell, Rex R., Johnson, Daniel M., and Stangler, Gary. 1974. "Return Migration of
Black People to the South." *Rural Sociology* 39.4 (Winter): 514-528.

CBS Television Network. 1960. "Harvest of Shame." Documentary prepared for the
Columbia Broadcasting Company for the program "CBS Reports" by Edward R.
Murrow in cooperation with Fred Friendly.

Chiswick, Barry R., and Mincer, Jacob. 1972. "Time-Series Changes in Personal Income. Inequality in the United States from 1939, with Projections to 1985." *Journal of Political Economy* 80.3, Part II (May/June): 34-66.

Costner, Herbert L., ed. 1972. *Sociological Methodology 1972* (London: Jossey-Bass).

Cowhig, James D., and Beale, Calvin L. 1964. "Socioeconomic Differences between White
and Nonwhite Farm Populations of the South." *Social Forces* 42.3 (March): 354-362.

Cronemeyer, Cora S. 1972. "New Ways of Helping Migrants." *Rural Manpower Developments* (March): 9-16 (Washington, D.C.: U.S. Department of Labor, Manpower Administration).

Cunningham, L.D. 1969. *An Economic Study of Regular Hired Labor*. Bulletin 1026, July
(Ithaca: Cornell University Agricultural Experiment Station, New York State College
of Agriculture).

"Current Labor Statistics: Household Data." 1979. *Monthly Labor Review* (August): 74
(Washington, D.C.: U.S. Department of Labor, Bureau of Labor Statistics).

Davis, Kingsley. 1949. *Human Society* (New York: MacMillan).

den Hollander, A.N.J. 1933. *De landelijke arme Blanken in het Zuiden der Vereenigde Sta-
ten: een sociaal-historische en sociografische studie*. Ph.D. dissertation, University of
Amsterdam (Groningen, Den Haag, Batavia: J.B. Wolters' Uitgevers-Maatschappij,
N.V.).

Dow, Kamal J. 1970. *Historical Perspective of the Florida Citrus Industry and the Impact
of Mechanical Harvesting on the Demand for Labor* (Department of Agricultural
Economics, University of Florida. Submitted to the U.S. Department of Labor, Manpower Administration).

Ducoff, Louis J. 1951. "Migratory Farm Workers: a Problem in Migration Analysis." *Rural Sociology* 16.3 (September): 217-224.

duFresne, Elizabeth J., and McDonnell, John J. 1971. "The Migrant Labor Camps: Enclaves of Isolation in our Midst." *Fordham Law Review* 40 (December): 279-304.

Dunbar, Tony, and Kravitz, Linda. 1976. *Hard Traveling. Migrant Farm Workers in America* (Cambridge, Mass., Ballinger Publishing Co.).

Dyer, William G. 1958. "Parental Influence on the Job Attitudes of Children from Two Occupational Strata." *Sociology and Social Research* 42 (January-February): 203-206.

Economic Report of the President. 1971. (Washington, D.C.: U.S. Government Printing Office).

——. 1976. (Washington, D.C.: U.S. Government Printing Office).

Economist. 1977. "The Problem that Won't Go Away" (13-19 August).

Eisenstadt, S.N. 1955. *The Absorption of Immigrants: a Comparative Study Based on the Jewish Community in Palestine and the State of Israel* (Glencoe, Illinois: Free Press).

Elder, Peyton. 1974. "The 1974 Amendments to the Federal Minimum Wage Law." *Monthly Labor Review* (July): 33-37 (Washington, D.C.: U.S. Department of Labor, Bureau of Labor Statistics).

——. 1978. "The 1977 Amendments to the Federal Minimum Wage Law." *Monthly Labor Review* (January): 9-11 (Washington, D.C.: U.S. Department of Labor, Bureau of Labor Statistics).

Elterich, G. Joachim. 1978a. "Coverage of Agricultural Workers under the Unemployment Compensation Amendment of 1976." *Journal of the Northeastern Agricultural and Economic Council* 7 (1 April): 23-33.

——. 1978b. "Estimating the Cost of Extending Jobless Insurance to Farmworkers." *Monthly Labor Review* (May): 18-24 (Washington, D.C.: U.S. Department of Labor, Bureau of Labor Statistics).

Ferman, Louis A., Kornbluh, Joyce L., and Haber, Alan. eds. 1956. *Poverty in America* (Ann Arbor: University of Michigan Press).

Fisher, Dennis U. 1974. "The Federal Wage-Hour Law and New York Agricultural Employment." *Rural Manpower Issues*, Mimeo. No. 2, 14 August (Ithaca: Department of Agricultural Economics, Cornell University).

——. 1975. "Highlights of the Farm Labor Contractor Registration Act of 1963 as Amended December 7, 1974." *Rural Manpower Issues*, Mimeo. No. 5, 31 March (Ithaca: Department of Agricultural Economics, Cornell University).

Fisher, Lloyd R. 1953. *The Harvest Labor Market in California* (Cambridge, Mass.: Harvard University Press).

"Florida Citrus Mechanization in the Seventies." 1970. *Farm Labor Developments* (November-December): 20-26 (Washington, D.C.: U.S. Department of Labor, Manpower Administration).

Fogel, Walter A. 1975. "Immigrant Mexicans and the U.S. Work Force." *Monthly Labor Review* (May): 44-46 (Washington, D.C.: U.S. Department of Labor, Bureau of Labor Statistics).

Frazier, E.F. 1949. *The Negro in the United States* (New York: MacMillan).

Friedland, William H. 1967. *Migrant Labor as a Form of Intermittent Social Organization and as a Channel of Geographical Mobility* (Ithaca: New York School of Industrial and Labor Relations, Cornell University).

——. 1969. "Labor Waste in New York: Rural Exploitation and Migrant Workers." *Trans-Action* (February): 48-53.

Friedland, William H., and Nelkin, Dorothy. 1971. *Migrant: Agricultural Workers in America's Northeast* (New York: Holt, Rinehart, and Winston).

Fritsch, Conrad F. 1976. "Development of Unemployment Insurance in the United States and its Relevance to the Agricultural Sector." In Seaver *et al.* 1976: 117-127 (Chapter X).

Fuller, Varden. 1967. "Farm Manpower Policy." In *Farm Labor in the United States*. Edited by C.E. Bishop (New York and London: Columbia University Press).

Gardner, B. Delworth, and Pope, Rulon D. 1978. "How Is Scale and Structure Determined in Agriculture?" *American Journal of Agricultural Economics* 60.2 (May): 295-302.

Genovese, Eugene D. 1965. *The Political Economy of Slavery: Studies in the Economy and Society of the Slave South* (New York: Pantheon Books).

Ginzberg, Eli, Ginsburg, Sol W., Axelrad, Sidney, and Herma, John. 1951. *Occupational Choice: an Approach to a General Theory* (New York: Columbia University Press).

Greene, Shirley E. 1954. *A Study of the Educational Opportunities and Experiences of Agricultural Migrants* (Washington, D.C.: National Council on Agricultural Life and Labor).

Griliches, Zvi, and Mason, William M. 1972. "Education, Income, and Ability." *Journal of Political Economy* 80.3, Part II (May/June): 74-103.

Haber, William, and Murray, Merrill G. 1966. *Unemployment Insurance in the American Economy* (Homewood, Illinois: Richard D. Irwin, Inc.).

Haller, Archibald O., and Woelfel, Joseph. 1972. "Significant Others and their Expectations: Concepts and Instruments to Measure Interpersonal Influence on Status Aspirations." *Rural Sociology* 37.4 (December): 591-619.

Hanoch, G. 1967. "An Economic Analysis of Earnings and Schooling." *Journal of Human Resources* (Summer): 310-329.

Harrington, Michael. 1962. *The Other America: Poverty in the United States* (New York: MacMillan).

Hirsch, Q.Z., and Segelhorst, E.W. 1965. "Incremental Income Benefits of Public Education." *Review of Economics and Statistics* 47 (November): 392-399.

Hickey, Joseph A. 1978. "Unemployment Insurance Covers Additional Nine Million Workers." *Monthly Labor Review* (May): 14-17 (Washington, D.C.: U.S. Department of Labor, Bureau of Labor Statistics).

Hodge, Robert W., Siegel, Paul M., and Rossi, Peter H. 1966. "Occupational Prestige in the United States: 1925-1963." In *Class, Status, and Power: Social Stratification in Comparative Perspective*. Edited by Reinhard Bendix and Seymour Martin Lipset. 2nd Edition (New York: Free Press).

Holden, Arnold G. 1968. "A Typology of Individual Migration Patterns." *Summation* (1 June): 15-28.

Holt, James S. 1976. "The Impact of Unemployment Insurance on Agricultural Workers' Income." In Seaver *et al.* 1976: 65-78 (Chapter VI).

Hribel, Amy S., and Minor, Gerri. 1977. "Workers' Compensation Laws. Major Amendments in 1976." *Monthly Labor Review* (February) (Washington, D.C.: U.S. Department of Labor, Bureau of Labor Statistics).

Husband, W.W. 1926. "Rational Immigration Policy." In *Population Problems in the United States and Canada*. Edited by Lois I. Dublin (New York: Houghton Mifflin).

Jansen, Clifford. 1969. "Some Sociological Aspects of Migration." In *Migration*. Edited by J.A. Jackson (Cambridge: Cambridge University Press).

———. 1970. *Readings in the Sociology of Migration* (Oxford: Pergamon Press).

Johnson, Michael P., and Sell, Ralph R. 1976. "The Cost of Being Black: a 1970 Update." *American Journal of Sociology* 82.1 (July): 183-190.

Johnston, J. 1972. *Econometric Methods*. 2nd Edition (New York: McGraw-Hill).

Jones, Danetta L. 1973. "Mobility Facilitator Units for Migrants." *Rural Manpower Developments* (March): 21-29 (Washington, D.C.: U.S. Department of Labor, Manpower Administration).

Jordan, T.D., and Dominick, B.A., Jr. 1968. "Mechanical Harvesting of Grape Varieties Grown in New York State." Paper presented at a Technical Seminar on Implications of Mechanization for Fruit and Vegetable Harvesting, 8-10 December 1968, Chicago, Illinois (sponsored by the Rural Manpower Center of Michigan State University in cooperation with the United States Department of Labor).

Koziara, Karen S. 1977. "Agricultural Labor Relations. Laws in Four States – a Comparison." *Monthly Labor Review* (May): 14-18 (Washington, D.C.: U.S. Department of Labor, Bureau of Labor Statistics).

Larson, Olaf F., and Sharp, Emmit F. 1960. *Migratory Farm Workers in the Atlantic Coast Stream: 1. Changes in New York, 1953 and 1957.* Bulletin 948, May (Ithaca: Cornell University Agricultural Experiment Station, New York State).

Lee, Everett S. 1969. "A Theory of Migration." In *Migration.* Edited by J.A. Jackson (Cambridge: Cambridge University Press).

Lijfering, J.H.W. 1968. "Selectieve migratie: een empirische studie van de samenhang tussen plattelandsmigratie en selectie naar intelligentie in Nederland" (Wageningen University, the Netherlands).

Lively, C.E., and Taeuber, Conrad. 1939. *Rural Migration in the United States.* Works Progress Administration, Division of Social Research, Research Monograph XIX (Washington, D.C.: U.S. Government Printing Office).

McWilliams, Carey. 1942. *Ill Fares the Land: Migrants and Migratory Labor in the United States* (Boston: Little, Brown and Co.).

Mangalam, J.J. 1968. *Human Migration: a Guide to Migration Literature in English: 1955-1962* (Lexington: University of Kentucky Press).

Mangalam, J.J., and Schwarzweller, Harry K. 1968/1969. "General Theory in the Study of Migration: Current Needs and Difficulties." *International Migration Review* 3.1: 3-18.

——. 1969/1970. "Some Theoretical Guidelines toward a Sociology of Migration." *International Migration Review* 4.2. 5-21.

Manpower Report of the President. 1971 (Washington, D.C.: U.S. Government Printing Office).

Marcson, Simon, and Fasick, Frank. 1964. *Elementary Summer Schooling of Migrant Children.* Cooperative Research Project No. 1479, Social Structure and Ignorance (New Brunswick, New Jersey: Rutgers, the State University).

Martin, Philip L. 1978. "Rural Employment Programs: the Case for Remedial Policies." *Monthly Labor Review* (April): 30-32 (Washington, D.C.: U.S. Department of Labor, Bureau of Labor Statistics).

Mattera, Gloria. 1971. "Migrant Education in the United States : Some Significant Developments." In *Migrant Children: their Education* (Washington, D.C.: Association for Childhood Education International).

Metzler, William H. 1955. *Migratory Farm Workers in the Atlantic Coast Stream: a Study of the Belle Glade Area of Florida.* Circular No. 966 (Washington, D.C.: U.S. Department of Agriculture).

Metzler, William H., and Sargent, Frederic O. 1960. *Migratory Farm Workers in the Mid-continent Streams.* Production Research Report No. 41 (Washington, D.C.: Agricultural Research Service, U.S. Department of Agriculture, in cooperation with the Texas Agricultural Experiment Station).

Migratory Labor in American Agriculture. 1951. Report of the President's Commission on Migratory Labor (Washington, D.C.: U.S. Government Printing Office).

Miller, Herman P. 1964. *Rich Man, Poor Man* (New York: Thomas Y. Crowell).

Mincer, Jacob. 1974. *Schooling, Experience, and Earnings* (National Bureau of Economic Research, New York: Columbia University Press).

Monsen, Joseph R., Jr., and Cannon, Mark W. 1965. *The Makers of Public Policy: American Power Groups and their Ideologies* (New York: McGraw-Hill).

Montero, Anne M. 1966. *Migratory Labor in New York State...Are There Alternatives?* (Washington, D.C.: National Consumers Committee for Research and Education, Inc.).

Moore, Truman E. 1965. *The Slaves We Rent* (New York: Random House).

Morgan, J.N., David, M.H., Cohen, W.J., and Brazer, H.F. 1962. *Income and Welfare in the United States* (New York: McGraw-Hill).

Motheral, Joe R., Thomas, Howard, and Larson, Olaf F. 1954. "Migratory Farm Workers in the Atlantic Coast Stream. Western New York, June 1953." A preliminary report, Department of Rural Sociology. Mimeo., Bulletin No. 42 (Ithaca: New York State College of Agriculture, Cornell University).

Myers, Robin. 1959. *The Position of Farm Workers in Federal and State Legislation* (New York: National Advisory Committee on Farm Labor).

Myrdal, Gunnar. 1944. *An American Dilemma: the Negro Problem and Modern Democracy* (New York: Harper and Bros.).

National Advisory Committee on Farm Labor. 1967. *Farm Labor Organizing 1905-1967: a Brief History* (New York).

National Sharecroppers Fund. 1971. "The Condition of Farm Workers and Small Farmers in 1971." Report to the National Board of the National Sharecroppers Fund by James M. Pierce, Executive Director.

Nelkin, Dorothy. 1969. "A Response to Marginality: the Case of Migrant Farmworkers." *British Journal of Sociology* 20.4 (December): 375-389.

———. 1970. *On the Season: Aspects of the Migrant Labor System*, ILR paperback No. 8, November (Ithaca: New York School of Industrial and Labor Relations, Cornell University).

Newsweek. 23 July 1973. "Immigration: Revolving Door," 24.

New York Times. 6 March 1973. "Typhoid Reported at Migrant Camp."

———. 4 May 1973. "Article on Removal of Aliens from U.S. Creates Furor in Mexico."

Noel, Daniel L. 1972. "How Ethnic Inequality Begins." In *Issues in Social Inequality*. Edited by Gerald Thielbar and Saul D. Feldman (Boston: Little Brown and Co.).

OECD. 1979. *Equal Opportunities for Women* (Paris).

Padfield, Harland, and Martin, William E. 1965. *Farmers, Workers and Machines: Technological and Social Change in Farm Industries of Arizona* (Tucson: University of Arizona Press).

Persh, Louis. 1953. "An Analysis of the Agricultural Migratory Movements on the Atlantic Seaboard and the Socio-Economic Implications for the Community and the Migrants, 1930-1950." Ph.D. dissertation (American University, Washington, D.C.).

Petersen, William. 1958. "A General Typology of Migration." *American Sociological Review* 23 (June): 256-266.

"Puerto Ricans on Contract." 1970. *NACLA Report on the Americas* 11.8 (November-December): 18-28.

Ravenstein, E.G. 1885. "The Laws of Migration." *Journal of the Royal Statistical Society* 48, Part 2 (June): 167-227.

———. 1889. "The Laws of Migration." *Journal of the Royal Statistical Society* 52 (June): 241-301.

Rees, Albert, and Shultz, George P. 1970. *Workers and Wages in an Urban Labor Market* (Chicago: University of Chicago Press).

Rose, Arnold M. 1958. "Distance of Migration and Socio-Economic Status of Migrants." *American Sociological Review* 23.4 (August): 420-423.

———. 1969. *Migrants in Europe: Problems of Acceptance and Adjustment* (Minneapolis: University of Minnesota Press).

Ross, Arthur M., and Hill, Herbert, eds. 1967. *Employment, Race, and Poverty: a Critical Study of the Disadvantaged Status of Negro Workers from 1865 to 1965* (New York: Harcourt, Brace and World).

Rubin, Morton. 1960/1961. "Migration Patterns of Negroes from a Rural Northeastern Mississippi Community." *Social Forces* 39.1 (October): 59-66.

Rushing, William A. 1968. "Objective and Subjective Aspects of Deprivation in a Rural Poverty Class." *Rural Sociology* 33.3 (September): 269-284.

———. 1972. *Class, Culture, and Alienation: a Study of Farmers and Farm Workers* (Lexington, Mass.: D.C. Heath and Co.).

Schmid, Calvin F., and Nobbe, Charles E. 1965. "Socioeconomic Differentials among Nonwhite Races." *American Sociological Review* 30: 909-922.

Schnore, Leo F. 1961. "Social Mobility in Demographic Perspective." *American Sociological Review* 26.3 (June): 407-423.

Schultz, Theodore W. 1967. "National Employment, Skills, and Earnings of Farm Labor." In *Farm Labor in the United States.* Edited by C.E. Bishop (New York and London: Columbia University Press).

Schwartz, Harry. 1945. *Seasonal Farm Labor in the United States: with Special Reference to Hired Workers in Fruit and Vegetable and Sugar-beet Production* (New York: Columbia University Press).

Seaver, S.K., Elterich, J.G., Bauder, W.W., Emerson, R.D., Holt, J.S., Warland, R.H., Wood, B.J., and Fritsch, C.S. 1976. *Economic and Social Considerations in Extending Unemployment Insurance to Agricultural Workers.* Bulletin 806, February (University Park: Pennsylvania State University, College of Agriculture, Agricultural Experiment Station).

Seaver, Stanley, and Holt, James S. 1974. "Economic Implications of Unemployment Insurance for Agriculture." *American Journal of Agricultural Economics* 56.5 (December): 1084-1092.

Sewell, William H., and Shah, Vimal P. 1958. "Social Class, Parental Encouragement, and Educational Aspirations." *American Journal of Sociology* 73 (March): 559-572.

Shabecoff, Philip. 1973. "Florida Cane Cutters: Alien, Poor, Afraid." *New York Times* (12 March): 24.

Sharp, Emmit F., and Larson, Olaf F. 1960. *Migratory Farm Workers in the Atlantic Coast Stream: II. Education of New York Workers and their Children, 1953 and 1957.* Bulletin 949, May (Ithaca: Cornell University Agricultural Experiment Station, New York State College of Agriculture).

Shepardson, E.S., Markwardt, E.D., Millier, W.F., and Rehkugler, G.E. 1970. "Mechanical Harvesting of Fruits and Vegetables." *New York's Food and Life Sciences Bulletin*, Bulletin No. 5, December. Physical Sciences, Agricultural Engineering No. 1 (Ithaca: Cornell University Agricultural Experiment Station, New York College of Agriculture, Cornell University).

Shostack, Albert Lawrence. 1964. "Migratory Farm Labor Crews in Eastern Maryland — a Preliminary Typology." Ph.D. dissertation (American University, Washington, D.C.).

Shotwell, Louise R. 1961. *The Harvesters: the Story of the Migrant People* (New York: Doubleday).

Siegel, Paul. 1965. "On the Cost of Being a Negro." *Sociological Inquiry* 35: 41-57.

Slocum, Walter L. 1967. *Occupational Careers* (Chicago: Aldine).

Sorkin, Alan L. 1969. "Education, Migration and Negro Unemployment." *Social Forces* 47.3 (March).

Startup, Richard. 1971. "A Sociology of Migration?" *The Sociological Quarterly* 12 (Spring): 177-190.

State of Florida Legislative Council and Legislative Reference Bureau. 1963. "Migrant Farm Labor in Florida." Mimeo.

Steinbeck, John. 1939. *The Grapes of Wrath* (New York: Viking Press).

Stewart, Judith Anne. 1968. "An Examination of the Social Boundaries of the Migrant Labor System of the Atlantic Coast Stream." Master's thesis (Ithaca: Cornell University).

Stouffer, Samuel A. 1940. "Intervening Opportunities: a Theory Relating Mobility and Distance." *American Sociological Review* 5.6 (December): 845-867.

Sturt, Daniel W. 1970. "Some Migrant Worker Needs." *Farm Labor Developments* (November-December): 3-11 (Washington, D.C.: U.S. Department of Labor, Manpower Administration).

Szymanski, Al. 1975. "Trends in Economic Discrimination against Blacks in the U.S. Working Class." *The Review of Radical Political Economics* 7.3 (Fall): 1-21.

Tarver, James D., and Mcleod, R. Douglas. 1970. "Trends in Distances Moved by Interstate Migrants." *Rural Sociology* 35.4 (December): 523-533.

Taylor, Lee. 1968. *Occupational Sociology* (New York: Oxford University Press).

Taylor, Lee, and Berkey, Arthur L. 1970. "Introduction." In *Workers in Agribusiness.* Edited by Lee Taylor and J. Paul Leagans. Bulletin 1029, March (Ithaca: Cornell University Agricultural Experiment Station, New York State College of Agriculture).

Ter Heide, H. 1965. *Binnenlandse migratie in Nederland*. Rijksdienst voor het Nationale Plan — Publikatie nr. 16 (The Hague: Staatsuitgeverij).

Thias, Hans Heinrich, and Carnoy, Martin. 1972. *Cost-Benefit Analysis in Education: a Case Study of Kenya*. World Bank Staff Occasional Paper Number Fourteen, International Bank for Reconstruction and Development (Baltimore: Johns Hopkins Press).

Thomas, Hendrik. 1973. "Personal Income Distribution in Yugoslavia: a Human Capital Approach to the Analysis of Personal Income Differences in the Industry of a Labor-Managed Market Economy." Ph.D. dissertation (Ithaca: Cornell University).

Tinbergen, J. 1975. *Income Differences: Recent Research*. Professor Dr. F. de Vries Lectures (Amsterdam: North-Holland).

U.S. Congress, Senate. 1961. *Children in Migrant Families. A Report to the Committee on Appropriations*. Submitted by the U.S. Department of Health, Education, and Welfare, Social Security Administration, Children's Bureau. 87th Congress, 1st Session (Washington, D.C.: U.S. Government Printing Office).

U.S. Congress, Senate, Committee on Agriculture and Forestry. 1965. *Importation of Foreign Agricultural Workers. Hearings before the Committee on Agriculture and Forestry*, 89th Congress, 1st Session, 15 and 16 January (Washington, D.C.: U.S. Government Printing Office).

U.S. Congress, Senate, Committee on Labor and Public Welfare. 1960. *The Migrant Farm-worker in America: Background Data on the Migrant Worker Situation in the United States Today*. Prepared for the Subcommittee on Migratory Labor by Daniel H. Pollitt and Selma M. Levine, 86th Congress, 2nd Session (Washington, D.C.).

——. 1961/1969. *The Migratory Farm Labor Problem in the United States. Annual Reports of the Subcommittee on Migratory Labor* (Washington, D.C.: U.S. Government Printing Office).

U.S. Department of Agriculture, Economic Research Service. 1970. *The Hired Farm Working Force of 1970: a Statistical Report*. Agricultural Economic Report No. 201 (Washington, D.C.: U.S. Government Printing Office).

U.S. Department of Commerce, Bureau of the Census. 1969. *1969 Census of Agriculture*. Vol. II: *General Report*; Chapter 3, "Farm Management, Farm Operators" (Washington, D.C.).

——. 1970a. *Current Population Reports, Consumer-Income*. Series P-60, No. 76, December 16 (Washington, D.C.).

——. 1970b. *United States Census of Population: 1970*. Vol. I: *Characteristics of the Population*. Part 1; United States Summary (Washington, D.C.).

U.S. Department of Labor. 1959. *Farm Labor Fact Book* (Washington, D.C.: U.S. Government Printing Office).

——. 1962. *The Day Haul Program: Suggested Standards and Practices*. Bulletin 245 (Washington, D.C.).

U.S. Department of Labor, Manpower Administration Bureau of Employment Security. 1972. *Comparisons of State Unemployment Laws*. BES No. U-141, January (Washington, D.C.).

Walsh, Denny. 1973. "Justice Officials Find Corruption Rife among Immigration Aides in Southwest." *New York Times* (Monday, 21 May): 1 (con'd).

Webb, John N. 1935. *The Transient Unemployed*. Works Progress Administration, Division of Social Research, Research Monograph III (Washington, D.C.: U.S. Government Printing Office).

——. 1937. *The Migratory-Casual Worker*. Works Progress Administration, Division of Social Research, Research Monograph VII (Washington, D.C.: U.S. Government Printing Office).

Webb, John N., and Brown, Malcolm J. 1938. *Migrant Families*. Works Progress Administration, Division of Social Research, Research Monograph XVIII (Washington, D.C.: U.S. Government Printing Office).

Weiss, Leonard W. 1966. "Concentration and Labor Earnings." *American Economic Review* 56.1 (March): 96-117.

Weiss, Randall, D. 1970. "The Effect of Education on the Earnings of Blacks and Whites." *Review of Economics and Statistics* 52 (March): 150-159.

Wilson, Mildred G. 1972. "Trends in Farm Wage Rates." *Rural Manpower Developments* (March): 21-26 (Washington, D.C.: U.S. Department of Labor, Manpower Administration).

Wonnacott, Ronald J., and Wonnacott, Thomas H. 1970. *Econometrics* (New York: John Wiley & Sons).

Wright, Dale. 1965. *They Harvest Despair: the Migrant Farm Worker* (Boston: Beacon Press).

Wyckoff, Florence R. 1965. "Migrant Children and Youth." In *Rural Youth in Crisis: Facts, Myths, and Social Change*. Edited by Lee G. Burchinal and prepared for the National Committee for Children and Youth (Washington, D.C.: U.S. Department of Health, Education and Welfare).

Zipf, George Kingsley. 1946. "The P_1P_2/D Hypothesis: on the Intercity Movement of Persons." *American Sociological Review* 11 (December): 677-686.

SERIES ON THE DEVELOPMENT OF SOCIETIES